PRAISE FOR

"A startling, clear-eyed, and unflinchi[...]
Jewish girl during the Holocaust."
—*Publishers Weekly*

"Ruth Kluger holds one's attention by the very nature of her story, and the story could hardly be better told, in a forceful, colloquial style."
—*New York Review of Books*

"Kluger reminds us in her astringent memoir, the Holocaust involved millions of people, but each of their experiences was in some way unique."
—*Wall Street Journal*

"A most remarkable memoir. It approaches familiar matters—the life of a Jew in Nazi Europe—in an unfamiliar way; it can leap from one part of Ruth Kluger's life to another, or narration to reflection, quickly and effectively, so that the reader feels the force of a single consciousness, the author thinking, judging, remembering. These are not mere literary conceits, but a voice worth listening to."
—Peter Gay, the author of *My German Question*

"Reflective, impassioned and uncompromisingly honest . . . *Still Alive* is not only about survival, but about the forging of character in extremity and the power of a fierce individuality to triumph over the impersonal machinery of destruction."
—Eva Hoffman, author of *Lost in Translation*

"*Still Alive* is not a sentimental book. It is a necessary one. Kluger calls upon readers to acknowledge the impossibility of knowing what happened behind the barbed wire and the imperative of trying to understand. The reward is in the passionate eloquence of the journey."
—Nancy K. Miller, author of *What They Saved*

"In the vast literature of the Holocaust this is a unique work."
—Walter Laqueur, coeditor of *The Holocaust Encyclopedia*

Still Alive
A Holocaust Girlhood Remembered

Ruth Kluger

Foreword by Lore Segal

THE HELEN ROSE SCHEUER JEWISH WOMEN'S SERIES

FEMINIST
PRESS
AT THE CITY UNIVERSITY
OF NEW YORK
NEW YORK CITY

Published by the Feminist Press
at the City University of New York
The Graduate Center
365 Fifth Avenue, Suite 5406
New York, NY 10016

feministpress.org

First English-language edition, 2001
First paperback printing, 2003
Reissued as a Feminist Press European Classics edition in 2012

Library of Congress Cataloging-in-Publication Data

Klüger, Ruth, 1931-
 [Weiter Leben. English]
 Still alive : a Holocaust girlhood remembered / Ruth Kluger ; foreword by Lore Segal.
 p. cm. — (The Helen Rose Scheuer Jewish women's series)
 ISBN 1-55861-436-2
 1. Klüger, Rugh, 1931– 2. Jews—Austria—Vienna—Biography. 3. Jewish children in the
Holocaust—Austria—Vienna—Biography. 4. Holocaust, Jewish (1939–1945)—Austria—Vienna—
Personal narratives. 5. Holocaust survivors—New York (State)—Biography. 6. Vienna (Austria)—
Biography. 7. New York (State)—Biography I. Title. II. Series.
DS135.A93 K58513 2001
940.53'18'092—dc21
                                                                                        2001040459

Stephen H. Scheuer, in memory of his mother and in celebration of her life and the hundredth
anniversary of her birth (1995), has been pleased to endow the Helen Rose Scheuer Jewish Women's
Series. *Still Alive* is the eighth named book in the series.

 Publication of this book is supported by public funds from the
ART WORKS. National Endowment for the Arts.

Publication is also made possible, in part, by a grant from the J. M. Kaplan Foundation.

The Feminist Press would also like to thank Mariam K. Chamberlain, Blanche Wiesen Cook, Freddi
and Joel Felt, Helene D. Goldfarb, Barbara Grossman, Nancy Hoffman, Frances Degen Horowitz,
Florence Howe, Joanne Markell, Kate O'Hanlan and Léonie Walker, Gloria Wiener, and Genevieve
Vaughan for their generosity in supporting this project.

In memory of my mother
Alma Hirschel
1903–2000

Supporter le désaccord entre l'imagination et le fait. Ne pas se refaire un autre système imaginaire adapté au fait nouveau. "Je souffre." Cela vaut mieux que: "Ce paysage est laid."

To put up with the discrepancy between imagination and fact. Not to invent another imaginary system that will agree with a new fact. Better to say "I suffer" than "This landscape is ugly."

—SIMONE WEIL

CONTENTS

Going on Living

On March 12, 1938, Hitler's Germany annexed its neighbor, Austria, and the Jews of Vienna looked abroad for escape. Yet when seven-year-old Ruth Kluger's mother learned about the *Kindertransport* that was to carry some ten thousand Jewish children—the writer of this foreword among them—to safety in England, she refused the opportunity. Children, she reasoned, belong with their parents. Consider these ironies: it was this same reasoning that permitted the United States Senate to kill in committee an initiative that would have brought Jewish children to America, and while the State Department multiplied the legalities that prevented Jews from coming in, the Nazi regime multiplied the difficulties that prevented Jews from getting out. "Vienna," writes Ruth Kluger, "was a city that banished you and then didn't allow you to leave."

Ruth and her mother did not get out of Vienna until their deportation, four years later, to Theresienstadt. The Nazis called it a "family camp"; Ruth Kluger calls it "the stable that supplied the slaughterhouse." From there the cattle cars eventually transported them to the extermination camp Auschwitz-Birkenau. The child noted "there was soot in the air." The chimneys of the gas chambers were the route of escape for inmates not selected to die in the work camps. Ruth Kluger survived by adding three years to her actual twelve and getting herself sent to camp Christianstadt shortly before the remaining Birkenau inmates were gassed. Her book goes on to describe a gutsy escape from the forced march of the last war weeks, two years in the chaotic landscape of a defeated Germany, and in her sixteenth year, the beginning of a new life in America.

The early chapters of the memoir chart every child's experience of contriving knowledge out of information half understood, information withheld. This child came into the knowledge that her fellow citizens wanted her dead, that her death was mandated by laws that made mercy punishable as a crime. Most children discover that their elders don't know how to operate the world. Little Ruth learned that her mother would not safeguard her, that her father could not save himself.

We yearn for our moral world, at least, to work properly. Let good and bad know their places and stay in them. Murderers are to be cold-blooded, victims innocent. We need to imagine the Holocaust's children rudely torn out of their warm nests, and so they were. But Ruth Kluger's need is for a purer, harsher truth. She levels her steady gaze at the troubles inside the nest.

Today a woman approaching seventy, she seems still to be figuring out her handsome, spirited, uncomfortable mother. The mother challenged the little girl. She essentially dared her to walk into possible danger and probable exposure in a movie house out of bounds to Jews. When the mother argued that children belong with their parents it was although —perhaps because—she was not in Prague with her son by an earlier marriage. (The boy did not survive.) In the camp she "adopted" the parentless Susi and, after war's end, provided for this sturdy three-woman family by working for the Americans. She got herself and the girls to New York, married three more husbands, went crazy: a splendid old woman and a pain in the neck.

One indigestible memory of Ruth Kluger's childhood is her father's inexplicable and unjust anger toward her when he returned from his first stay in prison, before he was taken to the camps. Her imagination requires her to envision how her doctor father, who joked that he had "no elbows," might, in his death throes in the gas chamber, have elbowed himself to the top of the heap of choking women and children.

Ruth Kluger's book asks what one is to do with such facts, memories, imaginings, how one is to live with knowledge "like a bullet lodged in the soul where no surgery can reach it." Will we ever stop wondering if Primo Levi died of his knowledge?

She worries that the very act of literature betrays what was experienced in the Holocaust: don't words make "speakable" what is not? The recollection of her mother physically punished and out of control is so "vivid and lurid," she thinks, "I can't write this down." Then she writes it down.

It is not Ruth Kluger's bent or her intention to dramatize. Her anecdotes are told not for their own sake but as the ground or illustration of her thought. Even as a young child Ruth was a consumer and producer of poetry, and it trained in her what biology calls "irritability," the organism's responsiveness to stimuli from within and without. Ruth Kluger responds to the extreme moment with eye, ear, nerve, and mind. And it is the habit of poetry, surely, that gives her prose its agility. When we ask what something "is like," the language uses an idiom demanding simile or metaphor. We are asking for an association of something we can't know with something recognizable, and we respond with shocks of recognition. What was fear in the camps like? Ruth Kluger answers, "the psychological equivalent of epileptic fits," "like a theater in which a fire alarm has gone off." What were the roll calls like? "Standing in rows of five, thirsty and afraid of dying," hours, above all, of boredom. "The awareness that you are a prisoner of time," she says, "is a close cousin of despair."

She makes us feel the child's heartbreaking vitality, the yearning to have the use of its youth. During a transfer from camp to camp she discovers "the secret of simultaneity." They pass a children's summer camp. A boy is energetically waving a red flag, "a gesture affirming the sunny side of the system that was dragging us along in the blood and excrement of its underside. So much light out there—how could that be?" After the escape there is "the countryside . . . freshly washed . . . full of gleaming objects." The young girl experiences "the unforgettable, prickly feeling of what it means to reconstitute yourself."

Of the tattooing of the number onto her arm in Birkenau Ruth Kluger writes that it "produced a new alertness in me . . . I was suddenly so aware of the enormity, the monstrosity, really, of my situation that I felt a kind of glee about it. I was living through something that was worth witnessing." The thirteen-year-old poet understood this was going to be copy: "Perhaps I would write a book . . ."

The book before us is Ruth Kluger's English version of her acclaimed autobiography *weiter leben: Eine Jugend*, published in Germany in 1992.

Challenging German readers to "face themselves in the mirror of their past," as she puts it, it provoked a new round of discussion about the Nazi era, brought out untold stories, and became a literary phenomenon. It won numerous prizes, including the Heinrich Heine Prize and Thomas Mann Prize. By now repeatedly translated and widely read, it enlarges our understanding of the Holocaust and calls on us to reexamine a basic principle: the right to live.

The English title *Still Alive* thumbs its nose at those who wanted Ruth Kluger dead, but loses perhaps a small nuance in the German *weiter leben*: "going on living" suggests it's a bit of a chore. The chapter that describes Ruth Kluger's arrival in America records her irritation in the ordinary sense of the word. She is capable of friendships with younger Germans, although here the usual wall between the generations is "barbed wire. Old, rusty barbed wire." Nevertheless, "Europeans who have sat in air-raid shelters have something in common with me that Americans don't." Americans, including Jews, including the New York cousins, listened to "the enormity, the monstrosity, really" that she had to tell, "as if I had imposed on them and they were graciously indulging me." She is suspicious of today's army of interviewers, who are not genuine partners in this conversation, giving nothing to it except their "implied superiority to suffering." She senses an "instinctive revulsion."

Ruth Kluger accuses us all of avoidance. She employs the metaphor of the museum. The camps, tidied up, cleaned out, and helpfully labeled, give the visitors an experience that is the opposite of what was suffered there by Ruth, her mother, Susi, the crowd of dead. Ruth Kluger means us to have to "rearrange a lot of furniture" in our "inner museum of the Holocaust." We are not to settle down in whatever attitude to the Holocaust we have created for ourselves. It is by revisiting and rethinking and refusing to ease away nuance or complexity that Ruth Kluger means to keep discomforting herself and her readers. She goes on probing her own understanding of the murderers, the guilty bystanders, and those of us who got away, and the victims including father, mother, the child she used to be, and the woman she has become. Her tool is language at once so fierce and precise it aims to understand all without the temptation to forgive anyone or mitigate anything.

Lore Segal
New York City
July 2001

Part One

VIENNA

Instinct picking up the Key
Dropped by memory –

—EMILY DICKINSON, FROM
"AFTER A HUNDRED YEARS"

1

Their secret was death, not sex. That's what the grown-ups were talking about, sitting up late around the table. I had pretended that I couldn't fall asleep in my bed and begged them to let me sleep on the sofa in the living room, which we called by the fancier French word *salon*. Of course, I didn't intend to fall asleep. I wanted to get in on the forbidden news, the horror stories, fascinating though incomplete as they always were—or perhaps even more fascinating for their opaqueness, that whiff of fantasy they had about them, though one knew they were true. Some were about strangers, others were about relatives, all were about Jews.

At the table there was talk of Hans, a younger cousin of my mother's, whom *they* had held temporarily in Buchenwald. The name means beech grove—a pretty name, the kind I liked because I read poetry about nature. The voices at the table, women's voices, indistinct and barely audible because I kept my head under the blanket, were saying *KZ*. Just the two letters, short for *Konzentrationslager*. In German they make an ugly sound; they spit and cough like "kah-tset." Hans was scared. They had bullied him into not talking, and he hadn't talked—or perhaps he had, maybe just to his mother? They had tortured him. What is torture, how does one stand it, how is it done? But he was alive and back, knock on wood, let's be thankful. Next question: How do we get him out of Austria?

Hans did get out, and I was to meet him again in England, when I was no longer eight years old, but the way I am now: impatient and absentminded, prone to drop things intentionally or through clumsiness, even breakables like dishes and love affairs; a woman who is perennially on the move, changing jobs and homes at the drop of a hat and inventing the reasons afterwards while she is packing; a person who runs away as soon as she gets nervous, long before she smells danger. Because running away was the best thing I ever did, ever do. You feel alive when you run away. It's the ultimate drug, in my experience.

So there I was with Hans in England, in his home, which he loved because he owned it. He was married to an Englishwoman, a gentile, and his children were visiting. I had come from America, together with Heinz, another cousin on my mother's side, who had survived the war in Hungary with false papers that declared him an Aryan and a Catholic. Heinz was lucky in that his overanxious mother had refused to have him circumcised, a fact that caused considerable embarrassment when he was a little boy playing on the beach in the nude, as was customary in Europe. ("Put some pants on him," my grandfather, though no prude, would say to his older daughter, my aunt, writhing in his beach chair with discomfort at the sight of that shameful piece of skin, a babyish indiscretion disgracing the family.) Nowadays Heinz assures me that that bit of skin came in handy in the Hungarian school lavatories and locker rooms. When Heinz's grandmother died in Budapest during the war, the family had to drag the Catholic priest away from the door of her room, for she would have vehemently rejected his promise of eternal life and thereby would have endangered the earthly life of the others.

Meanwhile our English cousin Hans—who had ended up liberating his homeland, Austria, as a soldier in the British army and surprising the natives with his ability to curse in perfect Viennese—was telling us indignantly how his rabbi hadn't wanted him to marry a gentile, and how he had left the rabbi and clung to his woman. I hadn't even thought of consulting a rabbi when I got married in Berkeley. Hans's father, killed in Auschwitz, had been the only observant Jew in the family. It was incongruous, and therefore amusing, that his son, who had been the earliest embodiment of my childhood's darkest and ever-expanding secret, should concern himself, let alone get angry decades after the fact, with some English rabbi's objection to the woman of his choice. That was the best part. The rest was tea and cakes, and I was shifting in my seat, eager to get up, do something, go for a walk, anything to escape the all-embracing envelope of boredom, the unrelenting regurgitation of details from everyday life. Heinz told me later, not without a touch of malice, that Hans had asked him if I suffered from hemorrhoids, since I wouldn't sit still for long.

But Hans wasn't your average English home owner: he had been tortured in Buchenwald when he was a teenager. And I was the little relative who kept her ears open under her blanket, determined to find out more about this extraordinary experience. Not so much from sympathy as from curiosity, because Hans was the center of an exciting mystery which concerned me, too, in some nebulous way. Though no one would tell me about it because I was too young. And now?

Now I was better informed and could ask all I liked, for those who had imposed the restriction were gone, dispersed, had died in gas chambers or in their beds, wherever. And still I can't get rid of the prickly sense that I am breaking taboos, searching for indecencies, like Noah's children uncovering their father's nakedness, that I am not supposed to know about death and dying. As if there were anything else worth knowing. The grown-ups pretended that only grown-ups die. But on the street, for all to hear, the Nazi boys were singing the song about Jewish blood spurting from their knives. That included my blood, didn't it? And they were carrying sharp little daggers, weren't they? You didn't have to be very smart to get their meaning; on the contrary, it required some mental agility to ignore it, to shrug it off. (A German colleague of mine—I have become a professor of German literature since—reads what I have just written and says, "You know, those knives weren't daggers. They were good for cutting bread, that's all. On excursions. They weren't even pointed." He takes a pencil and painstakingly draws the kind of knife he used to own as a member of the Hitler Youth. "I would have preferred a real weapon," he reminisces, then adds, "Our knives carried the legend 'Blood and Honor.'" That's a dagger for sure, I think. Blood and honor means a dagger, whether the knife is pointed or round.)

So now I have a chance to ask Hans about the old secrets, and I do. In graduate seminars you learn how to ask precise questions, and I have taught that skill to students. But the other guests in the stifling space of the tidy English living room want to be left in peace: the children assure us that they were about to leave anyway and had better go now; Heinz takes off his glasses, wipes them, and asks plaintively whether we have to go through with this. Hans's gentile wife leaves the room. She has heard it all before and more than she wanted. True, no doubt, but did she ever pay attention?

And Hans answers my questions and tells me his story. I want to know exactly what it was like, and with a certain groaning roundaboutness he tells me the minutiae, the contortion of the limbs. He can explain it well. He can even show me; he suffers from back pains dating from that time. And yet these details have a way of leveling the horror, as appeals from Amnesty International never quite get across what they are telling you because the familiar words, black ink on dry white paper, interfere with the mute and essentially wordless suffering—the ooze of pain, if I may so call it—they aim to communicate. Only in Hans's tone of voice is there a hint of the sheer evil, of radical otherness. For the sensation of torture doesn't leave its victim alone—never, not to the end of life. It isn't the pain per se, it's how it was inflicted. Consider how new mothers, by contrast, forget the great pangs of childbirth within days and so can look forward to their next child. What matters is not just what we endure, but also what kind of misery it is, where it comes from. The worst is the kind that's imposed by others with malicious intent. That's the kind from which no one recovers.

My head is a warehouse of such tales and reflections. And I crave more. I read them and listen to them. Though with the passing years many fervent convictions, and certainly all manner of faith, has drained out of me, I still seem to believe in the principle "Knowledge is power," which someone wrote in my little-girl poetry album (it had an enchanting tiny wooden horse for a bookmark). Occasionally I tell a few stories of my own, if someone asks. But that rarely happens. Wars, and hence the memories of wars, are owned by the male of the species. And fascism is a decidedly male property, whether you were for or against it. Besides, women have no past, or aren't supposed to have one. A man can have an interesting past, a woman only an indecent one. And my stories aren't even sexy.

This English cousin recently died, and I wondered why I hadn't visited him more often. One reason was my indifference to family relations, which it took me years to acknowledge. Wherever there are Jews, the world over, it has become customary to count the murder victims among our relatives, to insist that our children know these figures, and to compare them with the remnant of the *mishpokhe*, the extended family. They are horrendous figures, huge collective graves. "One hundred and five," says an uncle. The next one adds another dozen, while an aunt ticks off a few more names on her fingers. For a long time I participated in this counting and accounting and tried to persuade myself that I was in mourning for people whom I hardly remembered. But actually I never experienced the comfort of a *mishpokhe*. Mine fell apart at the time I became conscious, not later. I'd like to belong, but wishing won't do it.

Basically, I never did belong; the dispersion started too early. Yet who likes to be a monad, alone in space? Better to be a link in a broken—yes, even a broken—chain. Still, now that the Holocaust archives are doing the counting for us, I won't register with them as a survivor. The form lies where my son has put it for me, gathering dust in a corner of my desk. I can't overcome my resentful reluctance to fill it out, as if it were one more roll call in the shivering hours of the morning, or the merciless heat of noon, on the *Appellplatz* of some last concentration camp.

To complicate matters, the other survivors of my Viennese childhood irritate me like a powerful itch, and I prefer to avoid them. I guess the child in me suspects that the older ones deserted me and that the younger ones still would, if they had the opportunity. Perhaps these barriers are my fault, perhaps theirs. Who knows? We all splash in dark waters when it comes to the past, to this past.

But the real reason I always shied away from visiting relatives was my bad conscience. Hans's mother, my great-aunt, was one of those who died in the most pitiful way there ever was: the infamous death in the gas chambers. She was a relative I knew well, since Hans's parents shared an apartment with my mother and me after my father had been arrested and we could no longer stay in our home. In my memory she remains the person who wouldn't let me drink water after eating cherries, a superstition that undermined the authority of my absent father, the doctor in the family to whom nobody listened. She was the person who confiscated my collection of used streetcar tickets, one of the few amusements I invented for myself outside of reading, when so much else had closed down. She claimed it was unhygienic. (But it was mine, damn it. What right did she have to take it? I can still feel my eight-year-old indignation.) And she insisted that I eat all the food put before me in the dark hours of the morning at the kitchen table before going to school—a revolting, sticky mess washed down with a sweetish cocoa drink covered by that skinlike layer of milk which nauseates all children in the world, unless they are starving. She scolded me when I recited poems out loud, another private amusement, this one turning into a bit of an addiction to be sure: while walking the unsafe streets, I would mutter verses as if they were a magic spell. It was as much a neurotic symptom (I now say in retrospect) as an early sign of a literary turn of mind. But worst of all, she was the person who stood between me and my mother, keeping her at a distance from me so that after a day spent trying to get my father out of jail or looking for a job, she wouldn't be aggravated by her little daughter's demands for reassurance and affection in a world that was becoming ever more constricting and unfathomable.

So what could I say to her son, who loved her as a child loves his mother, when he questioned me, who hated her with a child's needle-sharp aversion, and who can't forgive her, even after a death that is as hard to imagine as it is impossible to forget? For it is not in our power to forgive: memory does that for us, and when memory refuses, the honey-eyed words that are meant to convey what we sincerely think we ought to feel turn sour with hypocrisy. I know of her death in my mind. But my childish resentments are more deeply ingrained, where the mind doesn't reach.

And anyway, what was so bad about reciting classical ballads on the street, the perfectly respectable kind of poems that older children were made to memorize in school? Why was nobody proud that I had learned them all by myself? "It makes a bad impression." "You shouldn't call attention to yourself in public." "Jewish children who have bad manners cause *rishes* [anti-Semitism]." But was that relevant, when the entire population had been incited to despise and persecute us? The older people repeated the litanies learned in their childhood and didn't, or simply couldn't, think far enough to revise them to fit present circumstances. But I had been born in 1931 and thought it ludicrous that the great storm raging around us could be increased or diminished by my good or bad manners. Or that anyone should think so. My aunt wasn't that stupid. So she just didn't like me, I figured. And since I had not lived through many pre-Nazi years, I understood instinctively, without having to read Sartre on the subject, that while the consequences of anti-Semitism were a considerable problem for us Jews, the thing itself, the hatred, was a problem of and for the anti-Semites, and for them alone. Deal with it as you can was my attitude: I'm not going to become a paragon of virtue or put on nice-girl manners in order to shame and convert you. As if you wanted to be converted. And I went on memorizing and reciting eighteenth-century verse about knights and dragons and ancient bards and heroes.

The grown-ups had lost their bearings, and not only with regard to their children's behavior: they were confused about how to conduct their own lives and by what standards. Mind you, these were not rich people. They were middle-class folk who, however solid, had to watch the bottom line. Yet now they fantasized that it could have made a difference if they and other Jews had acted differently—and this in a city which owed half its innovative thought and culture to Jews! What more could the Jews have done for what they thought was their country, too? Jewish women, for example, shouldn't have worn jewelry in public, in the restaurants and cafés that were Vienna's favorite gathering spots. (And why, I wondered, does one buy jewelry, if one isn't supposed to wear it? I didn't myself see much point to glittering stones, but if it's so despicable to own them, I thought, why don't they close the jewelers' shops?) My people knew of the pogroms of the past (they wouldn't have been Jews if they didn't), but these were dark, historical, preferably Polish and Russian matters—nothing to do with us. They also knew what had been going on in neighboring Germany for the past five years. Or didn't they read the newspapers? Maybe only the men did. At this point my understanding of my family falters, even at this late date. What *were* they thinking of? I ask with self-righteous hindsight. Their sudden and unwarranted self-criticism was a kind of psychological damage control, a way to find comprehen-sible proportions, recognizable parameters, for this new persecution. They turned introspective instead of getting out, legally or illegally, and regardless of destination. Just out. True, they didn't have as much time as the German Jews to leave their country, but more than the Polish Jews. I know I would have left, I say now, with the feel of disaster still and forever in my bones.

I complained to my mother about this aunt of hers, Irene. "She's a mother of boys," my mother said. "She isn't used to girls." What was there to get used to, I thought irritably. And thus, frozen in death, this woman embodies the most appalling generation gap, for I cannot bring myself to think of her and her husband, my great-uncle, with commiseration. I remember his resentment at having to give me lunch when I came back from school and the women weren't home. It wasn't a man's job, and he took out his humiliation on me. I realize that their murder shouldn't be framed by the petty complaints of my childhood anger. But that is where my uncle and aunt are lodged in my mind and won't budge. I remember that she would punish me when she found out that I had poured my breakfast cocoa into the sink. She would make me stay in the kitchen until I had eaten or drunk a second helping, more than my unwilling stomach could absorb, but only after it had done so was its owner permitted to leave the house for school. Which was unpleasant, because it meant I was going to be late. I reasoned that the grown-ups should get together and make up their collective minds and not impose punishments which other grown-ups considered cause for punishment, like making you late for school as a punishment for not eating your breakfast.

2

Yet ultimately it didn't matter whether I was on time or late for school. It was one of those things that had become irrelevant in view of a more important question: which and how many of my classmates had been arrested overnight. (The German word was *ausgehoben*, "lifted out," and the men who did the job were usually Jews who hoped to gain privileges by collaborating, and who justified their work as an improvement over leaving it to the Nazis. They were *Ausheber*, "lifters out," a curious euphemism.) Or maybe the missing classmates had gone underground or had managed to leave the country by some mysterious, or perhaps even legal, means. I entered the classroom and looked round. The missing children might be sick, but it was more probable that I wouldn't see them again. Every day there were fewer of us. When there were too few, the school was closed, and we were transferred to another school with the same problems. And then yet another one. The classrooms became older and more run-down. There was one with gaslight instead of electricity. On the dark winter mornings the teacher had to get up on a chair to light the lamp. There was something antique and venerable to this process, so I didn't mind that we had to do our work in semidarkness. The remaining children wore shabby hand-me-downs, and their language was the dialect of the outlying districts: one could see and hear that they were the children of the poor. For one could not emigrate without money. In all the countries of the world, poor Jews were even less welcome than wealthy Jews. The teachers, too, disappeared, one after the other, so that we came to expect a new one every two or three months.

I attended eight different schools in four years. The fewer schools there were for us, the longer it took to get to school. You had to take the streetcars and the underground train. The longer it took, the less likely it was that one could avoid hateful glances and encounters. I left the house and was in enemy territory. It was little consolation that not all passersby were hostile, as long as there were enough, or any, who were. (This part of my story coincides with what older blacks will tell me, and with what black writers such as James Baldwin have poignantly described: a child facing a sea of hostile white faces. No white can understand, they say. I do, I say. But no, you have white skin, they counter. But I wore a *Judenstern* to alert other pedestrians that I wasn't really white.)

When we had a male teacher, we recited the Shema Yisroel, the Jewish equivalent of the Lord's Prayer. We recited it in German, monotonously, and without the slightest indication that we felt even an inkling of that love of God which the prayer imposes on the faithful. The boys had to cover their heads; inevitably there were some who had left their yarmulkes at home. They were reprimanded by the teacher and made to use their dirty handkerchiefs as head coverings, tying a knot in each corner so they wouldn't slip. I was revolted by this quasi ritual, as I was revolted by the vulgar speech which had taken over, and which not only seemed inimical to the poetry I cherished but also ran counter to the more cultivated language of my bourgeois home, even though I didn't live anymore in a bourgeois home.

One day when the children were particularly rambunctious during recess, the teacher called us a *Judenschule*—an anti-Semitic term referring to the supposed lack of discipline in a Jewish shul or *cheder*. But we *are* a Jewish school, I thought. Why did a Jewish adult humiliate Jewish kids, as if our Aryan compatriots weren't doing their level best to take away our self-esteem? (I purposely don't put quotation marks around the word *Aryan*, for at that time it was hardly ever used ironically.) And suddenly, although I had felt like an outsider among my relatively illiterate and proletarian classmates and hadn't been one of the noise makers, I felt a new solidarity with the others and their quiet shame. The teacher, himself one of the downtrodden, had kicked those beneath him. Up until then I had had a bit of a schoolgirl crush on him. No longer: Jewish self-contempt wasn't for me. I had discovered the opposite: Jewish pride. The bit about the *Judenschule* was even worse than Aunt Irene's contention that bad manners cause *rishes*.

Soon afterwards, at the suggestion of my mother, I stopped going to school altogether. I had complained bitterly about how meaningless and depressing school had become, how I wasn't learning anything, and what a burden it was to get there. For a while I had private English lessons from an Englishwoman who admired the Nazis, and whom I accordingly mistrusted. Why did your mother ever employ such a woman? says a young friend. I reply that Nazis and non-Nazis weren't like apples and oranges, that it was rather a matter of more or less Nazi, and identities were constantly shifting. There were wild mood swings—were Austrians really Germans, as Hitler, himself an Austrian turned German, tried to persuade them, or something older and better? Opinions might or might not change into convictions ("Opinions lie in the street," Thomas Mann says somewhere. "Anybody can pick them up"). Today's fellow travelers of the regime could turn tomorrow into its opponents, or more likely, vice versa. My mother liked the woman's British accent and didn't think my teacher's political opinions were any of my business. She was wrong: the teacher didn't like Jew girls any better than I liked adherents of the New Order, and the lessons became an exercise in antagonism. It became a point of honor—Penelope's honor, as it were—to forget from one lesson to the next whatever I had learned.

In school there had been girl named Liesel who was a few years older and physically much more developed than I. For me, she was the incarnation of a streetwise kid. She liked to throw out knowing hints on matters of menstruation and sexuality, with an implicit claim to the social superiority of the school yard, which she had anyhow in my eyes, since she was ahead of me by a couple of grades, and therefore, in that immutable hierarchy, was someone to respect. She knew that I wrote and memorized poems, and she took every opportunity to make fun of me. "Don't you know such and such a poem by heart?" she would innocently ask. "Let's hear it." I would gladly oblige and begin to recite. Slowly but surely her face would turn into a sneer as she managed to distill some unintended indecency from the text. And I, in my poetic humorlessness, was upset and hurt when it dawned on me that I had been had and had walked into a trap. Liesel's mother was dead, her father poor and uneducated. I was yet to find out how much she loved him, and that Liesel herself would remain with me as an ineradicable and desperate memory of my shabby, shameful childhood Vienna.

3

The city of my first eleven years is not a place where I really know my way around. When I visit Vienna now, I walk the streets like a tourist, map in hand, and easily lose my way. "Oh, you are from Vienna," Americans like to say. "How lucky you are. What a charming city." That's what they said even in the late forties, as if they had promptly forgotten what the war was about, and I'd reply incredulously, "But I am Jewish." They would act as if that had nothing to do with the objective charm of waltzes and empresses with long hair and Mozart operas. And nowadays they think of *The Sound of Music* and of Schwarzenegger. But with the yellow Jewish star on one's coat, one didn't go on excursions or into museums. Even before we were required to wear it, half the city was forbidden, *verboten*, taboo, or out of reach for Jews. The signs telling Jews and dogs to stay outside were ubiquitous. If you had to buy a loaf of bread, you had to walk past a little sign which instructed Aryan customers: "Don't say hello, don't say good day / Heil Hitler is the German way." I would timidly use the familiar Austrian *Grüss Gott*, which translates roughly as "God's greeting." More often than not, I'd get no answer at all, only a harsh "What do you want?" I was always relieved when the simple two-word salute met with an echo and thought that perhaps the response was a small sign of resistance, as if the person was saying, "I am in God's hand, not in Hitler's."

Suddenly I had become a disadvantaged child who couldn't do the things that the children in our circle usually learned to do, like swim in the municipal pool, acquire a bike, go with girlfriends to children's movies, or skate. I did learn to swim in the Danube after the war, but not near Vienna; and after the war I also got on a bike elsewhere, not in Vienna. I never learned to skate, sad to say. I had just started lessons, staggering around the rink a couple of times, and then it was over. It was one thing after another: stuff one wanted to do and see and started to do and see, and then having to give it up for no good reason. It was sad and irritating. Vienna taught me to speak and read, but little else. (Still, isn't that all that is needed for a life of the mind?) Anti-Semitic signs and slogans were among my first reading materials, and here I had an early opportunity to practice critical discrimination as well as a sense of (Jewish) superiority. I happened to be the youngest child in our extended family, and hence the only one who couldn't grow into an expanding life, who couldn't swim, skate, or bike, and for whom the Austrian landscape was merely a series of sweet-sounding names: Semmering, Vorarlberg, Wolfgangsee, names of nearby places that seemed as idyllic as faraway ones. It was as if a whole generation lay between me and my cousins, and even today a gap yawns between me and those Viennese emigrants who have memories of moving freely and unselfconsciously about the city. Anyone who was just a few years older experienced a different Vienna than I, who at age seven wasn't permitted to sit on a park bench and instead could take comfort, if I so chose, in the thought that I belonged to the Chosen People. (In 1950, in Texas, the shock of recognition at the menacing signs of segregation, from water fountains to toilets, was like a slap in the face, though not meant for me.) Vienna was a city with no exit, a city that banished you and then didn't allow you to leave.

So Vienna became my first prison. As in all prisons, there was interminable talk about freedom and escape, meaning emigration. Our bags were always packed, we were always on the brink of moving to another country, and we were never comfortably settled, not even for the near future. I therefore couldn't afford to cultivate habits, and if I began looking forward to anything, such as reading the stories in the popular children's magazines *The Parrot* and *The Butterfly*, I immediately corrected my anticipation of such delights with the even more delightful hope that I would be in another country before the next issue appeared on the newsstands.

I had started first grade in September 1937, shortly before my sixth birthday and half a year before the German invasion. Before that, there isn't much I recall. Once we drove to Italy for a summer vacation, and when we had crossed the border, we had to continue on the other side of the street—how strange and funny!—for Austrians drove on the left-hand side until they became part of the German Reich. That was long before the plague of traffic congestion. Far south on a lonely, dusty road, a car with an Austrian license plate passed us, and we waved to each other. We don't know those people, I thought. At home we wouldn't have waved at them. I was enchanted by the discovery that strangers in a strange land greet each other because they are compatriots. I am from Austria (where the cars drive on the proper side of the street and people speak German). That is a valid statement about me, and here in Italy I realize how my origins are part of me. The place up north is where I belong and where I am at home with my family. I was soon to find out that it wasn't so, but not right away.

At the end of my first schoolday, when I stepped outside there was a crowd of children and parents all pushing each other. I didn't see my father at first. He stood in back, leaning against a fence, not yet forty years of age. It boggles the mind that I have grown so much older than he was ever to be. When I asked him with tears in my voice why he was waiting so far away from the building, making me wonder whether anyone had come to fetch me, he replied cheerfully: "Why push? What's the big hurry?" Right away he seemed to me the most distinguished of all the parents, and the others with their elbows were simply vulgar. I gratefully accepted the colorful bag of candy traditionally given at the successful completion of one's first day at school, took his hand, and went home, proud of him and in high spirits.

About a year later we again walked hand in hand through a part of our city. We lived in the Seventh District, fairly close to the center of town, on a street with the pretty name Lindengasse. It was November 1938, just after the infamous *Kristallnacht*. He pointed to the broken store windows and said only the obvious, his cold breath hanging in the air: "You can't shop there anymore. Of course not: it's closed. Why? The owners are Jews. Like us. That's why." I was overcome by fear and curiosity, sensing that this was all tremendously important. I would have liked to ask him more questions, and at the same time I felt that perhaps he didn't know more, and so I merely made a point of remembering his words. (See, I still know them.)

I have two photos of him. In the first he looks young and adventurous, an impecunious medical student in a city that had too many physicians. That is the period when he courted my mother, the daughter of a wealthy chemical engineer who insisted on giving her to a different man, supposedly a better provider. My mother went along, but her first husband was boring and stingy, according to family lore. They lived in Prague, but she was drawn to Vienna. The two cities were within easy reach of each other at that time, though a few years later there would be an unbridgeable distance between them.

My mother divorced her husband, a rather unusual step in those days. Her father forgave her and helped her out financially in her second marriage. She got custody of my half brother, Schorschi, as he was called in the Austrian vernacular. (He was Georg in German and Jiří in his native Czech.) He came to Vienna with our mother, who finally and for a few years had what she wished for: the dashing medical student from a poor family of ten siblings with a widowed mother. My father, the seventh child, now a full-fledged doctor, got a handsome wife with a dowry, and after a year they had a child. Just a girl, to be sure, but any child makes for happiness. They were well-off and presumably contented.

The dawn of memory: my brother, six years older than I, owned a flashlight, which he would turn on under the blanket so that you could clearly see everything, even though the big light in the room was turned off. (This was not exactly an approved game, because in Sigmund Freud's town brother and sister weren't supposed to play together in bed.) My brother read Jules Verne on the toilet when he was supposed to be on his way to school and got scolded. He played Indian games with his friends, which I could join only on rare occasions, given the limited number and subordinate nature of Indian girl roles (Pocahontas wasn't part of the Austrian Indian mythology). And in Grandfather's garden he turned into a patriotic Czech, fighting the good fight for President Masaryk, despite the assertion of Austrian friends and cousins that Chancellor Schuschnigg was "better." My brother had a bicycle and could ride it, while I didn't and couldn't. He also had a library of Czech children's books, which he actually was able to read. After he was gone, I sometimes leafed through them and marveled at the curly diacritical marks, in awe of Schorschi's secret knowledge. And I frequently annoyed him, and sometimes he would play with me.

That's all I know about my brother; all else is hearsay. He was my first role model, and I loved him with that peculiar craving of a small child to be more and bigger and someone else. One day I'd be like him, as far as a girl could be. One day he was gone.

My mother cried and berated her ex-husband, who hadn't let the boy come back after a summer vacation in Prague. The court there had reversed an earlier decision and granted custody to the father on the ground that no Czech child (even a little Jew) should be subjected to a "German" education in Vienna. As my mother said, resentfully and not incorrectly: "After 1918 the Jews became more Czech than Old King Wenceslas himself." Nationalism struck the small boy and the small country like one of the Egyptian plagues. In retrospect, I am pleased that Schorschi was on the right side in Grandfather's garden, when he defended Tomás Masaryk, the first president of the Czech Republic, a democrat and a liberal, against the Austro-Fascist Chancellor Schuschnigg, but I also know that his choice was accidental. The boys took sides solely on the basis of "my country, right or wrong," because they thought they had a country.

Schorschi was my first great loss, and every subsequent loss has seemed a replay of that first. I had not only lost a beloved family member but also a role: little sister. "He'll return," my parents comforted me. "You have to learn to wait."

Not so. If you wait long enough, death comes for you. Don't learn to wait, learn to run away. Once, in a meadow of dandelions in bloom, you said to me: "Look, little sister, they're lions, ready to bite us." (The pun is more obvious in German, which calls the flower *Löwenzahn*, lion's tooth.) So we started running until we were out of breath, yelling in pretended fear, and then we rolled in the grass, laughing our heads off. My dear dead brother, we should never have stopped running. Running from danger, a heady game.

My mother, later: "If it hadn't been for you, I would have saved him. I couldn't leave you alone in Vienna while I went to fetch him." So was it my fault? Or did she have a bad conscience because of her divorce, which had led to her separation from her older child? To be reunited with him became an obsession with her, but she did nothing to bring it about. Once I asked her the foolish question "Whom do you like better, him or me?" And she actually said, "Schorschi, because I have known him longer." I thought that was a fair enough reason and comforted myself that there was surely enough love left for me. Sixty years later, however, I still hear her say it.

4

In March 1938 I lay in bed with a strep throat and a warm compress. Below the window men were yelling in chorus. What they were yelling can be checked out in the history books. My nanny mutters, "If those guys lose their voices, they won't get any chamomile tea from me," as she brings me a cup. It's the first political joke I remember hearing. During the next days the first German uniforms appeared on the street. These soldiers spoke German, but with a funny, harsh accent, not like us, and initially I believed they didn't belong here as much as I did. My father came home with the new currency and showed it to me. No more schillings and groschen; marks and pfennig now. We enjoyed looking at the newly minted coins as he explained their value, and I admired the difference and glitter. It reminded me of my brother, fresh from a vacation in Prague, as he emptied his pockets and dubiously studied his Czech cash, wondering aloud with Slavic intonation about the exchange rate he could expect from his generous grandfather. My father explained the value of the new money and imitated the weird pronunciation of the invaders. In brief, we had fun. My mother indicated that this was scandalously childish behavior in desperate times. I didn't understand what she meant and wondered if she was right (if her concern was genuine), or if she was being a spoilsport.

My father refused to let worry eat at him. At first Aryan women still came to the door for treatment. We had to tell them that he was only permitted to treat Jews. Then it became fashionable among would-be emigrants to learn a new trade. My father learned to make sausages. We ate his journeyman sausages for lunch and made snide remarks about their lack of symmetry. He explained in perfect deadpan how you stuff the meat into the intestines, and I laughed so hard I couldn't swallow. No man was as witty as my father.

He must have imagined that the whole world was like Vienna, like his Vienna, and that everywhere there were too many medical doctors, too many specialists. We could have emigrated to India, where they definitely didn't have too many doctors. But the climate, he said, the climate would be unbearable, much too hot. In reality, he meant too foreign, inveterate Viennese that he was. Because as far as heat went, years before the German invasion of Austria he had announced: "We are sitting with our Jewish *tokhes* on a powder keg." He helped the second of Aunt Irene's sons reach Palestine via some elaborate detours. I met that cousin in Haifa in the eighties, shortly before he died, and he was still grateful to my father for his good advice, his high spirits, and of course, the help.

I keep wanting to celebrate him in some way, to find or invent an appropriate way of mourning, some ceremony for him. And yet celebrations and ceremonies are not my thing. I suspect them of mendacity, and often they strike me as ridiculous. Nor would I know where to start. In the Jewish tradition only men say the kaddish, the prayer for the dead. (Who is keeping you from saying any prayer you please? my friends ask. But it wouldn't count, couldn't be part of a prescribed communal ritual, so what would be the point?) My much beloved grandfather, who always had a welcome smile and his pockets full of presents for me, used to say with playful somberness to his (male) dog: "You are the only one around who'll be able to say kaddish for me." That's how he talked to his dog in front of his two daughters, because he had no sons, and my mother, who adored him, told me the story without the slightest criticism, accepting the humiliation like a good Jewish girl, for after all, it had been only a joke. If it were different, if I could mourn my ghosts in some accepted public way, like saying kaddish for my father, I'd have a friendlier attitude towards this religion, which reduces its daughters to helpmeets of men and circumscribes their spiritual life within the confines of domestic functions. Recipes for gefilte fish are no recipe for coping with the Holocaust.

Yet I am often told that I underestimate the role of woman in Judaism. She may light the Sabbath candles after having set the table, an important function. I don't want to set the Sabbath table or light candles; I don't live with tablecloths and silverware. And why do you want to say kaddish? the same people, who know me, ask in astonishment. We haven't seen you pray a lot, nor do you wear sackcloth and ashes in public. True, true, but the dead set us certain tasks, don't they? They want to be remembered and revered, they want to be resurrected and buried at the same time. I want to say kaddish because I live with the dead. If I can't do that, forget about religion. Poetry is more helpful.

So how shall I celebrate? I can call him by his name, which was Viktor. There was a small sign near the entrance of our apartment building that said "Doktor Viktor Klüger," and below that "Frauen- und Kinderarzt," gynecologist and pediatrician. It was one of the first signs I could read by myself, and I was amused at the double end syllable *tor*. The grown-ups didn't see the point; another surprise, this discrepancy of perception.

My mother says that my father was generous, that he used to give away money. To whom? I ask. Sometimes even to his patients, she says, when they didn't have any, but mostly to his family, all of whom were poor. My German friends claim that all Jews had money. To them Jews are wealthy by definition. All the Jews except the ones I have known, I think: my father's family, my classmates in Vienna (after the propertied Jews had emigrated to countries where Social Darwinism was a viable creed), and later my college friends in New York. Why have I known so many penniless Jews when there are supposed to be only rich ones?

My oldest son should have had my father's name, since Jews call their children after the dead. But in my ninth month of pregnancy—and I was very young—I was afraid to call a child after a murder victim, and what's more, the name was like a mockery: the victor as victim. So we gave the newborn an English name that had no significance for his parents. Sometimes I think that was a betrayal of the past. Or perhaps I wanted to pay him back his own betrayal, the fact that he left without me and never returned? And therefore refused to let him live on in his grandson, who is quite happy with the name he has got.

My father's generation didn't pay much attention to small children. My mother claims that he was crazy about me, but that's like staging and then retouching a family photo. I know better. When I had learned to read I began to interest him a little, and he brought me a few books from the public library. Once he took me to a bookstore where I could choose a volume. That was unusual; it stands out in memory. I picked the fattest book among those that were eligible, a choice, or rather a criterion, of which he approved. A book of Jewish legends, it became a favorite. When the Tower of Babel was built, God threw colored confetti into the crowd, thus damning them to their various languages and misunderstandings: God's wrath as a painted carnival of chance.

He was an enthusiastic, perhaps even a good, chess player, and when I was six he announced that he was going to teach me the rules. I was proud to be permitted to sit like him on a black leather chair in the *Herrenzimmer*, a room that smelled of smoke and had bookshelves. I tried as hard as I could to remember the moves and execute them to best advantage. But after a few lessons he got bored; I just wasn't gifted enough, or I was too young, he said. I was disappointed, and what was worse, upset at having disappointed him. I felt a little stupid and a bit ashamed. And yet the game had staying power, and though I never advanced beyond mediocrity, it has given me much pleasure over the years, with its aesthetic of pure cohesion, unspoiled by questions of means and ends, since the means are the end: a game like a dance. The rules themselves are beautiful, like the rules of a sonnet. There have even been weeks (not whole months, though) when I was a little (not a lot, I believe) possessed by or addicted to chess and bought books on the subject and replayed the games of the masters. It's part of my ongoing conversation with my father: "You see, you didn't waste your time with me in your *Herrenzimmer*. I haven't forgotten what you taught me. I have added to it, even though I still don't play as well as you seem to have expected. Sorry about that." Forever, this "you see." Once I even tried to play against a computer, and I thought of him, how he might have lived into the age of computer games. When I stumble with my tourist map through Vienna, I can see and hear him at my elbow: "If you are looking for the Herrengasse, you have to turn left, not right, for crying out loud." (Is it just the assonance with *Herrenzimmer* that makes his ghost appear on that particular corner?)

But I was also scared of my father, in the manner of children who aren't intimate with their parents and have difficulty gauging their moods. There was the incident with the typewriter. It stood on his desk, a manual of course, and my fourteen-year-old cousin Julia and I had the idea that we could use it for some game. He wasn't in, so we went and took it, my cousin fully confident that her jovial uncle wouldn't object. But the jovial uncle was pretty angry when he came home. It was a machine, he said, it was no toy. I was hypersensitive to reproaches from him and trembled all day with regret about having borrowed it. I can still see his annoyed expression. Once I asked my mother why he should have cared so much, given that a manual typewriter can hardly be damaged. "He came from a poor family," she said superciliously, "and for him a typewriter was a major purchase." The incident happened after the German invasion, so he was surely more thin-skinned than usual, and so was I, for the atmosphere in my first-grade class was changing. And yet I still resent his pettiness. "Why all the fuss?" I ask him, light-years later in our electronic age. "There, you see," I argue with his ghost, "who needs a worthless old typewriter? Look what I have instead: here a laptop, there a PC. I've always let the children try one out if they want to see how it works. And last year I even gave one of these things to your great-granddaughter, and you should have seen how happy it made her." (Is my life running circles round me? For all my many moves, shall I live forever in the Lindengasse in Vienna and give a computer to a child because I couldn't play with my father's manual typewriter? Everything to do with him is unfinished; nothing was ever resolved.)

I recount these childish trivia because they are all I have of him, and because I can't make them jibe with his death. Try as I may, I can't change these images or the feelings that go with them, and concentrate instead on what I know happened to him in the end. For I only *know* of his fate, I don't *recall* it, and imagined pictures have a lower priority than remembered ones. I see my father as an authority figure in the life of a small girl. That he ended in a cramped room, naked, swallowing poison gas, most likely struggling for an exit, makes all these memories singularly insignificant. Which doesn't solve the problem that I can't replace them or erase them. There is a gap between knowledge and memory, and I can't bridge it.

People say, okay, we understand that the murder of your father hit you hard, and we are ready to sympathize with you if you want us to (though we suspect that you can do without our pity). What we don't get is the problem. Your father led a normal life and died an unnatural death. Very sad—but where is the difficulty you mention?

The difficulty lies in the bad fit between facts and feelings, in the discrepancy between actual, normal, petty sentiments and the horrendous suffering of which childish memory is innocent. And then again there is the quaint nostalgia we experience when we think of the men and women we knew in childhood, which is mere self-love, the love of one's own roots. Witness the foregoing pages, where I dusted off the ramshackle mementos of my father and brother, enjoying my stay in the attic of memory. I recalled Schorschi's flashlight and could have added his penknife, which I found again after the war and carried with me for years as a souvenir. (God knows where and when I lost it.)

Normally we have a set image of a person we know and love and can visualize him or her within a stable mental frame; we don't have to cope with a dozen snapshots that split and turn like the images in a kaleidoscope. My memory presents my father as he politely takes off his hat to neighbors in the Burggasse, the nearest cross street to Lindengasse, but thanks to my informed imagination I see him die convulsively, murdered by the people whom he greeted on these streets or by their ilk. Nothing in between, no connecting links. And when we talk of a finished life we have known, we generally use a certain tone of voice, integrating the end with the beginning. We explain our premises and set up warning signals along the way, foreshadowing what is to come. I am trying to do this but I am failing, because memory is a prison of sorts, too: you can't shake or alter the images engraved there. Just as the viewer who looks at the famous drawing that both the art historian Gombrich and the philosopher Wittgenstein appreciated sees either a rabbit or a duck, but not both at the same time, so I can conjure up the "right" feelings for the living father or the dead, but what I can't do is bring them together into the single, undivided person he was.

The most precise memories are thus the ones that seduce us into lies, because they won't be budged by anything outside themselves. No matter what you propose to them by way of later judgment and better knowledge, no matter how you reproach them or cajole them, like stubborn dogs they just show you their teeth without giving an inch. There is no necessity that binds my disparate father fragments together, and so they don't make for tragedy, only for helpless and unconvincing combinations that end in a vacuum, or in sentimentality.

I can't do a better job of it. All I can do is demonstrate an insoluble dilemma, showcasing my own limitations. My father has become an unredeemed ghost. I wish I could write ghost stories.

5

I don't like to report what I only know from hearsay. Those chaotic times lie under a gray fog, and the voices in the fog are not clearly audible or reliable. What they say is, my father was arrested, the charge was an illegal abortion, the patient a non-Jew. My mother explains: "She was poor and young, and he felt *rakhmones* [pity] for her. She implored him. And then someone denounced him." There is no doubt that he performed abortions, especially in those days, when few families wanted children. He aborted a child of his own, which would have been a boy, my mother says, and he was "sad for days." (None of us would have survived if there had been a baby.) She says the SS, not the police, arrested him, and they put him not in a camp, but in prison. My mother sprang into action. She found a lawyer who "belonged to the party, but wasn't really a Nazi. Besides, he liked our money." In other words, an opportunist, not necessarily an Oskar Schindler.

She had to promise to stay in the country until she paid the infamous *Reichsfluchtsteuer*, literally a tax for flight from the Reich. The Reich wanted to be compensated when its unwanted citizens actually left. You were either the property of the state, or you were "stateless," which in turn meant that although you had unquestionably been born into the world, you were not allowed to live anywhere. These are the paradoxical alternatives with which my generation grew up. My father had to leave Austria within a week or two after he got out of jail, and he went to neighboring Italy. My mother made his emigration possible through her promise to stay. But she couldn't find the money to pay the tax, because Jewish real estate had been confiscated and Jewish bank accounts couldn't be accessed by their owners. So we got stuck, and he could escape. And yet we survived, and he didn't. This story moves in circles, and the more of it I tell, the less it makes sense.

Anyway, my father came home from prison. We had had to move in the meantime and now stayed in the house of my deceased grandparents, where we shared an apartment with my mother's uncle and aunt. It was 1940 and the war had started, though I don't remember the outbreak as a special event. I do remember the day the Germans invaded Czechoslovakia, almost exactly a year after they took over our little country. But that wasn't the beginning of war, since the Allies didn't honor their commitment to the Czechs. Cousin Heinz came running up to my mother full of the joyful excitement that children feel when they are the carriers of bad news that is not their fault. It gives them a sense of unaccustomed power to be able to upset the grown-ups, and my mother, with her son in Prague, must have been amply upset. The adults spoke of an impending war, but later when I remarked, "When the war comes . . . ," I was informed that the war was already with us, and I was ashamed to have spoken like a little dummy. The invasion of

Czechoslovakia overshadows the onset of war in my mind, because I couldn't imagine what war was like, except that it involved fighting, and there was no fighting where I lived. On the other hand, I could very well imagine that the Germans had now reached Schorschi, too. The grown-ups had told me that Papa, who was in jail, had had to go on a trip, but that didn't seem plausible. I had ears, so I guessed and wondered. You couldn't trust them: they insisted that children speak the truth, even about trivia, but they themselves lied without batting an eyelash, even about drastic matters like my father's whereabouts. The official lie I was given prevented me from gathering information by asking urgent questions; later my father's return made the matter a moot issue, without explanation, let alone an apology on their part.

There was a big luncheon, lots of family, and I had been allowed to invite my best friend to show her my newly released father. He was talking, and everyone was listening to him; he was the center of attention, and I wanted to be noticed by him, contact him, probably be reassured about the abrupt changes in our lives. All it got me was a thrashing such as I had never had before, in front of my wide-eyed friend—the humiliation of it!—and being banished from the family table. To this day I don't know why or how I made him so mad, and to this day I would like to know and make up for it. But that was not to be: it's my last impression of him, forever connected with terror, violence, injustice, and the deep regret of having been misunderstood. Again these incorrigible memories. So he mistreated his child for once, at a time of crisis, but a lot of parents do that. The problem is that there was nothing more to come. It's as if I resent his death because it deprived me of a chance for reconciliation. As if his uncompleted life had had no other purpose than to be patient with the demands of an eight-year-old, or to listen to the carefully prepared explanations and apologies of the teenager or the adult she turned into.

In prison he had learned one of the camp songs, the so-called "Buchenwaldlied." The lyrics translate roughly, "Buchenwald, I can't forget you, because you are my destiny. Anyone who has entered here becomes conscious of the wonders of freedom." It is a famous song, but the lyrics are not very good. No great poetry was composed in the concentration camps. If it were not so, one might entertain the idea that the camps were good for something, that they were, for example, a kind of catharsis, producing fine art. In fact, they weren't good for anything. Of course, right away I memorized the words of the song.

My father put off his farewell for a couple of days, as long as he could.

One evening he stood before my bed as I was about to go to sleep and said good-bye. I was still under the impression of the punishment I had received and couldn't imagine that he didn't, in truth, look forward to leaving me. I was afraid of him—not for him. In the second photo I have, he looks as he did on that last evening: serious, his hair a little thinned out, around the temples the first signs of baldness—but he didn't live long enough to go bald. I never saw him again.

My mother took him to the train station. She says: "He stood at the open window of the compartment and yelled, 'Alma, Alma, board the train, as you are, you and the child, now, or we won't see each other again.'" That can't be right, since I was at home in bed. As she got old, she forgot or invented. But it is true that I would have liked to come along to the station. And I thought, if he wanted to, he could take me along. But he doesn't want to, because I've had been a bad girl and would be in the way. There had been talk that he could take me on his passport. I had forgotten or repressed that idea, but decades later my mother confirmed it. "Viktor had you on his passport and wanted to take you." So why didn't he? Either she didn't want to let me go, or he didn't want to have me along. What other possibilities are there? And then I wasn't even permitted to come along to the station. Because it was nighttime, and children mustn't be up so late. A lame excuse. Maybe my mother was afraid he and I would leave together at the last moment. Instead I was in bed, yet another kind of prison, where one had to go if anything exciting happened. And I thought with tears of resentment how they'd refused all my wishes—even simple, modest wishes they had rejected—and I never knew beforehand when they'd say no.

My mother thought of her second husband as a weak, sensitive man. I see him as a person of absolute and yet phony authority, a tyrant with great charisma who was no last resort, for he didn't return. For me he is ambiguous: angry and impenetrable, then again funny and easygoing, and in all questions my oracle. His love of life and his ability to seize the day. His laugh: I can still hear it. He could shake with laughter. Sometimes I laugh like that, a belly laugh, very unfeminine, people say. But like my father's daughter.

If I could only have appropriated my mother's memory to flesh out the fragments I possess and thus reach back to my own beginnings. Or if she had only been more truthful. But she bent the world to her needs, the needs of her disturbed ego. And still I kept asking and asking the old woman, who had been alive for nearly thirty years before I was born. The walls of those early years: if I could only see what truly haunted her, not merely what she permitted to surface. If one could peek into the inner chambers of another person's mind, and reach behind what has been smoothed out and retouched and cosmeticized, behind those word pictures that dissolve the grainy resistance of what happened until it's unrecognizable in the retelling. Her picture of him seemed all of a piece, puppetlike, while mine has too many facets. She knew him well; I hardly knew him. And so he is merely an unmovable object in my mental household, by now drenched in the floods of later events, like a piece of rotting furniture which cannot be pushed aside and certainly can't be tossed out.

Yet once when she was in her eighties and still made a little sense now and then, we were talking on the telephone, both of us having a hard time because she wouldn't wear her hearing aid, and suddenly she says my father often claimed that he had no elbows, he wasn't pushy, he couldn't stand up for himself. Of course she had a whole attic full of memories of him, but the attic was locked to me. I stood outside and didn't know how to make her tell me more. I used to try, not just with her but with others who had known him—friends or supposed friends, and his relatives here in the U.S. But nothing came of it. Either they didn't understand the need of the orphan to know her origins, or maybe they resented this need. Or they simply didn't know how to talk about him, how to tell something, anything. So I picked up snippets like the one about the elbows. It sounds right, a piece from the jigsaw puzzle of truth. Out of the blue this detail.

For there is the mystery of the gas chambers. I couldn't face having my father die in a gas chamber. I wrote poems about his death. They had lines like

> My father drowned in every sea,
> Yet lifts his head at break of day
> Above the flood of memory.
>
> Oceans I crossed, yet cannot flee,
> For here in San Francisco Bay
> My father drowns in every sea.
>
> He turns his salt-washed face to me,
> The sockets of his eyes are gray
> Above the flood of memory.

And so on. Of course these were meant to be symbolic oceans, but they still sound more like echoes of Dylan Thomas, wanting his father not to go gentle into that good night, than of the Holocaust.

My father went first from Austria to Italy. And there he made the mistake of fleeing from a fascist country to a democracy, that is, to France. The Italians were much less prone to interfere with Jewish refugees than the French were, and in fact one of his brothers survived in Italy, for the Italians have a healthy disrespect for government. The French have only recently begun to remember how they collaborated with the Nazis; it was in France that my father was handed over to the Germans. After the war we learned that in 1944 he was transported from Drancy, the notorious holding camp for Jewish refugees, to Auschwitz, where he was presumably sent straight from the ramp to his death. But I stubbornly rejected that thought by fantasizing that he committed suicide on the train, for wasn't he a doctor with access to suicide pills? It took me half a life and more to come to the obvious conclusion that this is pure wish fulfillment. My German and English poems for him were a kind of exorcism, to gloss over the fact that he didn't drown in every, or even in any, sea, but was made to breathe poison in a cramped room full of people. The symbolic claptrap was a kind of security blanket, for since we have researched everything about the fate of the victims, we know how they died in the gas chambers. The strong climbed on top of the weak in that last agony, as they choked. So the men were always on top when they pulled out the corpses, and the women and children at the bottom.

That is what came to mind when I heard that he liked to say he had no elbows: the question of whether he trampled on those who were weaker. My father did this? On kids like me, when he died? Perhaps he didn't, since he had no elbows. But do you have a choice, or have you reached the limits of freedom, when you are choking on poison gas? These are the questions I cannot answer and cannot shed.

6

I had written the above account of my father's life and his death and my ongoing reaction, and how I feel that it's an ongoing story. It was published in German, translated into French, and a Frenchwoman read it. As if to prove how ongoing these stories, these deaths, really are, just as I finish translating my lament for him into English, she e-mails me that she has the list of names from my father's transport out of Drancy, transport number seventy-three of a total of seventy-nine. It was nine hundred men, and they didn't go to Auschwitz, but to Lithuania and Estonia, and who knows how they were murdered. The historians have paid little attention to this transport, though they acknowledge that it took place. She has his birthdate—it was on the list of deportees. She has edited a book which she distributes on her own, called *Nous sommes 900 Français*.

I should be relieved that he didn't die that ultimate nightmare of a death, in a crowded gas chamber, that it was a different, and perhaps a slightly lesser, nightmare. But now my mental furniture has to be rearranged, and it feels as if I am running through my house in the dark, bumping into things. How *did* he die then? I know so little about who he was, and now I don't even know this final, inalterable fact.

These stories have no end. As long as we live and care, they have no end. Why did they send these men to the Baltic states? It makes no sense—as if anything the Nazis did made much sense.

So here are the two versions, the one with which I have lived for more than half a century, and the other still new and undigested.

7

Vienna was settled early by the Romans and has had a vibrant history, embellished by folklore and extending over two thousand years. The Romans called it Vindobona, a name I associated in childhood with a thriving café. (Did the Romans enjoy their coffee there, or whatever they drank? I used to wonder.) The Danube, the surrounding mountains, and even ordinary houses in the city, provided they have a venerable age, are crawling with supernatural creatures, whose stories found their way into our school books. Learning to read was like eating candy. In comparison, the local history that my boys learned in California's grade schools seemed so much less interesting. (Even the Indian lore they were taught was about Spanish missions, that is, white expansion and colonialism.)

We were meant to become good, patriotic little Austrians, and so in first grade we learned a song celebrating the martyrdom of Chancellor Dollfuss, who had preceded the present chancellor, Schuschnigg, and who had been murdered by a Nazi, one fascist in effect killing another fascist. The song had a very short life, since in March of my first school year we were invaded, a happy-making event to a large portion of the citizenry. Schuschnigg, who had tried to resist Hitler, escaped to America, where he had nothing more serious to endure than the picketing of disapproving Jewish groups. Meanwhile I had to pack up as best I could my budding love of country, the country that had been renamed Ostmark, meaning "eastern border country," while its true name, Österreich, means "eastern empire."

The school principal came to our class, told us that we now had to use the Hitler greeting, and raised his right arm to show us how it was done—only the Jewish children weren't to use it. The class dutifully imitated him, while we five or six Jewish kids got to sit in back. Because the principal was friendly and the teacher visibly embarrassed, I was unsure at first—such is the touching optimism of the young—whether our special status was a privilege or an insult. After all, the grown-ups knew that Austria had been unjustly overpowered, and surely not all of them were Nazis.

In arts and crafts class the other girls learned how to cut and glue swastikas from colored paper. The Jewish girls were allowed to cut and paste what they liked, which was and wasn't like free playtime. One tried to enjoy it, but one didn't. On and off, Aryan girls would come over and let us admire their handiwork. They asked us to criticize and compare. It was only reasonable that this state of things couldn't continue: we were thrown out of school and went to a new one, just for Jewish children.

I have heard a Jewish woman who is about my age tell how she first experienced the Nazis in Vienna. It was the sandbox, she says. She was playing in the sandbox, and one of the Aryan mothers simply threw her out. She thought at first it was a new game and promptly piled back in. The "game" was repeated. After the third time she understood. Jewish children are notoriously good learners. But what, I wonder, went on in the head of the woman who did this? And yet being thrown out of our sandbox for no apparent reason by the parents of the other kids—that was the quintessential experience of my generation of preschoolers and first graders in Hitler's Vienna.

I had been very receptive to a nascent patriotism, and I loved all of my city's old stories. There was the river nymph in the Danube and the monstrous Viennese basilisk, which could kill you with a glance. There was the defeat of the Turks, who lay siege to Vienna in the seventeenth century. In triumph the bakers created the crescent-moon-shaped rolls which we called *Kipferl* and which the French took over as croissants. Even better was the story about Drunken August, who lived at the time of the Great Plague and wasn't scared but got drunk every night after entertaining the crowd with his bagpipe. One night when he was stumbling home, he fell into an open grave, full of corpses. He slept until morning and crawled out of this deadly ditch bright-eyed and not infected. A possible patron saint of the deported who returned, indestructible, lovable, and a little contemptible in the view of those who never got close to the plague of our time. But Jews have no patron saints.

Now that my tentative faith in my homeland was being damaged by daily increments beyond repair, I became Jewish in defense. Shortly before I turned seven years old, during the first week of the German occupation, I changed my first name. I had been called Susi, a middle name, but now I wanted the other name, my first name, the Biblical name. Why do I have it if I can't use it? I thought, and under the circumstances only a Jewish name would do. Nobody pointed out to me that Susanna is as much a part of Holy Scripture as Ruth is. Bible reading wasn't a pastime of ours. I tenaciously corrected the grown-ups when they used my old name, and miraculously they gave in, with either a smile or a frown—it didn't matter which, as long as I got what I wanted. It was the first time that I achieved something through sheer, dogged stubbornness, and so I got my proper name not even knowing then how right it was for me, that it means "friend" and belonged to the woman who left her country because friendship meant more to her than kinship. For Ruth the Moabite emigrated not because of her faith, but because of another woman, her mother-in-law, Naomi. She was loyal to a person who was not a beloved or betrothed male, though her "Whither thou goest, I shall go" is often misappropriated to that context. Hers was a freely chosen loyalty, beyond the limits of community and gender, from woman to woman. (No male theologian is going to rob me of my friendly namesake. I'll trade you the Book of Esther and throw in Maccabees. Those are stories I don't need, fables of tribal victory through sex and violence.)

Only my father's mother continued to call me Susi until the end of her life. She died in Theresienstadt, with not one of her nine children with her. Only her daughter-in-law was there, the spoiled child of wealth, my mother, who did everything she could to ease the misery of that death. The others had emigrated with clear consciences, firmly believing that nobody would hurt an old woman. Or a child, like her youngest granddaughter, Susi.

The first death I witnessed had been that of my grandfather's talking parrot. Her name was Laura, and I had always known her. She was no ordinary bird, but a confirmed member of the *mishpokhe* and a primordial creature, because her existence stretched back before memory began. She was killed in my presence by an overbred, neurotic wirehaired Scottish terrier, who had bitten me once from jealousy and now wreaked his vengeance on poor Laura, probably from the same motive, since she was popular with us children. The adults screamed and gestured and ordered the dog to drop the bird. Instead he dragged her under a sofa and wouldn't let go of his squealing victim until she was a heap of bloody feathers. I stood in the doorway and yelled.

We were emancipated, but not assimilated. The difference may seem hairsplitting, but to us it mattered. On Yom Kippur, a day of mourning and repentance, the grown-ups ate and drank nothing from dusk to dawn. Thus being grown-up was equivalent to having permission to fast once a year. Once I am thirteen, I may join them. Ten days before Yom Kippur was Rosh Hashanah, or New Year, when we celebrated the creation of the world. It was an exceptional day warranting an exceptional visit to the synagogue. I sat upstairs with the women, listened to the men below praying in a language I didn't understand, and was bored out of my wits. At home we ate pork and ham—but do me a favor and don't eat ham on matzoh in front of people who may be offended by this delicious combination. This humorous request of my father's or grandfather's was meant to instruct us about the existence of a certain variety of Jews and was received with appreciative giggles. Matzoh, the unleavened Easter bread, was good to eat once a year, but unlike the Orthodox, we didn't banish bread from our kitchen during the Passover week. We were of the opinion that the dietary laws weren't valid for us, that they hailed from a time and country where some foods were dangerous to eat. Hygienic measures imposed by Moses, the enlightened prophet, but nonsense today. See, we have always been an enlightened people.

So now I tried to become more Jewish, but how? What did it mean to be Jewish? In Austria public schools provided religious instruction, and I had been enrolled in first grade as a member of the "Mosaic" religion. I didn't know that word. But I did have a mosaic among my toys. No, no, no, little dummy, Mosaic has nothing to do with mosaic; it's got to do with Moses, the great lawmaker of our early enlightenment. No wonder the word was unknown to me. It was a euphemism, as if the word *Jewish* had been defiled by anti-Semitic venom. Our lessons in religion were a lot of fun. A dear old gentlemen told us Bible stories, and sometimes he let us act them out. We did Adam and Eve, and believe it or not, I was God. I stood between the blackboard and the wall in order to be invisible and told the first couple that they had sinned. When I described the scene at home, the whole household cracked up. (Sixty-two years later I am still smiling with glee, as memory spotlights that classroom.)

In December 1938 our maid must still have been with us, for she gave me a piece of candy from her little Christmas tree. She was soon to leave us because, as an Aryan, she wasn't allowed to work for Jews. When I found out where this present came from, I ostentatiously spat it out. Nothing Christian should touch my pure Jewish lips. But then I noticed that I had hurt the feelings of a person I liked a lot and was mortified and confused. I had wanted to make a point, perform a symbolic action, and learned that symbols are as volatile as weather vanes and point in every direction, depending on how the wind blows. I almost asked her for a second sweet to make up for the irretrievable first piece, which had been flushed down the toilet by my self-righteous, seven-year-old self. But that atonement would have required more humility than I had in me. I was left with the discomfort of a first discovery of the principle of moral ambivalence.

8

I must confess that my Jewishness is really nothing to be proud of. I can't remember a single religious celebration that I honestly enjoyed. I am thinking chiefly of Passover in Vienna and those ritual seder meals. Actually this celebration, which is so weighted with poetic and historical significance, was very timely, since it commemorates the salvation of the people through flight and exodus. Passover is an imaginative feast and appealed to a little girl who loved poetry, for it combines true events with fables and folklore and song and a table laden with carefully chosen foods. Even a modest seder is a thing of beauty. But in truth, it is all these good things for men and children, and scarcely for women.

Not even an inexperienced child, provided she was female, could overlook the gender diffe rence on this day of glory. The women in the family stood all day in the smelly, overheated kitchen to prepare the dishes without their usual household help, those dishes which the oldest uncle would then ceremoniously use for his interpretation of the end of our exile.

Naturally the aunts who did the cooking weren't usually in a good mood or even accessible. At one seder celebration my mother's sister cried with her arms on the table and her head on her arms. There were thirteen of us, and she was superstitious. My brother, visibly upset: "You have to lean back, not forward, Aunt. That's the law." My father gets up, takes his hat and leaves the house so that there'll be only twelve, and his sister-in-law can stop crying. Perhaps she had meant him to leave, or maybe he was glad to have the opportunity. Family antagonisms don't disappear on the High Holidays. Among those left at table, general consternation.

During another seder I clashed with an older cousin. Now that I could read, I was sure that it was my turn to ask the central question of the evening, a privilege of the youngest person present: "Why is this night different from all other nights?" I could even say this important sentence in Hebrew.

But I was only the youngest girl, and the next oldest child was a boy. (We have met him. He is the one who was to survive in Hungary.) Heinz insisted on his male prerogative, but I didn't give in, and we quarreled fiercely, each convinced that our cause was just. Finally one of the grown-ups said: "Leave her be, if she wants to say the *maneshtane*. You are a big boy, shame on you." The prayer book of the evening, the holy Haggadah, came sailing in my direction across the table, tossed by my angry cousin. I had won, but the pleasure of taking part in a meaningful ritual had been drained out of this victory.

And what is the answer to the question that was such an honor to ask and worth fighting for? How indeed was the night different from all other nights? God saved us, is the answer; he took care of his people. The analogy to the twentieth century didn't hold up in the event, and what little I had been taught of a Jewish faith in a Jewish God crumbled in the course of the years that ensued. I would have become an agnostic anyway, but the Nazis added to my disappointment the feeling of having grasped a rotten plank during a shipwreck.

9

In 1940, when I was eight or nine, the local movie theater showed Walt Disney's *Snow White*. I loved movies. I had been weaned on Mickey Mouse shorts and traded pictures of Shirley Temple with classmates. I badly wanted to see this film, but since I was Jewish, I naturally wasn't permitted to. I groused and bitched about this unfairness, until finally my mother proposed that I should leave her alone and just go and forget about what was permitted and what wasn't.

I hesitated a bit at this unexpected go-ahead, for it was a Sunday, we were known in the neighborhood, and to go to a movie right there in broad daylight was a kind of dare. My mother couldn't accept the absurdity of blatant discrimination. She assured me that no one would care who sat in an audience of children. I shouldn't think I was that important, and I should stop being a coward, because she was never a coward, not even when she was my age. So of course I went, not only for the movie, but to prove myself. I bought the most expensive type of ticket, thinking that sitting in a loge would make me less noticeable, and thus I ended up next to the nineteen-year-old baker's daughter from next door with her little siblings, enthusiastic Nazis one and all.

I sweated it out for the next ninety minutes and have never before or afterwards understood so little of what happened on the screen. All I could think of was whether the baker's daughter was really glaring at me, or if I was only imagining it. The wicked queen of the film merged with my neighbor, her fairy-tale malice a poor imitation of the real thing, and it was I, and no innocent princess, who was lost in the woods, offered poisoned apples, and in fear of glass coffins.

Why didn't I get up and walk out? Perhaps in order not to face my mother, or because any move might attract attention. Perhaps merely because one doesn't leave a theater before the film is over, or most likely, because this solution didn't occur to me, frightened as I was. Consider that I still wonder why my people didn't leave Vienna in time—and perhaps there is a family resemblance between that question and why I stayed glued to my seat.

When the lights came on, I wanted to wait until the house had emptied out, but my enemy stood her ground and waited, too. She told her little brothers to hush and fixed me sternly. There I was, trapped, as I had surmised. The baker's daughter put on her gloves and coat and finally addressed me.

She spoke firmly and with conviction, in the manner of a member of the *Bund deutscher Mädchen*, the female branch of the Hitler Youth, to which she surely belonged. Hadn't I seen the sign at the box office? (I nodded, what else could I do? It was a rhetorical question.) Didn't I know what it meant? I could read, couldn't I? It said "No Jews." I had broken a law. She was using her best High German—none of Vienna's easygoing dialect for this patriotic occasion. If it happened again she would call the police. I was lucky that she was letting me off this once.

The story of Snow White can be reduced to one question: who is entitled to live in the king's palace and who is the outsider. The baker's daughter and I followed this formula. She, in her own house, the magic mirror of her racial purity before her eyes, and I, also at home here, a native, but without permission and at this moment expelled and exposed. Even though I despised the law that excluded me, I still felt ashamed to have been found out. For shame doesn't arise from the shameful action, but from discovery and exposure. If I had got away with my transgression, I would have been proud of my daring. But I had been unmasked. W. B. Yeats writes of a man "among his enemies":

> How in the name of Heaven can he escape
> That defiling and disfigured shape
> The mirror of malicious eyes
> Casts upon his eyes until at last
> He thinks that shape must be his shape?

The common lot of the outcast is self-contempt. I might have felt better had I known this poem, which I committed to memory some ten years later.

It was over pretty soon. The girl had asserted the superiority of her Germanic forefathers as opposed to the vermin race I belonged to, and there was nothing more to say. I was in a state of shock. This was new and terrible. Tears welled up, but I held them back. The usher, an older woman, helped me into my coat and handed me my purse, which I was about to leave on the seat. She was sorry for me and said a few soothing words. I nodded, incapable of answering because I was choking on my tears of humiliation, but grateful for this bit of kindness, these alms for the poor.

It was still light outside, so I walked at random through the streets of my neighborhood in a daze. I had found out, for myself and by myself, how things stood between us and the Nazis and had paid for knowledge with the coin of pain. To be sure, I was overreacting to a minor incident, but that didn't change the fact that now I knew. I had had the feeling of deadly danger, and this feeling didn't leave me but escalated until it was justified. Without having to think it through, from now on I was ahead of the grown-ups.

I came home crying and furious, blaming my mother for what seemed a near catastrophe. She shrugged her shoulders. Who would think of bothering a child watching a fairy tale? To my exasperation, she acted as if what had happened hadn't happened, because it oughtn't to have happened. And even if it did, she implied, don't get upset. There are worse things. But that was exactly the problem. Wasn't this bad enough? Hadn't I almost been arrested? What were the worse things? How was I to learn the priorities of danger? It was easy for my mother, who presumably knew where you drown and where you can still barely tread water. But I didn't know and wanted explanations, instructions, directives. What was the worst, and could it be something other than death? Later I realized that the grown-ups around me didn't know much themselves, that they were entirely flummoxed by the turn of events, and that, in fact, I was learning faster than they. I got the impression that I shouldn't trust my mother, that she had only bad advice for me. This impression was wrong. Like other people's advice, my mother's varied between good, bad, and indifferent. Sometimes its source was paranoia, sometimes reason and evidence. Goodwill or malice might be part of it. Mostly, however, it came from an undifferentiated instinct, a mixture of unexamined experiences, a bubbling stew of indistinguishable thoughts and emotions. Some years later, in 1944, when she happened to be right, my lack of confidence in her, dating from that afternoon at the movies, almost cost me my life.

10

As of September 1941 we had to wear the yellow Star of David, the infamous *Judenstern*. I tend to think it was earlier, because discrimination was already rampant, both the legal kind and the joyous popular sort, and I have to check the history books to make sure I have the date right. I can't say that I was unhappy about that star. Under the circumstances it seemed appropriate. Let them see who we were, different and chosen.

We had to buy the yellow patches at the Jewish Community Center. The Nazis made a profit wherever they could, exhibiting a cynical commercialism that was identical to the vices they professed to see as typically Jewish. Wherever they could make a dishonest penny, they pocketed it, even if it was just the ten pfennig for each yellow Jewish patch they forced us to wear.

My mother came home with ten pieces and quickly sewed them onto our coats, jackets, and whatever we wore on the street. I watched her disdainful expression, which I admired and tried to imitate when it was directed against our enemies, but which drove me to despair when she belittled my friends or the things I thought beautiful, such as Friedrich Schiller's eighteenth-century blank verse.

We went out together, apprehensive of how people would react and on the lookout for other Stars of David. There were plenty, a new street life. One Jewish woman said quickly to my mother in passing: "It goes well with your blouse." I thought the remark plucky and witty; my mother could have done without it.

One day when I was standing in a subway car, I felt someone touch my hand as we were going through a tunnel. My first thought was, a man who wants to molest me; my second, a pickpocket. So I clutched my wallet. But no, this man pressed something into my hand, a gift. He wanted to show his pity for me, the child with the Jew star. I understood. To give gifts to Jews was forbidden. Those who did it were publicly branded as *Volksfeinde*, enemies of the people. That's why he had waited until we were in the tunnel. The gift was an orange. By the time we were back in daylight, I had stowed it in my bag and gratefully looked up at the stranger, who looked down on me with a benevolent smile. But my feelings were mixed, as in the case of the sweet from the maid's Christmas tree. I didn't like the role of the passive victim who could be comforted with small demonstrations of kindness. I wanted an assertive, oppositional role, at least in my thoughts. An orange, no matter what it stood for, was no help as my life became progressively more restricted and impoverished. It was a sentimental gesture, and I was a prop for the donor's good intentions. The piece of fruit was somewhat less useful than the comforting words of the lady usher at the movie theater. But I would have caused the giver embarrassment and perhaps got him into trouble if I had refused his charity in the crowded streetcar, if, for example, I had said loud and clear: "Take it back. Your gift is a cop-out." An unthinkable reaction.

That is how I explained the case to my mother when I came home with my unwanted orange and my story. But she was more radical: "What got into you to take presents from a stranger in a streetcar? Are we beggars? Don't you get enough to eat?" But hadn't I been in a quandary? Not to her mind, I hadn't. I met the familiar look in her eyes—rigid, vacuous—which meant that she had found a free run for her accumulated anxiety and rage. I was helpless before this moral double bind: my mother's disapproval, the stranger's goodwill. Should I have endangered him or made him look ridiculous? At the same time, admit it: didn't you enjoy the adventure, the game of conspiracy, the scene in which you skillfully played the role of grateful Jewish girl?

11

I could read as much as I liked, because with a book I wasn't a nuisance. Sometimes the grown-ups saw my addiction to books as a sign of intelligence, sometimes as just a bad habit. Once I got hold of a Bible in order to read the story of Ruth. I had just gotten to the part where my namesake uncovers Boaz's feet and wanted to ask my great-uncle—the one who presided at seder—how to interpret that strange scene. Instead he took the book from me. It was a holy book, not for entertainment. I tried to explain that I had all due respect for its holiness and only wanted to learn about my name, humbly and reverentially. If I had been a boy, he would have treated me differently, that I was sure of. Boys had to study for their bar mitzvah, their confirmation, and it was to their credit if they voluntarily read the Bible. But girls did not need that; they only used books to pass the time. My father, I figured, would have let me have the Bible—he had given me the book of Jewish legends—but he wasn't here anymore. I felt I had been unjustly treated, and I sulked.

This incident is fairly typical of how I fared with my reading. I deliberately tried to avoid forbidden books, or those that might be forbidden, because I hated to give up something I had started reading. And since it was mostly modern novels that were considered unsuitable, I came to the conclusion that colorful, attractive covers were for adults, and the monochrome volumes of the German classics were for children. The classics could easily be gotten: they stood on the bookshelves of every middle-class household, sometimes behind glass in cases with keys, but one could ask for them, because they were considered good for you, like cod-liver oil. They were difficult, but I had nothing else to do and got the hang of their language with much patience and some guessing. It was an odd kind of autodidactic training in syntax and logic, but it was a fair substitute for the regular schooling I wasn't getting.

There was, however, one kind of forbidden literature that I found irresistible, and that was Nazi publications. They were hard to get hold of, and paradoxically, equally hard to avoid. The political pornography of the *Stürmer*, for instance, a propaganda rag that featured lecherous Jews and their unspeakable sins, didn't merely enjoy a large circulation, but full pages of it were on exhibit on the street corners in special cages behind wire netting. That way no one could steal this precious prose. The educated classes professed to despise the *Stürmer*, but there is no denying that it flourished. I was powerfully attracted to its exuberant slime, wondering from week to week what the next outrage would be. I read with astonishment that the simplicity of Jewish burial rites (a plain coffin or just a sheet, so that the body can return to the earth from which it came) was due to Jewish avarice and to our dirty habits. The Decalogue, according to the *Stürmer*, was a list of such obvious moral commandments that only a deeply corrupt people needed to have them in writing. The Germanic tribes knew instinctively that you shouldn't kill, steal, or lie. The photographed faces of men who had committed the abhorrent crime of miscegenation looked like my uncles' faces, only a little more frightened, and I tried in vain to recreate a point of view that would have detected evil in their homely, trustworthy features.

In spite of the unforgotten terror of my first illegal movie experience, the cinema was a magnet, and on occasion I would simply go to a film without wearing the star. I didn't tell my mother and carefully chose theaters in the busy inner city, where no one would know me. The movies I wanted to see were Nazi propaganda films, which gave me the satisfaction of a double defiance: I was thwarting both the discriminatory laws of the state and the rules of my family, who had never permitted me to listen to a speech by Hitler on the radio, in spite of my argument that we needed to know "what we were up against." As if we don't know, was the irrefutable answer.

These films taught me the dominant ideology, which concerned me, I reasoned, and which I couldn't just ignore because it wasn't palatable. The attraction lay in the critical distance I had to maintain, the resistance against any temptation to identify or agree. I saw *Jud Süss*, a historical film with pretty costumes and ugly Jews; another film about German athletic prowess, with lovely horses and daring men, animals and humans in the service of the fatherland; and two films about Germans in Africa. One dealt with the Boer War: the Afrikaners had the souls of Germans, and the British were moneygrubbing capitalists. The other, which impressed me more, was set in the 1880s and dealt with the short-lived German colony in East Africa. The representative of German power was named Carl Peters (who was historically a particularly obnoxious type), and in a central scene he stood in his lily-white suit, whip in hand, in front of a group of barely clad and cringing black natives. You have to remember that it was decades before violence, realistically acted out, became part and parcel of common movie fare. In those days the symbols of brutality had a disturbing effect, which vibrated among the audience. They must have inspired the boys who were watching in their short pants and their Hitler Youth daggers (or bread knives with motto), just as they appalled the Jew girl with vague premonitions. That is, I felt personally threatened by the whip, the boots, and the racist black-white confrontation in black-and-white. I call up this remembered image from the flickering screen as meaningful background to my later experience of a power structure that involved real men with boots and whips, for the film tried to make sense of it—to which I could oppose my contrary sense—whereas the reality was clumsy chaos.

12

It should be obvious by now that these pages hardly deal with the Nazis. I didn't know any Nazis, but I knew the difficult, neurotic people whom they oppressed, families who hadn't had ideal lives anymore than their Christian neighbors had. When I tell people that my mother worried about my father's possible love affairs while he was a refugee in France, and that my parents had not been a harmonious couple in their last year together, or that my mother and her sister literally tore each other's hair in my presence, so that their aunt, my great-aunt Irene, threw herself between her nieces to separate them, or that I feel no compunction about citing examples of my mother's petty cruelties towards me, my hearers act surprised, assume a stance of virtuous indignation, and tell me that, given the hardships we had to endure during the Hitler period, the victims should have come closer together and formed strong bonds. Particularly young people should have done so, say the elderly. But this is sentimental rubbish and depends on a false concept of suffering as a source of moral education. In our heart of hearts, we all know the reality: the more we have to put up with, the less tolerant we get and the texture of family relations becomes progressively more threadbare. During an earthquake, more china gets broken than at other times.

I often wonder at the spontaneous intimacy I see in the families of my younger friends and envy them a bit. I didn't become an overtly affectionate mother, probably because I was revolted by my own mother's intrusive possessiveness, which would alternate with unforeseeable punishments and reprimands. It wasn't she whom I learned to trust, but my nanny, whom I called Anya, and whom I loved dearly. She was young and funny and never laid a guilt trip on you. I can still see her putting on a pair of silk stockings in preparation for going out with her boyfriend, Egon, and I watch her and hope that I, too, will grow up to have long, smooth legs like my Anya. Unlike my mother, she was never suspicious or thought I was lying. I remember walking with her in the country and her devout expression as she crossed herself before a crucifix. I watch her, curious, trying to understand this unusual behavior. Among my few olfactory memories is an association of Anya with cyclamen, the mountain violet.

Again, this is all. She couldn't stay with us because of the Nuremberg laws, but she visited us once, months later. I jumped with joy like a puppy, wanting to be held and cuddled: my very own Anya. My mother was embarrassed, or perhaps jealous of this display, which the young woman took for granted. I don't know what became of her. Probably she was sucked into the Nazi "Movement." I can't look for her because I don't know her real name, and I wouldn't know whom to ask, since for my mother she was simply an employee of long ago.

For in the beginning I didn't see much of my mother. I had to be careful not to bother her when she was taking a nap, and she made me wear uncomfortable clothes: woolen underwear, which felt like hair shirts; cute little dresses, which mustn't get dirty or wrinkled; and worst of all, heavy boots with laces, which absolutely never fit and made your feet sweat. I noticed that *she* didn't wear such underwear or shoes, but nice things in which she moved gracefully, and I looked forward to the day when I could do likewise. If my face was dirty, she spat on a handkerchief and rubbed my cheek with it. That was revolting: it made me want to puke and I would loudly protest, but to no avail. Once I cut up a handbag of hers out of sheer spite, because I was so mad at her. I wasn't even six then, and wasn't supposed to touch the scissors I used in this act of revolt.

And then there were my mother's birthdays: she expected presents, but any giver of gifts acquires in the act a certain authority, or at least there is a claim of equality when inferiors or dependents give gifts. If you reject a gift, it means that you won't make any concessions. My mother demanded that we solemnly acknowledge her birthdays, but then she reacted with exaggeration to her presents, often without having looked at them. She made it clear that she didn't so much enjoy the carefully chosen gift, as she wanted us to know that her ostentatious thanks were a gift on her part. Even my birthday poems for her were insufficiently admired, I felt, for she didn't feed my authorial pride by commenting on them.

This pattern never changed. Whenever I bought her something to wear, it was the wrong color or size, which she wouldn't tell me soon enough to exchange it; instead of flowers, she would want candy on Mother's Day, or the other way around, no telling in advance which. But she had to get *some* presents, or she would be hurt. I have to add in fairness that I am no better: her gifts were impossible, and I used to pass them on to the Salvation Army, especially those she made herself. Formal occasions for giving, like those ill-fated birthdays, can be a source of conflict which one can only escape by rejecting both gift and occasion. In our case, the symptoms of this flourishing mother-daughter neurosis were textbook-perfect, and it's amazing that not only the neurosis itself, but the symptoms go back so far. Yet this awareness was of little help. Freud was an optimist.

13

With the increasing isolation of the few Jews left in Vienna, my mother became dependent on me for companionship and tortured me with her anxieties. She alluded to the suicide attempts of unnamed women; she talked about fatal illnesses and the imagined destination of the ever more frequent transports of deportees. I didn't know what to believe, let alone how to cope with these veiled threats to my existence. Out there was a deadly secret, but I could only suspect, not fathom, what it was.

I was like a young dog without exercise, and she tried to keep me from the few games which were left. We were allowed to use the library and recreation room of the Jewish Community Center, and the Jewish cemetery was our park and playground. When I came home to our cramped quarters from a rare outing with other Jewish kids, happy and exhausted from running around in the open air, she'd paint the specter of deadly pneumonia, which I was very likely to have caught, she said. She persuaded me that I had flat feet (I don't) and massaged my soles to prevent a future limp. My mother would have been an admirable nurse for an invalid child. She confessed that she sometimes dreamt of sitting beside a bedridden daughter. Apparently it was not a disturbing dream. Psychiatric jargon speaks of castration when the hapless subjects are sons. The term is one-sided and therefore harmful, for it excludes the possibility that daughters can be just as much incapacitated and stunted by their mothers' maneuvers.

When I embraced my mother too vigorously at the end of a lonely day, she would assure me that I had just then almost strangled her, and that the hand of a child who has hurt her mother, even though inadvertently, grows out of the grave for all to see. She told me so much nonsense that I ceased to believe anything she told me. By insisting what a brave child she had been, she tried to make me timid and fearful. For a while she succeeded, but I became more and more alienated from her. She claimed to have gotten the better of six boys in a fistfight as a girl, and I was much relieved when a friend of hers discounted the credibility of that story with a smile, because my only impulse when Aryan boys taunted me on the street was to run away.

There was nothing that she hadn't done better than I, and my only recourse was to doubt her word. As a little girl she had written both stories and poems, but when I asked to see some, none had survived. She had composed her poems very quickly, she said. She must have worked much faster than I did, I had to admit, for she needed only half an hour per poem, while a single stanza sometimes took me whole days. And my lack of knowledge, compared to all the things she knew when she was my age! I stopped asking her for help to avoid these put-downs. She would often slap me or kiss me from sheer nervousness, simply because I was there.

14

My first two homes were bright and sunny, but after we had to leave my grandparents' house, we lived in two dark apartments which we shared with a couple of other Jewish families. My mother and I had a small room, which got its only light from an inner courtyard. I picture sadistic architects designing these holes deliberately to exclude the daylight in spite of existent windows. There were bedbugs. You turn out the light and imagine the bugs crawling out of the mattresses. Then you get bitten and turn on the light and complain bitterly that the repulsive vermin are indeed sharing your bed.

My scalp was itching. My mother dismissed my complaints, but when she finally listened, she realized that I had lice. What to do with lice had not been part of the curriculum at her girls' finishing school in Prague. One of our co-tenants advised a kerosene cure. I didn't like the idea because the stuff stank. I begged, "Can't we wait until tomorrow?" but the two women had already found what they needed, made me bend my head with its long, unruly hair over a washbasin, poured on a generous amount of the liquid, tied my head in a towel, and sent me to bed.

I couldn't sleep. My head seemed on fire. Since I shared the room with my mother, I didn't give her much rest either. In spite of all my whining, I couldn't get her to take the towel off my head or allow me to take it off. Would I please stop sniveling? She needed her sleep; she had to go to work in the morning. Next day, when my tormented head finally got some air, the lice were gone, but so was much of my scalp. I was shaved clean and got ointment for the sore skin, but it was weeks before the burns were fully healed. What really haunted me, though, was why she hadn't paid attention to me when I was so obviously in pain. And while she admitted her fault, she didn't seem all that sympathetic even afterwards. I began to doubt that adult cruelties were wholly fortuitous or for the good of the children, as they always maintained. It's essentially the question we ask when we observe civilizations, alien to our own, that practice exorcism by inflicting harm on the bodies of the women and children who are said to host devils and demons.

My mother turned superstitious and regularly frequented a fortune-teller, much as she had employed a seamstress to make her dresses in the good old days. She talked about a miracle-working rabbi who had been an ancestor of hers and whose spirit protected the family in times of need. She implored me never to marry a goy, because all goyim beat their wives. "All of them?" I asked. "You think even Goethe beat his wife?" Goethe not only is Germany's greatest poet but also is traditionally invoked as a role model for all kinds of conduct. For a moment my mother was nonplussed. Then she said, yes, of course he must have beaten his wife. After all, he was a goy.

The catastrophe seemed to have come out of the blue sky, even though, with hindsight, everyone recited the forewarnings with relish. Politics was not meant to be a feminine domain, and in my mother's Czech finishing school they didn't teach the girls how to read a newspaper critically any more than they instructed them on how to delouse the heads of children. Neither did her social experience prepare her for the harsh realities we faced, since by definition anti-Semites didn't move in

Jewish circles. And didn't we live in an enlightened country, unlike Russia or Poland, the traditional lands of pogroms? Before the German invasion there were enough worries that were closer to home than politics, such as family disagreements, inheritance feuds, and in the aftermath of her divorce, the Czech-Austrian custody case. In addition she had started what we would now call a small fitness program, where housewives who were beginning to put on weight could take some of it off by means of light workouts. But after the German invasion nothing mattered more than politics.

Once when she and I were at the Jewish Community Center, a young man asked us whether she would consider sending me by myself with a children's transport to Palestine (or was it England? I am not sure). It was a last chance he said, just in the nick of time. Very advisable. My heart pounded, for I would dearly have loved to leave Vienna, even if meant betraying my mother. But she didn't ask me and didn't even look at me as she answered in an even voice: "No. A child and its mother belong together." On the way home I fought down my disappointment without mentioning it, since there was no point in hurting her. But I never forgot that brief glimpse of another life which would have made me a different person. What kind of a person? Who knows? Should she have asked my opinion? Not have treated me exclusively as her property? In her last years, when she was a broken old woman who had seen most of the century, with her faculties failing, I still now and then got a glimpse of this powerful claim to ownership, disguised as love and expressed as criticism. ("Why can't you visit me tomorrow?" "Do you *have* to travel?" "Where is your coat? It's too cold to go without." "You are wearing the wrong shoes.")

But in those years she had so little and was deprived of all that had made her life worthwhile. When my children left me, they went to college, not into a Nazi concentration camp, and I had a profession and friends, a sprawling country, and a free life. She was so nervous that she developed a tic, an automatic twitch of her leg. I found this tic appealing, because it was part of my mother. She fantasized about what else she could lose, and typically for the women of her generation, she didn't worry that her husband might be murdered, but that he might be unfaithful. There is a story that he had a girlfriend in France. Maybe. Who cares? After the war she got some letters from people who knew him in Drancy, the French camp from which he was deported, and they said that he was helpful and full of jokes to the end.

She made me her confidante in this matter of marital infidelity, though I was hardly the right person for it and had no idea how to respond. She had some mail from him (I never did, much to my chagrin), and later she would say: "Your papa wrote me such a loving letter from Drancy. I still had it in Auschwitz and lost it there." She said "lost," as if it disappeared inadvertently, as if she could have taken anything along from that hellhole. And she acted as if she had forgotten her Viennese jealousy, as she probably had.

I was a nuisance and often in the way, useless and lazy, yet all that was left. In the course of three or four years she had been uprooted, her life had shrunk, and she was engulfed in the isolation of the persecuted. Her husband was on the run, her son in an occupied country, her sister's family underground in Hungary. Her circle of friends had emigrated to America, England, and Palestine, or had been deported to Theresienstadt or "to Poland," a vague phrase, but much in use. And here she was with her *Reichsfluchtsteuer*, the tax she couldn't pay. Then came the news that my half brother and his father had been deported to Theresienstadt. My mother received a few postcards from there. The prospect of seeing him again made her own impending deportation acceptable.

And still I ask: Why didn't we get out in time? When others ask, I get irritated and answer that it's a stupid question: don't look at the émigrés who were lucky or rich or both; think of the hundreds of thousands of German and Austrian Jews (the Polish ones didn't have a chance in the first place) who perished. We happened to be among those who were pulled into that vortex. But I did ask *her*, many times, when she was still of sound mind: "Why? You had connections, you are pretty savvy, what happened to you?" She came back to that tax. (And I think, could it have been your neuroses, your cumulative madness, aggravated by the mad new social order, that prevented you from finding a way to save us?) "And I couldn't leave Schorschi alone in Prague." "So why didn't you go and get him?" "That would have been dangerous, and I would have had to leave you behind." The snake biting its own tail. A vicious circle.

There came a point where nothing could be done. She tried to remain in Vienna as long as possible. She had a job as a nurse and physical therapist at the Jewish hospital. She left early. I slept late, read in bed, walked over to the hospital, where I got a meal and could take a shower. Then I spent the rest of the day alone with a book in the hospital yard. We were pretty much among the last Jews to be deported from Vienna to Theresienstadt, on the so-called hospital transport of September 1942.

15

After the war my mother and I went back to Vienna for a couple of weeks to see what was left of our relatives, of our property. It was like entering the original slime, or perhaps cesspool, from which life developed. I was surprised that the city was still there at all, for I had left it so far behind. The Russian occupation forces were everywhere, and people told horror stories about them, women in particular tried to avoid them, but I didn't fear them, though they probably deserved to be feared, because by this time I didn't scare easily.

There was a joke current in postwar Vienna about two people to whom Jews had entrusted their things before deportation. One says to the other: "You are lucky, your Jew didn't return. Mine did." I didn't want to own anything, since I didn't understand that having more translates into living better. That hadn't been my experience. We had been middle class, and what good had it done us? I just wanted out and not to have to turn back.

Vienna was awash in self-pity. I was unmoved and noticed that the city wasn't nearly as devastated as the Munich from which I had just come. Everyone felt they had been victims of the Nazis, whereas to me, *they* had been the arch-Nazis. Statistics bear me out. Percentage-wise more Austrians than Germans were involved in the more gruesome tasks performed by the Nazis, in guarding concentration camps, for example.

And there was my cousin Heinz and his mother, back from Hungary. His father and grandmother had died, but of natural causes, and I felt a strange twinge of envy and also something like reassurance that normal deaths, too, were still possible. I visited the old house and the park where I used to play and felt only an incommensurable distance, out of all proportion to the few years I had been absent.

Only the language was what it had always been, the speech of my childhood with its peculiar inflections and rhythms, a sense of humor that Germans often don't get, and a wealth of malicious half tones that would be obscene in any other tongue; also an intense lyricism that easily degenerates into kitsch. I understand this language, but I don't like it. I speak it, but I wouldn't have chosen it. I am hooked on it, and it's the reason I go back for visits, though I have no relatives or friends of relatives, only a few new friends: writers, feminists, socialists, who sit in cafés and argue. I get depressed after a while and clutch my American passport, eyeing the taxis that will take me to the train station or the airport. But it is the city where I learned to speak, listen, and read, all the basics for a human life. I remain its reluctant child. The trouble is that it was a city that hated children—Jewish children, to be precise.

Part Two

THE CAMPS

Til there was no place left where they could still pursue him
Except that exile which he called his Race.
But, envying him even that, they plunged right through him

Into a land of mirrors without time or space,
And all they had to strike now was the human face.

—W. H. AUDEN, FROM "THE DIASPORA"

Today, more than half a century after the liberation of the camps, Germany is dotted with their carefully tended, unlovely remains: tourist attractions like the ruins of medieval castles. The same people who gather at noon in front of Munich's municipal hall to watch the pretty wooden figures emerge from the bell tower to do their jousting and dancing will take the bus to Dachau in the afternoon, somberly follow a guide, and pay obeisance to the old remains of Hitler's first concentration camp. If you are in the least interested in German literature, you'll want to travel to Weimar, Goethe's town, and once you are there, you feel obligated to trudge up the steep hill of nearby Buchenwald in a show of awe and consternation. The camps are part of a worldwide museum culture of the Shoah, nowhere more evident than in Germany, where every sensitive citizen, not to mention every politician who wants to display his ethical credentials, feels the need to take pictures at these shrines or, even better, have his picture taken.

Yet to what purpose? Of course one is glad that the Germans, who had been in denial for so long that we thought they would never face themselves in the mirror of their past, finally did face up, and once they started, did so with the proverbial German thoroughness. And yet I feel something is missing. In the eighties I happened to spend time at the University of Göttingen, and one afternoon I invited a colleague's class to visit me at home. As I listened to two likable first-semester graduate students who were talking animatedly about Auschwitz, it dawned on me that they were using the name not as shorthand for the Holocaust in general, as has become customary, but concretely, for a place they seemed to know well. I questioned them without letting on that I had a previous acquaintance with the camp, and learned that they had done their alternative national service, their *Zivildienst*, there. Instead of serving in the military, they had whitewashed the fences at Auschwitz. I associate Tom Sawyer and his friends with whitewashed fences, and I wondered aloud whether this cheerful activity made any sense in an extermination camp. My doubts astonished them in turn. Preservation was a form of restitution, they argued. Not that they liked the tourists (all those Americans!), and they were less than enthusiastic about the noisy schoolchildren with their know-it-all teachers. Nevertheless, the site of suffering has to be preserved.

And I ask myself: Why?

Drunken August, the darling of Viennese legend, spent a besotted night in a ditch full of dead bodies and awoke with only a hangover. He staggered out of the ditch, left it behind him, and continued to play his bagpipe. We are different. We don't get off so cheaply; the ghosts cling to us. Do we expect that our unsolved questions will be answered if we hang on to what's left: the place, the stones, the ashes? We don't honor the dead with these unattractive remnants of past crimes; we collect and keep them for the satisfaction of our own necrophilic desires. Violated taboos, such as child murder and mass murder, turn their victims into spirits, whom we offer a kind of home that they may haunt at will. Perhaps we are afraid they may leave the camps, and so we insist that their deaths were unique and must not be compared to any other losses or atrocities. Never again shall there be such a crime.

The same thing doesn't happen twice anyway. Every event, like every human being and even every dog, is unique. We would be condemned to be isolated monads if we didn't compare and generalize, for comparisons are the bridges from one unique life to another. In our hearts we all know that some aspects of the Shoah have been repeated elsewhere, today and yesterday, and will return in new guise tomorrow; and the camps, too, were only imitations (unique imitations, to be sure) of what had occurred the day before yesterday.

In today's Hiroshima, a busy industrial city, there is a memorial site to the great catastrophe which ushered in the atomic age. It is a park with flowers and temples, where Japanese children, in their English school uniforms, seem to have a thoroughly good time. The Japanese are as frustrated in coping with past horror as we are, because they, too, can think only of the mantra "Never again." It's easier to recognize this helplessness in a strange city. The children, with their history teachers in tow, hang origami toys, cranes, and other symbolic paper objects, on various bushes and trees dedicated to the goddess of peace, and then they romp about the park, screeching and chasing each other. There is the soothing sound of water, so typical of the aesthetics of Japanese landscaping, and tape-recorded messages with humanistic content are released at regular intervals. In the very midst of these efforts to propitiate and tranquilize the visitor, there is *the* monument, the ugliest ruin in the world: the building, we remember, wasn't hit by a bomb in the usual way; the bomb exploded above the building and disfigured it through heat, so that it looks as unnatural as a human face which has been ravaged by fire.

During a discussion with some youngsters in Germany I am asked (as if it was a genuine question and not an accusation) whether I don't think that the Jews have turned into Nazis in their dealings with the Arabs, and haven't the Americans always acted like Nazis in their dealings with the Indians? When it gets that aggressive and simple, I just sputter. Or I sit in the student cafeteria with some advanced Ph.D. candidates, and one reports how in Jerusalem he made the acquaintance of an old Hungarian Jew who was a survivor of Auschwitz, and yet this man cursed the Arabs and held them all in contempt. How can someone who comes from Auschwitz talk like that? the German asks. I get into the act and argue, perhaps more hotly than need be. What did he expect? Auschwitz was no instructional institution, like the University of Göttingen, which he attends. You learned nothing there, and least of all humanity and tolerance. Absolutely nothing good came out of the concentration camps, I hear myself saying, with my voice rising, and he expects catharsis, purgation, the sort of thing you go to the theater for? They were the most useless, pointless establishments imaginable. That is the one thing to remember about them if you know nothing else. No one agrees, and no one contradicts me. Who wants to get into an argument with the old bag who's got that number on her arm? Germany's young intellectuals bow their heads over their soup plates and eat what's in front of them. Now I have silenced them, and that wasn't my intention. There is always a wall between the generations, but here the wall is barbed wire. Old, rusty barbed wire.

And yet they could easily have objected. Don't I often insist that I learned something in the camps about what happens to us in extreme situations, which was good to know later on and was usable precisely because I don't reject all comparisons? And don't I resent those who would deny me this knowledge and those who assume, without further inquiry, that we all lost our minds and morals there?

In the late sixties, when I was teaching in Cleveland, a young Jewish political scientist, engaged to a German woman, said to my face, without flinching: "I know what you survivors had to do to stay alive." I didn't know what we had had to do, but I knew what he wanted to say. He wanted to say, "You walked over dead bodies." Should I have answered, "But I was only twelve"? Or said, "But I am a good girl, always have been"? Both answers implicate the others, my fellow prisoners. Or I could have said, "Where do you get off talking like that?" and gotten angry. I said nothing, went home to my children, and was depressed. For in reality the cause of survival was almost pure chance.

So we few survivors are either the best or the worst. And yet, as Bertolt Brecht was fond of saying, the truth is concrete, meaning specific. The role that prison plays in the life of an ex-prisoner cannot be deduced from some shaky psychological rule, for it is different for each one of us, depending on what went before, on what came afterwards, and on what happened to each during his or her time in the camps. Though the Shoah involved millions of people, it was a unique experience for each of them.

The museum culture of the camp sites has been formed by the vagaries and neuroses of our unsorted, collective memory. It is based on a profound superstition, that is, on the belief that the ghosts can be met and kept in their place, where the living ceased to breathe. Or rather, not a profound, but a shallow superstition. A visitor who feels moved, even if it is only the kind of feeling that a haunted house conveys, will be proud of these stirrings of humanity. And so the visitor monitors his reactions, examines his emotions, admires his own sensibility, or in other words, turns sentimental. For sentimentality involves turning away from an ostensible object and towards the subjective observer, that is, towards oneself. It means looking into a mirror instead of reality.

In contrast, a German psychiatrist of my generation, who is a good friend, tells me that right after the war she organized a group of other children and took them on an excursion to a nearby concentration camp. The camp was deserted, but the traces of the prisoners could still be seen: rusty objects, bits of clothing, and of course, the living quarters. It had been quickly abandoned after the liberation and had not been revisited. My friend says that there she got a whiff of the Shoah, and it wasn't a Shoah museum. Years later the teachers would shepherd their flocks to the same place, and if possible, steer their reactions along the right channels. But when my friend was there with her group, everything was still fresh; the blood had been shed but hadn't congealed yet. I imagine these children, open-mouthed, giggling with embarrassment, as they held up a tin spoon or stroked a straw mattress. They must have enjoyed the innocently guilty feeling of having pulled one over on the adults, having lifted a curtain and discovered a Bluebeard type of secret, led and seduced by a plucky fellow student.

Or there is Claude Lanzmann, director of the unforgettable documentary *Shoah*, pursuing his tortured search for what happened where, his obsession with place the guiding principle of his film. "Was it three steps to the right or to the left of here?" he asks the natives. "In this or that spot?" "When were these trees planted? Were they part of the old site?" It's a fetish with him, I think, watching him on screen in the dark theater, half of me admiring him while the other half feels ahead of him. You need the places, I tell his image; I need only the names of the places. Yet what is the difference? We are entangled in the same web, only in different meshes.

I once visited Dachau with some Americans who had asked me to come along. It was a clean and proper place, and it would have taken more imagination than your average John or Jane Doe possesses to visualize the camp as it was forty years earlier. Today a fresh wind blows across the central square where the infamous roll calls took place, and the simple barracks of stone and wood suggest a youth hostel more easily than a setting for tortured lives. Surely some visitors secretly figure they can remember times when they have been worse off than the prisoners of this orderly German camp. The missing ingredients are the odor of fear emanating from human bodies, the concentrated aggression, the reduced minds. I didn't see the ghosts of the so-called *Muselmänner* (Muslims) who dragged themselves zombielike through the long, evil hours, having lost the energy and the will to live. Sure, the signs and the documentation and the films help us to understand. But the concentration camp as a memorial site? Landscape, seascape—there should be a word like *timescape* to indicate the nature of a place in time, that is, at a certain time, neither before nor after. Lanzmann's greatness, on the other hand, depends on his belief that place captures time and can display its victims like flies caught in amber.

It's all right to believe in ghosts, but you have to know to whom you are praying. One of my two Tom Sawyers is a good Christian and found plenty of opportunity for prayer in Auschwitz One—the core of the sprawling death facility—but he definitely didn't know the difference between the Good Lord and a ghost. For the former is personified serenity and holds all creation in the balance of his imagined hands, whereas the fence in need of refurbishing stood at best in limbo, the realm of the unredeemed. So it is only fitting that on this site a religious war has been raging, Jews against nuns, our victims against your victims. Church dignitaries have a say, but there is no dignity here for the living or the dead. A stalking ground for ghosts, not God's acre.

These two students, who took an unintentional yet voluntary interest in my childhood, refused stubbornly to admit the difference between Poles and Jews and to include Polish anti-Semitism in their meditations on good and evil. The Poles had been invaded and mistreated, so they must be good. How else are we to tell victims from victimizers? The camp sites hide as much as they communicate. At Auschwitz the Jewish victims have been so coopted into the Polish losses that my two Tom Sawyers couldn't handle the difference. They believed everything, even the worst, of their own grandfathers, they had unkind thoughts about the Allies, but they couldn't cope with criticism of the victims. That is, they were convinced that the grandparent generation was still in denial, and that the Allies hadn't liberated the concentration camps soon enough, although they could have, or at least bombed the rails that led to the camps. But they categorically refused to believe that the Poles weren't all that averse to getting rid of their Jews. They both energetically rejected my objection to tossing Christian and Jewish Poles into the same kettle, although I pointed out that it was mainly the Jews who went to the gas chambers, and the murdered children had all been Jewish and Gypsy children. I was amazed how sure they were, these thoughtful and excellent specimens of what is best in the new Germany. And yet I hadn't even voiced my nastiest suspicion, about the hard currency which Jewish pilgrims, especially the American variety, bring to Poland and which has presumably made the Auschwitz museum into a lucrative venture for nearby Cracow. But I admit that I am more hard-boiled than I want others to be.

It won't do to pretend that we can evoke the physical reality of the camps as they were when they functioned. Nevertheless, I want my timescapes. Evocations of places at a time that has passed. I first wanted to call this book *Stations* and tie my diverse memories to the names I connect with them. (It seemed a modest title, until Catholic friends reminded me of the stations of the cross. Cultural differences: I hadn't even thought of it. Once it was pointed out, I was appalled at the unintended hubris.) Now I ask myself, why place names, when I am a woman who has never lived anywhere for long? These are not the names of present or former homes; they are more like the piers of bridges that were blown up, only we can't be quite sure of what these bridges connected. Perhaps nothing with nothing. But if so, we have our work cut out for us, as we look out from the old piers. Because if we don't find the bridges, we'll either have to invent them or content ourselves with living in the no-man's-land between past and present. We start with what is left: the names of the places.

Remembering is a branch of witchcraft; its tool is incantation. I often say, as if it were a joke—but it's true—that instead of God I believe in ghosts. To conjure up the dead you have to dangle the bait of the present before them, the flesh of the living, to coax them out of their inertia. You have to grate and scrape the old roots with tools from the shelves of ancient kitchens. Use your best wooden spoons with the longest handles to whisk into the broth of our fathers the herbs our daughters have grown in their gardens. If I succeed, together with my readers—and perhaps a few men will join us in the kitchen—we could exchange magic formulas like favorite recipes and season to taste the marinade which the old stories and histories offer us, in as much comfort as our witches' kitchen provides. It won't get too cozy, don't worry: where we stir our cauldron, there will be cold and hot currents from half-open windows, unhinged doors, and earthquake-prone walls.

GHETTO

1

The muse of history has a way of cracking bad jokes at the expense of the Jews. For example, the fortress of Theresienstadt was built by, of all people, the Emperor Joseph II, revered by Austrian Jews for emancipating them. In my time there, September 1942 to May 1944, some Czech Jews who had been stationed there as army recruits were now "drafted" a second time as prisoners. Inside the walls, the town was built on a grid, with intersecting streets for the civilian population and barracks for the soldiers. It was not much of a place for entertainment, certainly no spa like Karlsbad, and we have evidence from the turn of the century that the officers who had to spend time there were bored out of their wits.

During the Nazi period, Theresienstadt was called a ghetto, though today it is counted among the concentration camps. I, too, called it ghetto, in contrast to Dachau, Buchenwald, and Auschwitz, the camps whose names I knew. First we had been driven from our homes and forced to live in "for Jews only" houses, and now we were to resettle in a kind of all-Jewish shtetl. That was the logic behind the word *ghetto*. But it's obvious why the term was misleading: a ghetto doesn't normally mean a prison, but that part of town where Jews live. Theresienstadt, however, was the stable that supplied the slaughterhouse.

In Auschwitz-Birkenau I understood that I was in a concentration camp. (That word had long been part of my vocabulary, though not in connection with children.) The term *extermination camp* didn't exist yet. My third place of internment, whose name nobody can remember, was

Christianstadt, which was called a work camp and was an extension, an *Aussenlager*, of another concentration camp, Gross-Rosen. There were many of these work camps, or *Arbeitslager*. Hitler's Europe was dotted with them, but there is a great reluctance to pay attention to their names. Even in the circle of my own family and friends, no one could ever remember where I'd been held, and the reason is probably that we would like to put a common roof over the whole business with a few well-worn names, and not have it spill all over the house like Captain Shotover's dynamite in Shaw's *Heartbreak House*, or like the oil spilled from a damaged tanker in Alaska while the captain was drunk. Juggling a few names is less demanding than juggling many and doesn't require the differentiations that I am imposing on the reader right now. Yet I insist on them at the risk of alienating my readers (most of them likely to be female, since males, on the whole, tend to prefer books written by fellow males), because we need to break through the curtain of barbed wire with which postwar sensibility has surrounded the camps, neatly separating us from them. A visitor to the old camp sites is at a greater distance from the victims than I am sitting at my desk, and perhaps separation is a hidden function of these peculiar museums, though it runs counter to their ostensible purpose. The death camps seem easier to comprehend if we put them all into the basket of one vast generalization, which the term *death camps* implies, but in the process we mythologize or trivialize them. Even terror and deprivation are different from case to case. Not everyone was equal behind the barbed wire curtain, and no camp was like any other. No man is an island, and yet each of us occupies her own place on the map.

Back to the so-called ghetto of Theresienstadt. (By the way, the Czech name is Terezin, but I use the German for the same reason that we say Auschwitz, and not Oświęcim. The Slavic names should continue to denote harmless little towns.) Over the years many people have asked me: "I knew X or Y, who was interned at Theresienstadt. Surely you remember him or her?" Not once have I been able to give a positive answer. Theresienstadt wasn't a village of friendly neighbors and social interaction. It was a transit station. Almost 140,000 people were deported to that ghetto, and less than 18,000 were liberated at war's end. I was part of a population of 40,000 or 50,000, where at most 3,500 soldiers and civilians should have resided.

And so Theresienstadt was first of all a massive sampling of humanity. My life during my last months in Vienna had been reduced to solitary afternoons with a book in a hospital yard. Suddenly I had arrived in an overcrowded place where everyone wore the yellow star, and where the streets were therefore safe. But safety is a relative concept, and the ghetto was a hotbed of epidemics, one after the other. Encephalitis, or the sleeping sickness, was waning when we arrived. Then came jaundice, and my mother caught it. I still see her lying in her upper berth in the room she shared with several other women—not in the hospital barracks, where she didn't want to go. Her face was incredibly yellow, as yellow as a lemon. And there was always gastroenteritis. Transports arrived, transports left, the beds emptied out and filled up again. In times of peace and prosperity, every death announcement comes to us as a shock, as it should. There is time and space to mourn each individual loss, and that is perhaps the ultimate luxury. We got used to a steady stream of names whose owners were gone—or what you might euphemistically call "got used to," since there were no shock absorbers.

Among the aged and infirm who died in large numbers was my Grandmother Klüger, my father's mother. She had brought up nine of her own children and a stepson. Of those who had emigrated, no one thought of taking her along. To be sure, that wasn't unusual. My father hadn't taken us along either. The old idea, or rather the old prejudice, that women are protected by men was so deeply ingrained in that society that they overlooked what was most obvious, that is, that the weakest and the disadvantaged are the most exposed. Why would the Nazis, with their racist ideology, refrain from harming women? Did the concept of chivalry so outshine that of racism in the minds of our people? It didn't make sense. But even Theodor Herzl, the founder of political Zionism and our hero and guru, who hailed from my part of the world, believed that it was the duty of Jewish wives to be especially supportive of their husbands, because only men had to put up with anti-Semitism. You can find this startling idea in his play *The New Ghetto*—not a very good play, incidentally, but it premiered on a Viennese stage.

My grandmother died a prisoner in a large room crammed with other sick people who were doomed to die because of the circumstances. My mother, who is otherwise quick to disparage her fellows, admired her mother-in-law as the epitome of human warmth. She may have seen in her the opposite of her own mother, who was always dependent on men and money, and who developed a tortured self-love which reached pathological proportions as she advanced in years. My father's mother, on the other hand, was there for children, for her own and those of relatives, and was generous in spite of poverty. She welcomed all who came and fed them, reasoning that if there was enough for ten, there would be enough for a few more. After the children were grown and the worst was over, because the sons had jobs and helped support her, she died too early, abandoned and in a deeper misery than she had ever experienced. Of all the many people whom she had served food in the course of her life, my mother and I were the only ones who were with her near the end. My mother said the last words she heard from her were "Go to bed, child."

Theresienstadt wasn't all that bad, the German wife of a Princeton colleague said to me. This woman, whom I shall call Gisela, felt smug about belonging to a younger generation of Germans who couldn't be blamed for anything. She was always well groomed, her thoughts as immaculate as her dresses, and her tastes equally impeccable. She looked down on my enthusiasm for popular movies and stressed her preference for the opera. In contrast to my two Tom Sawyers, who don't trust their own people and glorify the victims, she was determined to reduce the past until it fit into the box of a clean German conscience that won't cause her countrymen to lose any sleep. Some Germans, it would seem, are caught up in a kind of chamber of horrors cum melodrama, where the nuances of reality and its gritty surfaces disappear in a fog, and you can't make out any details, so why try? Most Americans fit this pattern, too. They don't want to hear that for me life was better in Theresienstadt than it had been during the last months in Vienna, because to digest this bit of admittedly subjective information would mean that they'd have to rearrange a lot of furniture in their inner museum of the Holocaust. And others, like the aforementioned Gisela, refuse to get up from their uphol-stered sofas to look out the window. Unmoved by information, that is, by fresh air from outside, or by reflection, that is, by taking stock of the inventory and perhaps removing some shoddy pieces, they don't notice how much unadmitted guilt weighs down their conclusions. Gisela's remarks were a provocation and unmistakably aggressive. I am sure she resented that in warm weather I didn't wear long sleeves to cover up the Auschwitz number tattooed on my arm or try to hide it in some other way, with bracelets or cosmetics, to mention two of the suggestions I received in the course of fifty years. "Theresienstadt was a ghetto for old people and Jewish veterans," she says, reciting a bit of German folklore. She would undoubtedly react to my evaluation of the ghetto with a tri-umphant: "There you are! You admit that Theresienstadt was even nicer for you than the lovely city of Vienna."

Looking back, I see Theresienstadt as a broken chain of memories. Lost friends, threads that split off the spindle. Theresienstadt was hunger and disease, a small military village of straight lines and right angles, with a border I couldn't step across and an overpopulation that made it almost impossible to find a quiet spot for a private conversation. So that it was all the more of an achievement if, with some effort, you did find a corner where you could talk one-on-one. No freedom of movement beyond a square kilometer, and within the camp you were at the mercy of an anonymous will, which could, and would, send you on to some vaguely perceived but frightening destination. Theresienstadt meant the transports to the east, which occurred in irregular intervals as surely and unpredictably as earthquakes do in California. That was the framework of our existence, this coming and going of Jews who could make no decisions, had no influence on what was decided for them, and didn't even know when and how a decision regarding them would be made. Let alone what it would be.

We arrived and learned about housing conditions: several people were put in a smaller room and many in a larger one. A young man from the Jewish camp administration materialized and suggested I should live in a children's barracks. My mother could visit me whenever she pleased, I could go see her, and I would be with children my age. She agreed, a little to my surprise.

The children's barracks were the former officers' quarters—two large yellow buildings flanking the church, which was closed in our time. They had numbers: L410 and L414. The Jews who ran the camp had put the Czech children into the first building and the German-speaking children into the second. I came to live in L414, in a room for the youngest group of girls. L414 is the only one of my many addresses which I have never forgotten. We were assured that I had been lucky to get in, because there wasn't enough space for all the eligible children.

At first, however, I didn't feel all that lucky. We were thirty girls in a room where two or three would have been comfortable. This wasn't our dormitory, it was our home, the only place we had. We even washed there with cold water which we fetched from the hallway in basins. Soap was scarce and treasured. In cold weather our teeth chattered in concert. There was a warm shower in the basement, and every two weeks we could use it. The hot water would barely come on before it would go off again. You had to be on the ball to make use of it. We slept in three-tiered bunks on straw mattresses, one or two girls per berth, depending on the width of the bed. Those were my first weeks of protracted hunger; in Vienna I had had enough to eat. There is little to say about chronic hunger: it's always there and is boring to talk about. Hunger gnaws at and weakens you. It takes up mental space which could otherwise be used for thinking. What can you do with your food ration to stretch it? We acted as if the skim milk we were rationed was whipping cream and beat it into foam, a popular pastime. (I think of this pastime dreamily when I order a latte.) It could take hours, because it's difficult to make skim milk foam with a fork. We were not sorry for ourselves: we laughed a lot, we were noisy and full of beans, like other children our age, and we thought we were stronger than the "pampered" free kids.

There was always a long line in front of the toilets, for there were only two on each floor, in a building that held hundreds of children. I tried to figure out when there was the least traffic, but the problem—everyone's perennial problem—was diarrhea. During the first weeks I was the outsider, the newcomer who had few social skills. I was stupid and clumsy, and the other girls laughed at me. I don't know which of my reclusive habits made me the butt of their jokes, for who knows how she appears to others? I must have seemed peculiar, coming out of my enforced company with hospital patients, nurses, and the grown-ups who shared our apartment. I was used to amusing myself, mostly with books, and mostly adult books at that. I wasn't used to adapting to a group of peers and coevals, and at first I just wanted to go back to my mother. When she came to visit, I ran after her and desperately begged her to take me along. But she simply left, very quickly, without explanation or advice, leaving me to cope as best I could with my disappointment.

So I turned to the group, and soon I learned to become part of it. At bottom I wasn't too unhappy to escape from my mother's contradictory demands, and it soon dawned on me that it might be easier to live with other kids. I observed the behavior of the girls around me and saw that it wouldn't be too hard to please them. In the end I developed a gift for friendship, which I believe I still have.

No, I reply slowly to Gisela's words, it wasn't so bad. Should I get into an argument with this German woman, and does she expect that I'll respond to her insolence with a weepy story of suffering? We had sat next to each other on a plane from Newark to Frankfurt, and I rashly told her about the mood that overcomes me whenever I am about to land on German soil. It's a slight dizziness, not quite nausea, but a trace of a headache, all of it so slight, I explained, that it could be interpreted as a metaphor and not a symptom, or it could be shrugged off altogether, except that it doesn't happen when I land in Manchester, Brussels, or Newark. What did she want? Should I agree with her, and thereby disown my childhood friends who left a lasting mark on me, or defensively remind her that in the ghetto we sat in a trap with no hope except the military defeat of Germany, afraid of the next transport, unprotected by any civilized law? I hear my father say, "Don't mix or meddle," a favorite expression of his, or, "Don't get involved." We deplane, she goes one way, I another.

The administration of L414 was in the hands of youngsters who employed other youngsters. A sixteen-year-old was in charge of our room. These half-grown children made a point of creating some group spirit and turned our forced community into part of the youth movement, be it Socialist or Zionist. Either one was an antidote to fascism, but Zionism was the be-all and end-all of our political awareness, and I was swept up in it, because it simply made sense. It was the way out of an unendurable diaspora, it had to work, and besides, my father had been a member of a Zionist youth organization back in Vienna when he was a student. A land without a people for a people without a land—a catchy motto. Turning Jew boys into young Jews—a phrase from our prophet, Theodor Herzl, who was not above using the derogatory lingo of our enemies, if it served his cause. To till the soil and become a beacon for mankind. Show the world an example of a just commonwealth. We learned all we could about the history of Zionism and about the land of Palestine, which we called Eretz Israel. We sang Zionist songs and danced the hora for hours on end in the barracks yard. Our elders (by a few years) addressed us as *haverim* and *haverot* (comrades, male and female) and when going to bed we didn't wish each other *Gute Nacht*, but *leila tov*, one of the few Hebrew tags we had learned.

Because we lived in this children's home and had ideas about the future, we thought of ourselves as an elite. We formed haughty groups and were proud of our commitment to each other and our ideals. And yet I have largely forgotten my *haverot*. Sometimes a name floats to the surface from the depths of forgetfulness where my roommates lie buried: there was a German girl, Renate, and I learned that the name means born again, and that she owed the name to a sister who had died as an infant. She was dark and tall. Another girl from Germany was petite and delicate and knew how to step dance. She was as sweet as her name, Melissa.

Of course I haven't forgotten Hanna, who today lives in Australia. She was from Vienna and we became best friends. Her father was a mathematician, had wild hair, and was the author of unpublished mythological stories. Hanna showed me one of them about an earth goddess, Hertha. I was impressed by his ability to write so many pages in a rather impenetrable language, and by the fact that he was both a scientist and a writer. I envied Hanna for having a father.

It was common for two girls to bond and share everything. Food was precious, and bread was therefore a kind of currency. Sometimes in a supermarket I have a flashback and marvel that bread is so cheap. My mother traded her wedding ring, soon and without much ado, for bread. She has never been sentimental, except to impress an audience, not when it really mattered. (She was so right: it was the murder of a husband, not the loss of a ring that ended her marriage. And at least she got something for it before the Nazis took it.) Once she brought me some extra food, and I shared it with Hanna. When she found out, she was angry: she had saved it from her own ration. "It was for you, just for you." "But you told me that it was extra." "I said that only so you would take it." Once again, a guilt-producing double bind. I had not only eaten my mother's food, which she needed as much as everyone else, but I had spread it around and felt good about it. Again, an insoluble dilemma: what belongs to you absolutely, so that you can give it away, and what is yours with strings attached? Such questions change in quality, not just quantitatively, where no one has much to give. Gift giving is a human impulse, generosity a function of social behavior which doesn't disappear when you have virtually nothing to give. My mother knew this, she liked to give, and she was actually quite fond of this girl. She helped her after the war and wrote to her as long as she was still able to write letters.

We stored our few belongings either in our bunks or in small, open pigeonholes. Theft was virtually unheard of. We were far too well socialized, and besides, it could get you expelled from L414. In which case you would have had to move in with your parents, a depressing prospect, given how the parents lived. You could also get expelled for drinking the contaminated water from the pump in the yard, but I did just that a few times when I was thirsty, and was more afraid of being caught than of getting sick. Later in life, nothing offended me more than the generalization that the camps turned us all into brutal egotists, and whoever survived them must be morally defective. Again, the blithe refusal to look closely, to make distinctions, to reflect a little.

The Jewish camp administrations are today a stone of contention among historians and others. Was it necessary that the prisoners help the Germans maintain order, or wasn't it collaboration with the enemy? From my child's perspective, I say, "What would have happened to us if the Jews had done nothing to reduce the chaos, if there hadn't been these children's homes which they organized and ran within the purview of Nazi directives?" At the same time, I add that Jewish criticism of the forced community at Theresienstadt is nothing new and began in the ghetto itself. The outsider's tendency, presumed innate to Jews, to judge, to question, to uncover hidden motives, which has been a thorn in the side of gentiles for centuries, not because it is immoral (the Nazis called it degenerate and corrupting), but because it is irritating, was as present in the ghetto as discontent with the Chosen People is present in the books of the Biblical prophets. You can bring up children to develop the critical spirit, which is how I was educated. Very early in my childhood there were some brothers and friends of my father who would come in the door and immediately provoke me with jokes and comments just barely comprehensible to a child. These guys didn't expect me to be a good, shy little girl, they expected me to answer with quick repartee. If I succeeded, they would give me credit with some brief phrase, like "just so." License to be impertinent, or education for egalitarian thought? Take your pick. In Theresienstadt criticism was not only permitted but a matter of course. So I was not surprised that there were critical voices about the children's homes. Some said our games were too similar to the games of the Hitler Youth. You had to ponder this disturbing charge, and you might not come to any conclusion, but it kept you awake and alert. There were stormy open discussions, a boiling kettle without a lid.

Looking back, the treatment of the children in Theresienstadt seems to me to have been exemplary, with one exception. That was the separation of the Czech children from the German speakers. The Czechs in L410 looked down on us because we spoke the enemy's language. Besides, they really were the elite, because they were in their own country, and many Czechs had connections to the outside, which we didn't have. I know some Czech survivors who claim they were never hungry in Theresienstadt, while I never got enough to eat. I think the young Jews in charge should have made an effort to reduce the hostility of one group of Jewish kids towards another. I felt particularly hurt by it because I had the idea that, as Schorschi's sister, I was a kind of honorary Czech. But he wasn't there and I couldn't speak his language. So even here we were disdained for something that wasn't in our power to change: our mother tongue.

2

Auschwitz, says Gisela, that's another matter. From all she has heard it must have been a pretty tough place for a young girl, but then I wasn't there all that long, was I? I got off lightly, she continues, for I was able to emigrate to America after the war and was spared the first terrible postwar years in Germany. Compared to her mother, who lost her husband on the Russian front, my mother was lucky, Gisela continues, for she found two more husbands in America, while in Germany there weren't enough men to go around. Perhaps my mother was more attractive than yours, I want to say, but such cattiness would be off the point. And the point is that my mother had no luck in her life. Strength and energy, yes, though late and sporadic. Generosity, yes, although rarely coupled with kindness. Much courage and an astonishing fearlessness, though balanced by compulsions and paranoia. But luck, no, she was never blessed with luck.

That is what I want to tell you to make you understand why Gisela's comparison is inappropriate, why the relatives of anonymous murder victims can never be lucky, especially the victims' mothers. I want to tell you about my brother's ghost.

I had so looked forward to seeing him again: my Schorschi, my Czech brother, who had sent us a few postcards from Theresienstadt. But he wasn't there when we arrived. He had been deported during the winter of the previous year to Riga, according to rumor. Rumor was for once correct. He was shot there.

As time passed, my mother went on to repress what she once knew about the death of her oldest child. Or perhaps the news had been a hot iron, which, when they put it into her outstretched hands, she had to drop. I took her to an early conference on the Holocaust, and during the discussion she got up and asked a distinguished historian whether he could tell her how and when her son had perished. The audience was moved by the old woman, and the speaker was, too. Only I was embarrassed. She knows more than he, I thought. He can't remember every transport from every camp, but she must have kept that one stored in her mind. How can she have forgotten it? She is playing the mater dolorosa in public. What is the point? The speaker eventually told her, with considerable sympathy, that he thought she had lost her son in Auschwitz, where most transports went. But after the conference I tell her once more: Riga, he was shot. Did she listen to me? What do I know about what was inside of her tortured mind? I guess she did remember—she wouldn't really have forgotten—but it blurred and blended with other information, and probably it was easier to live with the indistinctness. Perhaps she was haunted by all the different deaths Schorschi might have suffered and had become old with the weight of these images. And didn't want to pin down the right one.

She waited too long for him, searched all the lists after the war, asked the right organizations. Then she forgot. And suddenly she'd say to me: "You can't know this, but I think of him every day." She never asked whether I thought of him, whether he meant something to me. And I confess, I was so suspicious that I mistrusted the full extent of her grief and speculated to what extent she was playacting. Perhaps I was simply jealous of her greater right to mourn him.

And so I could never tell her how I would sit in front of the TV decades later, when things got rough in Prague, and quite automatically start to look for Schorschi on the screen. I would ask: "Could he be the plump bald guy in the corner, or perhaps the thin one who is giving the Russian soldier a piece of his mind?"

Where there is no grave, we are condemned to go on mourning. Or we become like animals and don't mourn at all. (I know that even some animals mourn.) By a grave I don't necessarily mean a place in a cemetery, but simply clear knowledge about the death of someone you've known. For my mother there was never a day on which she could be sure that the two, her husband and the boy, had *not* escaped. Hope was like a limited quantity of liquid which gradually evaporates.

But I remembered everything, as I can tell from my old poems. My verse is my logbook. I have always written verse, sporadically. If I quote some of it here and there, it's not because I think these effusions are particularly good (though I wish I could write good verse, and I dream of an obituary that'll say "She wrote half a dozen memorable poems," knowing that this is not to be) but because they are another way of bearing witness. So here is one that I wrote when I had children of my own and was leading the life of a suburban housewife in the fifties:

HALLOWEEN AND A GHOST

I.

Unlike real people, ghosts are obvious,
Thinly disguised and come when most expected.
Must you stand at my door on Halloween,
With a sheet over your head like the other kids,
Asking for candy, brother?

Ripples of water where you were swimming,
Your questioning voice saying "Ampersand?"
These I recall and your sailor hat and
In a wintry schoolyard the shape of your breath.
But I never found out the shape of your death,
There being so many ways of killing.

Dead boys shouldn't walk the streets.
Real ghosts shouldn't wear real sheets.
The heart may break of tricks and can't give treats.

II.

You are the skipped sentence in the book I'm reading.
You are the kitchen knife that slips into the thumb.
Memory: the autonomous twitch of an aching muscle.
You are the word that is always mistyped
And, erased, defaces the page.

Tonight your two nephews play host here.
Candy and cookies are theirs to bestow
With shrieks of delight, for they do not know
That it's always you who is ringing the bell—
And the house turns into a pumpkin hell—
("There is no such thing as a ghost, dear").

Spilled ink I give.
Tears have run through a sieve.
Wine and milk are for lovers and children who live.

Another blending and blurring: it's not only my mother's mind that works this way. In my poem the old reality invades the new one, crossing over the unconscious layers that are straddling both when I least expect it, during a harmless children's event. That was the intent of my poem—to show this blurring—and it was so well understood by the few people to whom I showed it that it outraged them. The poem seemed as out of place, as unappetizing and indiscreet, to them as an account of sexual details had seemed a couple of decades earlier. No one even attempted to look at it as a construct of words; they just sent me packing with my rhymed grief. I went on writing, but I kept my poetry to myself. That was the fifties, and that's how it was the world over, so let's not get nostalgic for that period of repression and pretense.

In the late forties, when I was sixteen and seventeen, I took long nightly walks through the streets of Manhattan, oblivious to what nice girls should or shouldn't do. I tried to imagine what it was like to be killed at the age I had reached. I knew the fact of my brother's murder, but not the details, and it was these unknown details that haunted me. I couldn't talk to my mother about his death. That would have been too intimate, too embarrassing, and would have turned into a phony demonstration of appropriate emotions. Thus I had only my poems to fall back on.

More than thirty years after the end of the war, when I least expected it, I found out more. I was dining with some colleagues from the university in Princeton's best restaurant. Except for me, they were all historians, including the guest of honor, whose lecture on problems of Nazi ideology we had just heard. As so often when Jews talk about the Holocaust, we wondered about the mental state of the murder victims, as if they were required to show us their credentials and justify us as we go about our business. We asked why no panic broke out during executions, a question that's another way of asking why there was no resistance, and that in turn implies that there should have been. I said that it seemed to me impertinent of the living to ask of the dead that they should have acted or behaved in a certain manner that suits us, that makes their death more bearable to us, either offering the heroic gestures of a senseless fight or displaying the equilibrium of martyrs. They didn't die for us, and we, God knows, don't live for them.

The company at La Hiére's was much too smart to need my lessons, and yet not ready to drop the matter. There was a short silence. Then a well-known woman historian said: "There is some evidence that they tried to comfort one another, and wouldn't that be better than resistance?" Again the silence.

"But when all is said and done, there is still a residue which passes beyond our comprehension, something that is incompatible with the human psyche as we think we know it," said the visiting lecturer, who was born a Czech and had been hidden in France. "For example the death of a transport to Riga." He described what had happened to this particular transport from documents he had studied. We know that there are such reports—I don't have to repeat his words for the sake of the details, which seemed remarkable to him, and which captivated me because they were about my brother. He couldn't know that his example mattered to me not because of its general validity, but because of its unique application. And so I had the facts of that death served up with the cognac after a Princeton dinner, and the narrator, without knowing it, undid my New York undergrad fantasies of how Schorschi died. There it was again, the discrepancy between the social life of American academe, where I had carved out a niche for myself, my home, so to speak, and these excessive stories which shouldn't even exist to be told, like the horrors which in fiction, even the best of fiction, for example in *Macbeth*, seem a bit too much of a gruesomely good thing. Naked, freezing ghosts at the banquet. That night I got drunk on cognac, walked home in a daze, awoke hours later, turned on the light, leafed through some books, and found everything on first try. It was all as the man had said. It had been his transport. Groaning, I went back to bed and dreamt of a landscape where a few people wave at, or threaten, each other silently from a great distance.

One of my brother's nephews in my poem, my older son, has George for a middle name—but it didn't help. People aren't reborn. They live, or they don't live, their one inalienable life. Schorschi's had been taken, and there is no substitute such as "living on in memory." We don't want to be pious thoughts in the minds of others; we want the robust substance of our own lives. So throughout the years I felt that I had something which he should have, too, that one of us was the other's shadow, and I was never quite sure which was which. Then one day I woke up to the fact that it would have been his seventieth birth-year. And I said to him, with the logic of our long, one-sided relationship: "Even if you had lived, it would be essentially over by now. Granted you didn't have the years that were due you, but they would be used up by now. I can go into my own old age and no longer feel that I am feeding off a patrimony of time that was meant for both of us. Good-bye, brother."

Regular instruction for the children of Theresienstadt was illegal. I was amazed. Wasn't Jewish intellect held in contempt? So how could it be dangerous in the shape of schoolwork for imprisoned children? There was a daily schedule that the Jews who ran L414 imposed, but I have forgotten what it was. Since we weren't allowed to study, studying became a forbidden, desirable fruit.

Theresienstadt was brimful of the men and women of the Jewish intelligentsia, representing all the ideas and ideologies of Europe, which they continued to discuss vehemently. They were quite happy if some children sat at their feet and listened to them talk about Culture (with a capital *C*, of course). When a German inspection team was on the calendar, the bits of printed paper disappeared, and a few times, when the men in uniform turned up unexpectedly, we had to disperse in haste and just in time. And yet it was only at one of those irregular "classes" where a university professor or someone else who was overqualified talked to us. In Theresienstadt I didn't study any subject continuously and in depth. That was impossible under the circumstances.

There were few books, and accordingly they were highly valued, treated with care, and passed from hand to hand. I remember an art historian who had a volume with reproductions of famous paintings which he showed and explained to us: Albrecht Dürer, a hare with all its hairs separately visible, facial features, dimensions, proportions, the four apostles. It was all new to me; I had never been inside a museum. There was a teacher who, from time to time, taught a few of us who were interested a bit of literary history. The lessons were at night in a broom closet. I remember a boy who knew what the *Edda* was. I didn't and was ashamed of my ignorance. How would I ever catch up with all there was to know? Sometimes I visited an old lady who tried to teach me how to read poems correctly in the overcrowded room where she lived. We practiced on Romantic poems dealing with nature's power to expand the mind. She was very satisfied with me. I think spring and summer of 1943 were gorgeous seasons in Theresienstadt. I wrote nostalgic poems about home and freedom and the desire for both.

Rabbi Leo Baeck talked to us in the attic of L414. We sat close to each other, because everyone had come to listen to the famous Berlin rabbi. He explained to us how we didn't have to discard the Biblical account of creation in seven days in favor of the scientific version of millions of years.

Relativity of time. God's day is not like our days with their twenty-four hours. But when it comes to the order of creation, tradition and science are at one: first God created the inorganic world, then living things, and in the end he created man and woman. I was all ear, moved by the festive mood that prevailed as we sat crowded beneath the naked beams and impressed by these simple and clearly understandable ideas. It was the first lecture I had heard, and I was enthusiastic. This rabbi offered us our heritage like a gift: the Bible in the spirit of the Enlightenment. One could have both the old myth and the new science; life was going to be a wonder and a joy. Baeck must have been a highly gifted preacher—how else would I have remembered these details?—and yet he was also a naïve, law-abiding German citizen who insisted on paying the gas company while his captors stood in the doorway to take him away. Did he want to reduce *rishes* before they deported him? There is a story about a village of simpletons, *Schildbürger* in German, who built a town hall without windows and then packed the sunlight in large bags and poured it into the dark hall. It could be a parable about the futile idealism of German Jews.

In August 1943 a group of children came to Theresienstadt. I didn't see them, and hardly anyone did. They were supposed to continue on a special transport to Switzerland, or to some other foreign country, and only a few caretakers were permitted to interact with them during their short stay in the ghetto. In spite of their isolation, a rumor circulated that these children went into a panic when they were to take a shower. And the reason for their refusal. The grown-ups thought, or at least said, that the story about showers that dispensed poison gas instead of water was a product of the children's fertile imagination. But children like myself took it seriously. Why not? Children are still learning how the world works. So that was it. I began to see my Jewish surroundings as an unreliable cushion against the uniformed men's universe outside, running its obscene and secretive business, which one couldn't talk about because it turned into porno in your mouth, and was therefore a taboo subject.

I try to find out more about this children's transport—it's not difficult, everything is documented—but I can't get over a sense that I shouldn't. There's an itch, a discomfort, as if I'm doing something that is improper, not kosher (as if I cared about kosher and proper), like uncovering a sacrament or its opposite. Is there still a ban of silence governing the fate of these children? I read that they came from Poland—from Bialystock, to be precise—where the Jews knew about the Nazi methods of extermination. And that they were sent on in October with fifty-three

Jewish "caretakers," all assuming that they were traveling to a safe haven. But the journey was to Auschwitz and death. Among these caretakers was Kafka's favorite sister Ottla, not famous yet, for her late brother's books hadn't become the most widely read German works in the world. His sixtieth birthday had been celebrated in Theresienstadt that very summer, and she had participated. The ghetto believed in culture.

There were stand-up comedians, musicians, well-known actors, directors—you name it. I attended a classical theater recitation infused with contemporary allusions. It was exciting to realize that old texts could be put into the service of new ideas. In applauding I saw myself as an active member of an opposition.

Sometimes a mother would sit at the communal table in our room and instruct her daughter in ancient Greek history. That was more than my mother could do. I sat down next to her without asking, and she let me pick up a few hors d'oeuvres of Western civilization, fragments of school learning.

In a way, I loved Theresienstadt, for the nineteen or twenty months which I spent there made me into a social animal. Vienna had treated me as an outcast. It had made me into an eccentric oddball of a child who had no idea how to be a team player. In Vienna I suffered from neurotic compulsions and had tics; in Theresienstadt I overcame my obsessions by means of human contacts, friendships, and conversation. It's amazing how talkative we become when we have nothing but our tongues to distract us from our misery, though of course, the misery must be halfway bearable. So the German wife of my colleague was right, after all, when she said Theresienstadt wasn't all that bad? But where did she get off lecturing me on this place from my past, where everything that came from the Germans was pure malice and the good had its only source in us, the prisoners? Whose voices are still lodged in my brain—they had to be strangled to silence them—and blessed be their memory. Most of what I know about living with others (and it's a good deal; I have become a dependable person) I learned from the young Socialists and Zionists who took care of the children in Theresienstadt, looking after them until they had to deliver them up to destruction and were themselves destroyed. Where there wasn't enough of anything, and only the limitations imposed on us had no limit. To call that "not so bad." The only good was what the Jews managed to make of it, the way they flooded this square kilometer of Czech soil with their voices, their intellect, their wit, their playfulness, their joy in dialogue. The good emanated from our sense of self. And I learned for the first time who we were, what we could be, this people to whom I belonged, or had to belong, according to our oppressors, and now wanted to belong. When I ask myself today how and why an unbeliever like me can call herself a Jew, one of several possible answers runs: "It's because of Theresienstadt. That is where I became a Jew."

And I hated Theresienstadt: it was a mudhole, a cesspool, a sty where you couldn't stretch without touching someone. An ant heap under destructive feet. If I am introduced to someone who has spent time in Theresienstadt, I am ashamed of our common fate and immediately tell him or her that I didn't last there to the war's end. Then I break off the conversation in order to prevent any gestures of chumminess. Who wants to have been an ant? I see the other guy standing before the toilet, waiting for me to come out, no privacy anywhere. Life in a big stable. The owners occasionally show up in their ominous uniforms to make sure that the cattle behave. Makes you feel like the scum of the earth. Which is exactly what we were. To belong to a powerless people who are either arrogant or self-critical to the point of self-hatred. To know no language other than what those who thought us subhuman spoke. To have no opportunity to learn another language, to learn anything. All energy and enterprise drained away. An ever more impoverished, limited life. Like treading water, waiting for time to pass and getting older in the process. Having to stay there. Decades later I sat in an automobile driving out of Theresienstadt, and it was like a bitter euphoria, if I may be allowed the oxymoron, that belated fulfillment of a childhood dream.

For Theresienstadt proved a magnet: hadn't I grown up there? Long after the end of the war I went back, an American tourist in a Communist country, walking the streets of a small Czech town. It seemed nearly empty, and it had been so crowded. I went to the officers' building where we had lived, L414, and knocked on the door. The woman who opened understood right away that I wanted to see the room where I had camped with thirty other girls. It was now her living room, and it was rather smaller than my American living room. And I went up to the attic where I had heard the young Zionists and the old Rabbi Baeck from Berlin, and I thought it must have been Rosh Hashanah, since he talked about the creation of the world. Then I went for a walk and watched the children play on the street. I saw my ghosts among them, clearly outlined and recognizable, like silent silhouettes, while the living children were solid and loud. I was at peace when I left: I had not been to a museum; I had seen a reestablished normality, as comfortable and commonplace as the human habitat should be.

DEATH CAMP

1

If only the war would end! During the entire Hitler period I never heard a Jew voice the opinion that the Germans could be victorious. That was a possibility which was really an impossibility, a taboo sentence, an unspeakable thought. To hope was a duty.

The word *hope* will appear several times on the next pages. In Hebrew hope is *hatikvah*, which includes the article and so means "the hope," as if there were only one, which encompasses all other, minor ones. It is also the name of a song which some of the condemned sang on the trucks that took them to the gas chambers, because it was the Zionist hymn, and today "Hatikvah" is the national anthem of Israel. There is a saying that where there is hope, there is life. Or is it the other way around: where there is life, there is hope? No matter. But if hope is the reverse of fear, I think it is fear rather than hope that can give you the impression of life, of a vibrant vitality, for fear feels like sand on your tongue and courses through your veins like an exciting drug.

Tadeusz Borowski, a talented young Polish writer who after the war gassed himself to death in his kitchen, having escaped the gas chambers, thought that only despair gives us courage, while hope makes cowards of us all. In *This Way for the Gas, Ladies and Gentlemen*, he wrote about hope in Auschwitz:

> Do you really think that without the hope . . . that the rights of man will be restored again, we could stand the concentration

camp even for one day? It is that very hope that makes people go without a murmur to the gas chambers, keeps them from risking a revolt, paralyzes them into numb inactivity. It is hope that breaks down family ties, makes mothers renounce their children, or wives sell their bodies for bread, or husbands kill. It is hope that compels man to hold on to one more day of life, because that day may be the day of liberation. Ah, and not even the hope for a different, better world, but simply for life, a life of peace and rest. Never before in the history of mankind has hope been stronger in man, but never also has it done so much harm as it has in this war, in this concentration camp. We were never taught how to give up hope, and this is why today we perish in gas chambers.

Come to think of it, it is odd that we weren't constantly in the grip of fear, that in a way we got used to this unholy situation. Maybe there are two types of despair, the kind that enables you to take risks, as Borowski thought, and which he held in higher esteem than hope, and then the kind of despair that makes you listless, sluggish, impassive. There was a type of prisoner who had given up, whose will to live had been destroyed, who acted and reacted as if sleepwalking. I don't know the source of the moniker *Muselmänner*, Muslims, which was used to describe them, but no racial slur was implied, since Islam wasn't an issue either for the Nazis or for the inmates of the camps. The *Muselmänner* were walking dead men who wouldn't live long, I was told. I composed poems about them and the camp with slick rhythms and rhymes which were inappropriate for the subject but good for memorizing—an important asset, since I couldn't write them down, lacking pencil and paper.

I never gave up hope, and today it seems to me that the explanation is simply childish illusion and denial of death. In my case, hope was justified as it turned out—a satisfying result, to be sure, but not one that refutes the improbability of such an outcome anymore than naming a sweepstake winner refutes the fact that most gamblers lose their stake, or that it is just as unlikely that a particular player will win as it is certain that one player will. Don't make the mistake of confusing the laws of statistics with Providence, for laws don't choose and evaluate. From a statistical point of view, some of us were bound to get through alive, since the Nazis were losing the war. But to ask for the characteristics of the lucky dogs who crawled away from that murderous madness is to depart from numerical probability into a fairy tale forest of success stories. I can hear you ask: "Then why do you tell such a story?" Yet another dilemma, is my answer. Take old-fashioned tragedy (I think in these terms, because the study of literature is my living, and yes, my life, too), where you get the mutually related, attractive concepts of fate and necessity. The spectator can rest reassured, because whatever befalls the characters in that framework was meant to happen, for better or worse. Statistics has usurped the place formerly occupied by these tragic twins—fate and necessity—but statistics falls a little short of human interest and is not exactly prodigal with the details of individual lives. Statistics doesn't enter into our terrors and joys. And yet all human stories are about terror and joy—mine, too. All I can do is warn the reader not to invest in optimism vouchers and not to give credit, much less take credit, for the happy end of my childhood's odyssey—if indeed simple survival can be called a happy end.

2

Even today freight cars give me bad vibes. It is customary to call them cattle cars, as if the proper way to transport animals is by terrorizing and overcrowding them. Of course that happens, but we shouldn't talk as if it is the norm, as if abuse were our only option in treating animals. In any case, the problem with the transport from Theresienstadt to Auschwitz wasn't that cattle or freight cars are not meant for transporting people; the problem was not the type of car or wagon, but that it was so crowded. Later that same year I had to take another ride in such a wagon and didn't mind—on the contrary. But on the road to Auschwitz we were trapped like rats.

The doors were sealed, and air came through a small rectangle that served as window. Maybe there was a second rectangle at the back of the car, but that was the place for the luggage. In fictional accounts of such transports, whether in films or books, the hero and others often stand pensively at the little window, or someone holds up a child to see the landscape move by. But in reality only one person could stand in this privileged spot, and he was not likely to give it up. Rather he was apt to be someone who knew how to use his elbows. There were simply too many of us. We had been told to take along everything we owned. (So that it could be more readily confiscated on arrival, a kind of special delivery in which we unwittingly collaborated, and yet another example of the unsurpassable cynicism of greed from men who accused their victims of being too money-conscious.) Coming from Theresienstadt we didn't own much, but still too much for a freight car that held sixty or eighty persons. Soon the wagon reeked with the various smells that humans produce if they have to stay where they are.

If I look at a map today, I see that the distance from Theresienstadt to Auschwitz is not very great. Yet it was the longest trip I have ever taken. The train stood around, it was summer, the temperature rose. The still air smelled of sweat, urine, excrement. A whiff of panic trembled in the air. It's from this experience that I think I have an idea what it must have been like in the gas chambers. The feeling of having been abandoned, which is not the same as having been forgotten. We knew we hadn't been forgotten, because the railroad car stood on rails, had a direction, would arrive. But abandoned in the sense of discarded, separated, trashed, and tossed in an old crate, like last birthday's worn-out toys. An old woman who sat next to my mother gradually fell apart: first she cried and whimpered, and I grew impatient and angry with her, because here she was adding her private disintegration to the great evil of our collective helplessness. A defense reaction: I could not face or assimilate the reality of a grown-up losing her mind before my eyes. Finally this woman pushed herself onto my mother's lap and urinated. I still see the tense look of revulsion on my mother's face in the slanting twilight of the car, and how she gently pushed the woman from her lap. Not brutally and without malice. At that moment my mother became a role model for me, which she generally was not. It was a pragmatic, humane gesture, like a nurse might employ to free herself from a clinging patient. I thought my mother should have been indignant, but for her the situation was beyond anger and outrage.

I have just described an unforgettable event in my life, and yet I hardly ever get a chance to speak of it. It doesn't fit the framework of social discourse. For example, after I had written this, while in Germany, I visited friends and we talked about claustrophobia. People mentioned incidents where they had gotten stuck and described feelings of panic or near panic. There was talk about the Chunnel, the rail connection between Britain and France, which wasn't quite finished then, and whether the average person would be able to stand the confinement or freak out. There was a man who once couldn't get out of an elevator, and half the company remembered the air-raid shelters of their childhood. And meanwhile I had this transport to Auschwitz on my mind, but didn't contribute it, because if I had, it would have effectively shut up the rest of the company. They would have been bothered, troubled, sympathetic, and thoroughly uncomfortable. There would have been no further discussion of the way space affects us, which had been our subject. They would have resented me as a spoilsport. It had been an occasion for reminiscing, but there are limits. And so my childhood falls into a black hole.

So what do you expect of us? my friends say. Should we treat a transport to Auschwitz like a stuck elevator, or even like an admittedly more dangerous night in an air-raid shelter? And again I am stumbling through the labyrinth of conflicting comparisons and asking the question how we can understand anything if we can't relate to it. Some comparisons work better than others, to be sure. An execution is not like a fatal car accident, though for the victim the result is the same. It's a comparison where the dissimilarity is instructive. For which of us would want to live in a country where as many innocent people were randomly executed as now die on the road? The accident rate is a social problem; an equal rate of arbitrary executions would mean a nightmare regime. You emigrate from the latter, not from the traffic toll in a country. And yet people like my friend Gisela from Princeton equate disparate events by focusing on the one conspicuous point of comparison. That, in turn, provokes others to insist on the uniqueness of each event, which, these others say, will brook no comparison. And I feel that if I open my mouth, you'll all look at me as if I had jumped into a seething cauldron as though it were a swimming pool. So I listen in bored silence to speeches about the Holocaust with the usual self-enclosed phrases that don't engage anyone's attention, let alone imagination, and when I am with company, I let others talk. (You might not invite me back if I didn't.) And yet that evening we had a lot in common, those Germans and I: we had a common language, a common culture, and an old war that had destroyed much of both. We were articulate and knowledgeable. But the bridges had been blown up; we squat on piers that don't connect anything, though our houses are postwar and the equipment is state-of-the-art. But if there is no bridge between my memories and yours and theirs, if we can never say "our memories," then what's the good of writing any of this?

People who have experienced fear of death in cramped quarters have a bridge to understanding the kind of transport I have been describing.

As I believe myself to have some understanding of dying in gas chambers from having lived through such a transport. Europeans who have sat in air-raid shelters have something in common with me that Americans don't. Isn't all reflection about the human condition (or conditions) a process of deducing from ourselves to others? What tools are left if we don't compare?

I used to think that after the war I would have something of interest and significance to tell. A contribution. But people didn't want to hear about it, or if they did listen, it was in a certain pose, an attitude assumed for this special occasion; it was not as partners in a conversation, but as if I had imposed on them and they were graciously indulging me. The current craze for oral history and interviewing harbors a related flaw of one-sidedness, even though the interviewer is doing the imposing: he or she contributes nothing except an implied superiority to suffering. Beware of the kind of awe which easily turns into its opposite, disgust. For we like to keep the objects of both emotions at arm's length, in instinctive revulsion.

Shortly before the stickiness became truly unbearable, the doors were unsealed, and within minutes we were unloaded. My mother grabbed the bundle on which she had been sitting—she has always clung to things, as I cling to words—and then we were pushed from behind or pulled from the front; in any case, I fell out of the wagon, which was too high for stepping down. You had to jump. (When we were loaded in at Theresienstadt there had been a couple of wooden steps for climbing in.) I got up and wanted to cry, or at least sniffle, but the tears didn't come. They dried up in the palpable creepiness of the place. We should have been relieved—and for a few moments we were—to be outside the sardine box where we had been suffocating and to be breathing fresh air at last. But the air wasn't fresh. It smelled like nothing on earth, and I knew instinctively and immediately that this was no place for crying, that the last thing I needed was to attract attention.

So I swallowed the terror which filled my throat like vomit and concentrated on the hope for a little rest, a cup of water, a chance to recover. None of these were to be. We were surrounded by the odious, bullying noise of the men who had hauled us out of the train with the monosyllables "raus, raus" (get out), and who simply didn't stop shouting, as they were driving us along, like mad, barking dogs. I was glad to be walking safely in the middle of our heap of humanity.

During the following weeks I was to hear this hate-drenched tone all the time, and every time I cringed. It was a tone which stripped the person it addressed of her or his personhood, and at the same time held her like a lifeless thing; it was a tone no one should ever get used to, designed to intimidate and thereby deaden the sense of self. We are usually not aware of the courtesy in the sound of a normal conversation, or how much consideration there is even in controversy and anger. You argue with your peers, more or less; we Jews were subhumans, *Untermenschen*, hence not even enemies. Authority in Auschwitz meant disrespect for the prisoners to the point of rejecting their existence, their right simply to be. Primo Levi has a scene in his classic Holocaust memoir *Is This a Man?* where a German wiped his hands on him as if he were not a man, but a dirty rag. But Levi could take it, because he came to Auschwitz with the self-esteem of a grown European, a rationalist, at home in Italy, secure in his identity. For a child it was different, for in the few years that I had lived as a conscious person, my rights had been removed piece by piece, so that Auschwitz had a kind of logic to it. It was as if I had invaded a stranger's property and was told that my presence there was undesirable. As my presence had been undesirable in Aryan stores a couple of years earlier, according to the clearly marked signs in the windows. Now the wheel had turned one further cog, and the soil on which you stood wanted you to disappear.

That ramp proved to have staying power, I have never stopped falling onto it. Waking after surgery in the recovery room of a hospital, I fall, relieved and horrified at the same time, from the suddenly opened door of a sealed wagon onto an unknown pavement that has since become infamous. Blind alley of a civilization gone berserk. A moment like a monstrous insect in amber, petrified into an ever repeated sense of falling. From the frying pan into the fire, from the cattle wagon onto the ramp, from the transport into the camp, from a closed space into the pestilent air. Falling.

3

Buchenwald and Birkenau mean beech grove and birch forest respectively. Did the Germans deliberately bestow these pretty names on their camps, reversing with macabre irony their Romantic poets' benign view of arboreal beauty, or did they simply follow the dictates of their mendacious sentimentality? For the main characteristic of sentimentality is deception, including self-deception: the inclination to see something other than what's in front of you. These camps were a wasteland. Their names have a lyrical quality, as if they belonged in folk songs, and they conjure up images of natural bliss. And yet: on my way to a conference in Krakow, I suddenly notice from my train window (traveling first-class this time around!) how the roads are lined with birch trees as we approach Oświęcim, where the camp Auschwitz-Birkenau was located, and which is now a museum site that I won't visit. So the name Birkenau was not a fantasy name, as I used to think. The slender, elegant white trunks, flecked with black spots, lose their beauty as we pass them and become oddly menacing in my eyes. Innocence, too, is in the eye of the beholder, it would seem, and this beholder had an undigested story on her mind.

Birkenau was the extermination camp of Auschwitz and consisted of many smaller camps and subdivisions. Each had a main street, lined on both sides with wooden barracks. The barracks were backed by barbed wire, which divided them from a similar subdivision on the other side. B2B was an exception, inasmuch as it warehoused men, women, and children—babies, too. Hence its heartwarming name, Theresienstadt Family Camp.

Each building had two rows of three-tiered bunk beds along the walls. Between them stretched a brick structure called the chimney (not to be confused with the crematoria), which divided the room in two. On our first evening in the camp, the block eldest, herself a prisoner, stood on this structure, while we cowered in our bunks, and screamed, cursed, and gave orders which I don't remember, words whose purpose was intimidation and nothing else. We know this trick in talking to animals: what is said doesn't have to make sense, since it's the tone that carries the meaning, and I listened that way, like a puppy. But one sentence struck me: "You are no longer in Theresienstadt." She made it sound as if we had just been expelled from paradise. It occurred to me that this woman treated us as inferiors because she had been in Auschwitz longer than we. I felt confused: wasn't she an inmate like us? I learned the hierarchy of the numbers: those with the lower numbers were socially above those with the higher ones, because they had had to live for more days, weeks, and months in a place where no one wanted to live. A topsy-turvy world.

The same evening, when we finally lay down to rest in the middle row of the bunk, five to a row, my mother explained to me that the electric barbed wire outside was lethal and proposed that she and I should get up and walk into that wire. I thought I hadn't heard correctly. If to love life and to cling to it is the same, then life has never been dearer to me than in the summer of 1944, in camp B2B in Birkenau. I was twelve years old, and the thought of dying, now, without delay, in contortions, by running into electrically charged metal on the advice of my very own mother, whom God had created to protect me, was simply beyond my comprehension. The idea of it! I couldn't grasp it. I fled into the comfort of believing that she couldn't have meant it. Persuaded myself that she was only out to frighten me. Resented that she was up to bad tricks. Hadn't she often scared me for nothing? My mother accepted my refusal nonchalantly, as if she had merely offered me a walk in the country in peacetime. "Okay, whatever you say." And she never returned to her suggestion.

I knew my mother no better than most children know their parents, which isn't very well. Perhaps a certain wild, destructive pleasure was at the root of her proposal. But more probably she was quite serious and quite desperate. As I think back, I ask myself if I have ever forgiven her that worst evening of my life. Of course I have: but who can count the sparks in the ashes? We never talked about this exchange again, not in all the years that passed before her death at ninety-seven. Yes, there were moments when I had the urge to say: "That first evening in Birkenau, did you mean it or not?" But then I pulled in my feelers like a snail that has learned a bit more than it needs to about the outside world and is happy enough in its shell. I figured she was not going to give me an honest answer but would say whatever happened to suit her at the given moment. Besides, I detested any intimacy with my mother, and what could be more intimate than such a question?

Only when I had children of my own did I realize that one might well decide to kill them in Auschwitz rather than wait. I now believe that I would have had the same thought and perhaps carried it out more efficiently. For to kill oneself is a relatively familiar idea, especially if you come from a country like Austria, where the suicide rate is high, "doing oneself in" is a common topic of small talk, and a remarkable number of people have tried to do just that, one or more times. Committing suicide is a homespun, almost cozy, idea for many cultures, and certainly more acceptable than the prearranged death at Birkenau.

The next day we got our ID numbers tattooed on our left arms. A few female prisoners had been installed outside the building at a table with the necessary equipment, and we stood in line waiting our turn. The women knew their job, and they were fast. At first it looked as if the black ink would easily wash off, and indeed, water took most of it away, but then the fine points of my number remained: A-3537. The *A* was an abbreviation for a high number, a stenographic sign for many previous killings. The victims' skin saved the Nazis producing dog tags. Strange that the armpits of the SS were also decorated with tattoos. The same procedure for honor and shame, if one chose to choose these perspectives.

The tattoo produced a new alertness in me. Thanks to the dog tag under my skin, I was suddenly so aware of the enormity, the monstrosity, really, of my situation that I felt a kind of glee about it. I was living through something that was worth witnessing. Perhaps I would write a book with a title like *A Hundred Days in a Concentration Camp*. (Books and pamphlets with such titles did crop up after the war.) No one would be able to deny that I was one of the persecuted who had to be respected for their unusual and dangerous experiences, unlike those who had been simply neglected or pushed aside, the average downtrodden. I would have to be taken seriously with my tattooed number, as my cousin Hans was taken seriously by the family. It tells you something about how beaten down and stripped of a sense of self I already was that I thus invented for myself a future based on the experience of the most abysmal humiliation yet, a future where precisely that abyss would appear honorable.

One of my younger readers shakes his head and says that this is a bit unbelievable, even in a girl who was as hung up on the written word as I was. The horror, the panic, must have been too violent to allow such sublimation—if you'll forgive the term—of what was happening to me. But I counter that hope is by definition future-oriented. Hope says, "Now I am afraid. Later I'll be able to talk about my fear." I am only reporting my own well-remembered variation on a widespread strategy: comfort through projection. We didn't want to live in the present, where time itself was a prison. We'll be witnesses, we thought, meaning there'll come a future when this will be over, and the number will be a piece of incontrovertible evidence, proof of what had been. Add to this every child's wish to have adventures, especially when life is boring—and nothing is as boring as a day in prison. Hunger, thirst, and a steady sense of discomfort are boring, inasmuch as you want them to be past and the future to come, please, ASAP. This number was something entirely novel and amazing, and didn't so much terrorize as astonish me. Who would think up what the Nazis thought up when they dealt with the Jews! And so, in the intervals between attacks of fear, I managed to doubt that the camp's business was mass murder, simply by dint of a youthful will to live. I wouldn't perish here, not I.

4

Liesel, the lower-class kid who had spelled trouble for me at school in Vienna, had been a nuisance in Theresienstadt as well. I can't figure out why we bothered with one another. In her presence I always, overtly or covertly, reminded myself that I had read more than she, and that I was a doctor's daughter. To be sure, this arrogance was a reaction to her far more direct superiority, for not only was she older, she also was streetwise and knew her way around. In Theresienstadt she let me know with a little girl's leer that in Vienna my mother had had an affair with a married physician. "Yeah, and Mrs. W found out here in the ghetto and put your mother through the wringer." I dismissed the matter. Right or wrong, it was one more piece of dirty laundry I didn't want to touch.

When I met Liesel again in Birkenau, there were several reasons to hang out with her. She had come with an earlier transport, had been there for a while, had a lower number, and was on good terms with the "runners" (young messengers who went between the camps) and other privileged personnel. It was she who told me the facts of life, as she had always done, only this time they were the facts of death. Her father was part of a special work group, a *Sonderkommando*, whose task was to remove dead bodies. She talked as unaffectedly about the details of this work as street kids talk of sexual intercourse, but with the same subterranean challenge, the same sneaking offer of corruption. So I was educated in the perversities of murder and the desecration of corpses. From her I learned that the gold fillings of Jewish teeth weren't permitted to stay in dead Jewish mouths, and much else that is common knowledge today, can be researched in many reference books, and need not be repeated here.

Her father trusted her and told her everything. I saw him once or twice—a large, squarely built man with coarse features. His face had the ruined, decayed look of a madman's. When I watched his broad back from a distance, he seemed to walk out of the world, like someone who had been called into the devil's kitchen to sweep up the ashes. I feared and avoided him. Liesel had changed. She was depressed and looked hunted. But when I bugged her, begging for a drop of hope, for a hint that maybe the crematoria weren't like what she said they were, she simply shook her head.

Liesel wasn't a sentimental girl. Illusions were as wasted on her as German poetry. But she was also a child, and what she dished up for me was more than she herself could digest, even if she still got some kick out of knowing so much more than I did. Once a truck filled with bodies came through the camp in broad daylight, and she ran away screaming.

5

Hunger was less of a problem than thirst. Those who have never been thirsty repeatedly or for a long time are apt to have more sympathy for the starving. But you only have to consider how long it takes for a person to die of hunger and how quickly he dies of thirst. You can live for weeks, even months, without food, but you die of thirst within days. Accordingly, thirst is more nagging, harder to put up with, than hunger. In Birkenau our food, our daily nondescript soup, must have been very salty, for I was always thirsty, especially during the hot, hour-long roll calls in the sun. "What did you children do in Auschwitz?" someone asked me recently. "Did you play games?" Games indeed! No, we had roll call instead. In Auschwitz I stood in rows of five and was thirsty and afraid of dying. That's it, that's all, that's the sum of it.

Central Europeans in Birkenau. There was a woman high school teacher who shortly after her arrival, in the face of the smoking, flaming crematoria, lectured us with touching conviction on how the obvious wasn't possible, for this was the twentieth century and we were in Europe, that is, at the heart of the civilized world. And I recall how ridiculous she seemed to me. Not because she didn't believe in genocide—that refusal was comprehensible, for this business wasn't plausible (why kill all the Jews?), and every objection was welcome to my twelve-year-old love of life, or fear of death. But her reasons were ridiculous—the bit about culture and the heart of Europe. I, too, liked culture, what little of it had been accessible to me through books, but I didn't believe that it compellingly mandated a certain line of conduct. Put differently, I had no reason to believe that culture meant community. The humanist heritage, those fragments of German classical literature that floated through my mind, had been worth reading, but I wasn't surprised that the Germans hadn't taken them to heart. The idea that culture imposes an obligation, that literature ought to influence conduct, was a problem which I only tackled when I was grown and well-off. In those earlier days

I didn't know such claims. They seemed too much to ask of entertaining books—and they still do. Poetry wasn't connected with the outside, the real, world. Its value lay in the comfort it provided, in that profound consolation that could fill the mind when a malevolent environment tried to suck it dry. But I didn't expect it to teach and convert. Not for nothing had I walked hand in hand with my father along Mariahilferstrasse the day after *Kristallnacht*.

Today everyone recognizes the phrase over the gate of Auschwitz— *"Arbeit macht frei,"* "Labor liberates"—as the ultimate motto of a murderous irony. There were other proverbs written in large capital letters on the cross beams of our barracks. I used to stare in cold desperation at the nonsensical "SPEECH IS SILVER, SILENCE IS GOLD" and in utter disbelief at "LIVE AND LET LIVE." An earlier transport, which had been wiped out, had had the task of decorating our living quarters. I looked at these pearls of wisdom every day, revolted by their absolute claim to truth, which, in the face of the reality in which they were inscribed, exposed them as absolute lies. German proverbs nauseate me; I can't hear any of them without seeing its cynical application in the death factory. Some pious soul will quote one of these gems, and right away I make a derogatory remark, which I am sure is offensive to those who don't associate such life-enhancing maxims with willful extermination.

Sketches from Birkenau. A schoolteacher, whom I remember with some emotion but no respect. He would collect stalks of grass, of which there wasn't much, but he found what there was and patiently identified the grasses by their various names, commenting, "You see, even here in Auschwitz something can grow. There is life." But Liesel's accounts offered a more vivid reality than all the greenery of Upper Silesia, as that part of Poland was called by the occupying Germans, and for me there was no comfort in the thought that the grass would outlast me.

Second sketch. Two men are fighting in front of a barracks. One of them says, "What are you yelling about? No point getting excited. The chimney burns the same for you as for me." He is not resigned, he is angry, he shouts, and yet the gas chambers were a subject of everyday banter. There were discussions about whether it was technically possible to cremate as many people as rumor had it. The optimists thought that the crematoria, the "chimney," took care only of those who had died of more or less natural causes. Chitchat about one's own prospective slaughter.

Third sketch. A German guard on the other side of the barbed wire preens with a walking stick that has a loaf of bread at the end. The idea is to show the starving prisoners that one has the power to let bread spoil in the dirt. I was used to hunger and don't particularly associate it with Auschwitz. My physical recollections of the camp are mostly of heat (the glaring sun during roll call, which went on and on), of the stench from the death factory, which pervaded the camp, and of thirst. But the loaf of bread at the end of a stick hit me like a blow in the diaphragm, because it was such a crudely sarcastic expression of undifferentiated hatred.

Another sketch with a walking stick. This time it belonged to a naked two-year old boy who paraded it in the washroom and was happy because he had finally scared up a plaything. A man says to my mother, "What a shame that the kid won't get a chance to grow up." "What did the man tell you?" I ask her. My mother repeats his words.

D-Day. The news reached us in Auschwitz: the Americans had landed in Normandy. Wherever that might be, but it was somewhere in Europe. They had come out of the water and the air—in Auschwitz there was never enough water for me, and there was soot in the air. They had waded out of the ocean and leaped out of their airplanes. I imagined them landing. Now it can't last much longer. Later I was married for some years to one of those paratroopers, and probably chose him mainly because he had jumped out of the clouds and into the legendary land of Normandy during the leaden summer of 1944 to liberate me.

My mother carries soup. The enormous barrel is suspended between two poles. All together four women carry it, two in front, two behind. The weight is too much for my mother. I am stunned to see her this way, her face red and the veins protruding. She must have volunteered for the extra bowl of soup. For me. I don't want that. Don't do this to me!

Two old women arguing. They stand in the glaring sun, gesticulating with emaciated fingers. A third woman joins them, a prisoner with some authority, and knocks their heads against each other, hard. The brutality of the scene strikes me with full force, a sensation of deep terror: I am witnessing the dissolution of the social structure, which I had known at least sketchily. Later I used to think this horror was a little naïve—there was so much that was worse. But still later I came around to thinking that I was not simpleminded, and that my reaction was right as rain. Old women in Auschwitz, their nakedness and helplessness, the needs of old people, their exposure. Old women on the mass latrines, where at least a dozen women at a time were dealing with their constipation or diarrhea, in full view of each other. The old don't take physical functions for granted as children and young women do, especially the generation I have in mind, that of my grandmother, who had been born in the nineteenth century with its rigid standards of modesty.

And the naked corpses, heaped on a truck, piled up any which way, and molested by flies. The disfigured features that had faced the ultimate violence, the hair on their heads disheveled, sparse pubic hair, all in the glaring sun. Liesel runs away in a panic. I stand and stare in fascination.

It was the time of the transports from Hungary. The camp next to ours was suddenly full of Hungarian women. They had come directly from home and were uninformed. We talked to them through the barbed wire in fast, hectic sentences, without telling them much. I noticed how far ahead of them I was, with my experience of Theresienstadt. There was a woman who spoke excellent German and her daughter, about my age. It was evening, both of them were cold, though the days were very warm. My mother identified right away with this other mother, who worried about the whereabouts of her husband and son. They had been separated at the ramp, she said. My mother remembered that she still had a pair of woolen socks, ran to fetch them, and prepared to toss them over the wire. I interfered: I can throw better than you, give them to me. My mother refused, threw the socks, and they fell short, ending up stuck on top of the wire, where no one could reach them. Regrets on both sides. A futile gesture. Next day the Hungarian women were gone, their camp empty like a ghost town, our socks still impaled on the wire.

6

Selection, there was to be a selection. At a certain barracks at a certain time, women between the ages of fifteen and forty-five were to be chosen for a transport to a labor camp. Some argued that up to now every move had been for the worse, that one should therefore avoid the selection, stay away, try to remain here. My mother believed—and the world has since agreed with her—that Birkenau was the pits, and to get out was better than to stay. But the word *Selektion* was not a good word in Auschwitz, because it usually meant the gas chambers. One couldn't be sure that there really was a labor camp at the end of the process, though it seemed a reasonable assumption, given the parameters of the age group they were taking. But then, Auschwitz was not run on reasonable principles.

My mother had reacted correctly to the extermination camp from the outset, that is, with the sure instinct of the paranoid. Her suicide proposal of the first night is evidence of her understanding. And when I wouldn't go along with her then, she managed to take the first and the only way out. Time has proved that she was right all along, and yet I still think it was not her reasonableness but an old and deep-seated sense of being persecuted which enabled her to save our lives. Psychologists like Bruno Bettelheim have tried to persuade us that a sane person who hasn't been spoiled by a disabling bourgeois education should be able to adjust to new conditions, even if they are as outlandish as those of a concentration camp. The saner, the better the chance of survival is the bottom line of this type of argument. I think the opposite is true. I think that people suffering from compulsive disorders, such as paranoia, had a better chance to pick their way out of mass destruction, because in Auschwitz they were finally in a place where the social order (or social chaos) had caught up with their delusions. If you think that your mind is the most precious thing you own, you are right, because what have we got that defines us other than reason and love? But in Auschwitz love couldn't save you, and neither could reason. Madness, perhaps. There are no absolute means of salvation, and there are times when even paranoia may work. It wasn't the last time that my mother thought she was pursued, and maybe it wasn't the first time. But it took the Shoah to prove her right for once.

But isn't the price she paid too high: this madness that she carried inside her, like a sleeping tomcat? The cat would occasionally stretch, yawn, arch his back, softly case the joint, suddenly chatter with his teeth, reach with sharp claws for a bird, and go to sleep again—leaving the bloody feathers for me to clean up. I don't want to carry such a predator inside of me, even if he could save my life in the next extermination camp.

Two SS men conducted the selection, both with their backs to the rear wall. They stood on opposite sides of the so-called chimney, which divided the room. In front of each was a line of naked, or almost naked, women, waiting to be judged. The selector in whose line I stood had a round, wicked mask of a face and was so tall that I had to crane my neck to look up at him. I told him my age, and he turned me down with a shake of his head, simply, like that. Next to him, the woman clerk, a prisoner, too, was not to write down my number. He condemned me as if I had stolen my life and had no right to keep it, as if my life were a book that an adult was taking from me, just as my uncle had taken the Bible from me because I was too young to read it. Later I saw the selector's image in Kafka's door keeper, who won't grant a man entrance to his own space and light.

My mother had been chosen. No wonder: she was the right age, a grown-up woman. Her number had been written down, and she would leave the camp shortly. We stood on the street between the two rows of barracks and argued. She tried to persuade me that I should try a second time, with the other SS man in the other line, and claim that I was fifteen.

The month of June 1944 was very hot in Poland, and therefore both the front and the rear doors of the barracks stood open. The back entrance was guarded, but the detail consisted of inmates, and my mother felt I could sneak by and take another turn. And this time, please don't be a fool and tell them your real age of twelve. I got angry and was half desperate. "I don't look older," I remonstrated. I felt she half wanted me to step in a pile of shit, like the time a few years earlier when she had urged me to go to the movies despite the legal prohibition. (I repeat: my mother and I were very unfair to each other.) The difference between twelve and fifteen is enormous for a twelve-year-old. I was to add a quarter of my entire life. In Theresienstadt, in L414, they had put the different age groups into different rooms. A mere difference of one year had meant another room, another community. The lie which my mother proposed was so transparent: three years! Where was I to find them?

I was anguished and frightened, but this was not the profound fear that overwhelmed me when I looked at the chimneys, the crematoria, spitting flames at night and smoke by day. When that fear gripped me, it was like the psychological equivalent of epileptic fits. The fear I felt now was more like the bearable fear of malicious grown-ups, a fear with which I could cope. For what would become of me if I had to stay in Birkenau without my mother? Well, that was out of the question, she assured me. If I wouldn't try the selection a second time, she would stay, too. She'd like to see who could separate her from her child. Only it wasn't a good idea, and would I please listen to what she was telling me, she said, without paying attention to my conclusive counterarguments. "You are a coward," she said half desperately, half contemptuously, and added, "I wasn't ever a coward." So what could I do but go in a second time, but with the proviso that I would try thirteen, never fifteen.

Fifteen was preposterous. And if I get into trouble, it's your fault.

The space between the barracks I was to invade in order to reach the back door was guarded by a cordon of men. My mother and I watched them carefully for a minute or so. "Now!" we realized, and I sneaked by as the two men in charge happened to call out to each other. I bent over a little to appear smaller, or to make use of the shadow of the wall, turned the corner, and entered through the door, unobserved.

The room was still full of women. A kind of orderly chaos reigned which I associate with Auschwitz. The much-touted Prussian perfection of camp administration is a German myth. Behind every good organization is the presumption that there is something worth keeping and organizing. Here the organization was superficial, because there was nothing valuable to organize or retain. We were worthless by definition. We had been brought here to be disposed of, and hence the waste of *Menschenmaterial*, human substance, as the inhuman German term has it, was immaterial, to use another inhuman term. Basically the Nazis didn't ca re what went on in the Jew camps, as long as they were no bother. The selecting SS officers and their helpers stood with their backs to me. I went unobtrusively to the front door, took off my clothes once more, and quietly went to the end of the line. I breathed a sigh of relief to have managed so far so well, and was happy to have been smarter than the rules. I had proved to my mother that I wasn't chicken. But I was the smallest, and obviously the youngest, female around, undeveloped, undernourished, and nowhere near puberty.

I have read a lot about the selections since that time, and all reports insist that the first decision was always the final one, that no prisoner who had been sent to one side, and thus condemned to death, ever made it to the other side. All right, I am the proverbial exception.

What happened next is loosely suspended from memory, as the world before Copernicus dangled on a thin chain from Heaven. It was an act of the kind that is always unique, no matter how often it occurs: an incomprehensible act of grace, or put more modestly, a good deed. Yet the first term, an act of grace, is perhaps closer to the truth, although the agent was human and the term is religious. For it came out of the blue sky and was as undeserved as if its originator had been up in the clouds. I was saved by a young woman who was in as helpless a situation as the rest of us, and who nonetheless wanted nothing other than to help me. The more I think about the following scene, the more astonished I am about its essence, about someone making a free decision to save another person, in a place which promoted the instinct of self-preservation to the point of crime and beyond. It was both unrivaled and exemplary. Neither psychology nor biology explains it. Only free will does. Simone Weil was suspicious of practically all literature, because literature tends to make good actions boring and evil ones interesting, thus reversing the truth, she argued. Perhaps women know more about what is good than men do, since men tend to trivialize it. In any case, Weil was right, as I learned that day in Birkenau: the good is incomparable and inexplicable as well, because it doesn't have a proper cause outside itself, and because it doesn't reach for anything beyond itself.

I can't keep SS men apart—to me they are all the same uniformed wire puppet with polished boots. Even when Eichmann was tried and executed, I was embarrassingly indifferent to the whole process. These people were one single phenomenon, as far as I was concerned, and their different personalities were irrelevant. Hannah Arendt offered the counterpart to Simone Weil's reflections on goodness when she pointed to the simple fact that evil is committed in the spirit of mental dullness and narrow-minded conformity—what she called banality. Her reflections on evil caused much indignation among men, who understood, though perhaps not consciously, that this deromanticization of arbitrary violence was a challenge to the patriarchy. Perhaps women know more about evil than men, who like to demonize it.

The line moved towards an SS man who, unlike the first one, was in a good mood. Judging from photos, he may have been the infamous Dr. Mengele, but as I said, it doesn't matter. His clerk was perhaps nineteen or twenty. When she saw me, she left her post, and almost within the hearing of her boss, she asked me quickly and quietly and with an unforgettable smile of her irregular teeth: "How old are you?" "Thirteen," I said, as planned. Fixing me intently, she whispered, "Tell him you are fifteen."

Two minutes later it was my turn, and I cast a sidelong look at the other line, afraid that the other SS man might look up and recognize me as someone whom he had already rejected. He didn't. (Very likely he couldn't tell us apart any more than I had reason to distinguish among the specimens of his kind.) When asked for my age I gave the decisive answer, which I had scorned when my mother suggested it but accepted from the stranger. "I am fifteen."

"She seems small," the master over life and death remarked. He sounded almost friendly, as if he was evaluating cows and calves.

"But she is strong," the woman said, "look at the muscles in her legs. She can work."

She didn't know me, so why did she do it? He agreed—why not? She made a note of my number, and I had won an extension on life.

Every survivor has his or her "lucky accident"—the turning point to which we owe our lives. Mine is peculiar because of the intervention of the stranger. Virtually all those still alive today who have the Auschwitz number on their left arm are older than I am, at least by those three years that I added to my age. There are exceptions, like the underage twins on whom Dr. Mengele performed his pseudomedical experiments. Then there are some who were my age, but who were selected at the ramp to be sent immediately on to the labor camps, and who were thought to be older because they wore several layers of clothing, by way of transporting a wardrobe. They were not tattooed because they weren't in the camp. To get out of the camp, you really had to have been alive longer than twelve years.

I have always told this story in wonder, and people wonder at my wonder. They say, okay, some persons are altruistic. We understand that; it doesn't surprise us. The girl who helped you was one of those who likes to help. A young American rabbi says that after my buildup he expected a more heroic tale. Maybe he has seen too many action films or read too many Bible stories, the kind that tout male virtues, muscle over mind, noise over quiet resolve. But don't just look at the scene. Focus on it, zero in on it, and consider what happened. There were two of them: the man who had power he could exert on a random object, for better or for worse. He probably didn't believe that the labor of a starved little girl would promote the German war effort considerably or retard the final solution to a noticeable extent. He had to decide the case one way or the other, list or not list my number. Just then it suited him to listen to his clerk. And she is the other. I think his action was arbitrary, hers voluntary. It must have been freely chosen, because anyone knowing the circumstances would have predicted the opposite, or at least shoulder-shrugging indifference. Her decision broke the chain of knowable causes. She was an inmate, and she risked a lot when she prompted me to lie and then openly championed a girl who was too young and small for forced labor and completely unknown to her. She saw me stand in line, a kid sentenced to death, she approached me, she defended me, and she got me through. What more do you need for an example of perfect goodness? Never and nowhere was there such an opportunity for a free, spontaneous action as in that place at that time. It was moral freedom at its purest. I saw it, I experienced it, I benefited from it, and I repeat it, because there is nothing to add. Listen to me, don't take it apart, absorb it as I am telling it and remember it.

But perhaps you are of the opposite camp and claim that there is no such thing as altruism, that every action is motivated by some kind of selfishness, even if such egotism is no more than the consciousness of free choice. In that case, of course, freedom itself is a mere illusion as well. And perhaps you are right, and there is no absolute in these matters, but only approaches to goodness and to freedom. The main characteristic of freedom is its unpredictability. And no one has been able to predict human behavior with the same accuracy as, for example, the behavior of amoebas. Dogs, horses, and cows are semipredictable, but with humans there is never more than a certain degree of probability. People can change their minds at the last moment, and even if we knew everything about a person and stored it in the most advanced computer system, we could still not foresee the mental movement of a woman whom I didn't know, whom I never saw again, deciding to save me and succeeding.

And therefore I think it makes sense that the closest approach to freedom takes place in the most desolate imprisonment under the threat of violent death, where the chance to make decisions has been reduced to almost zero. (And where is the zero point? The gas chambers are zero, I believe, when the men in their final contortions are forced by a biological urge to step on the children. But how can I be sure?) In a rat hole, where charity is the least likely virtue, where humans bare their teeth, and where all signs point in the direction of self-preservation, and there is yet a tiny gap—that is where freedom may appear like the uninvited angel. If a prisoner passed on the beatings he received to those even more helpless than he, he was merely reacting as psychology and biology would expect him to. But if he did the reverse? And so one might argue that in the perverse environment of Auschwitz absolute goodness was a possibility, like a leap of faith, beyond the humdrum chain of cause and effect. I don't know how often it was consummated. Surely not often. Surely not only in my case. But it existed. I am a witness.

7

Liesel remained true to her father. He couldn't get out, she explained to me, because he had seen too much. Therefore the chance of a labor camp wasn't for her, though they would have taken her more readily than me, since she was a few years older. She didn't even try. She wanted to stay with him, and so she was killed with him.

She had no illusions about her death. I wouldn't have sacrificed myself for my mother, though I would have considered it natural if *she* had stayed with *me*. Liesel was a child who loved her father literally more than her own life, and my own moral mediocrity precludes me from commenting on, let alone analyzing, what went on in her. All I can do is mention her here once more in order to tell the end of this aborted, short life. When I think of Liesel, whom I never liked and therefore don't admire (you can't admire without liking), my own rescue from those flames seems even less significant than at other times.

8

From the small family camp, we, the selected ones, walked over to the larger women's camp. There we stayed a few more days, crammed together as usual, only more so, five to each bunk, three decks high, waiting for the transport. Deep anxiety, nothing to occupy us but fear, no place to go amidst the overflow of people in a tiny space except these beds and the everlasting roll calls. Meanwhile, outside, the chimneys had plenty to occupy them. The death machinery was running at full power in the summer of '44. In the women's camp the "politicals" seemed to be in charge, at least in our barracks. They were proud of having been honored by the Nazis with red triangles, not yellow ones like ours. The block elder screamed at us with contempt; she was good at it, despite all the humanistic claims which I had learned in Theresienstadt to regard as the core of a socialist weltanschauung. To the Socialists and Communists in the camps, the Jewish prisoners were inferior beings: they had learned this much from the Nazis.

At some point my mother lost her head, or to see it more positively, she stopped being a sheep and yelled back. As punishment she had to kneel on those bricks I have mentioned before, the "chimney" that divided the room. Her position became a torture after a very short while. She was in terrible condition, completely out of control, on her knees, still shouting at the woman who had done this to her. I stood next to her, helpless, witnessing something indecent: my mother being punished. This scene is perhaps my most vivid and lurid memory of Birkenau. And yet I have never talked about it. I thought, I can't write this down, and planned instead to mention that there are events that are indescribable. Now that I have written it, I see that the words are as common as other words and were no harder to come by. Moreover, I have described something that is in many ways a common sight to the children of wife beaters and was common to the children of slaves in the nineteenth century, though with the threat of imminent death added to it, in my case. The memory is connected with an overwhelming sense of shame, as if a superego had been dragged into the ditch water of the id.

The waiting got to me. I stopped believing in the labor camp, and fear infected me like a poisonous illness. My mind was like a theater in which a fire alarm has gone off and panic has broken out, I couldn't think of anything other than that I would be dead in a day or two.

I spent the night before we left sleepless with terror and taking refuge in a last bout of religiosity: surely God had other plans for me; God would let me live, or he wouldn't have let me make poems. Perhaps I had composed poems mainly to ingratiate myself with God, so he would make an exception of me. (Good thing that I lost my faith, or I would have to ask Him to forgive me for such hubris.)

Five of us were sitting on our bunk, and we had a bowl of water, which we were to share among us. I was the last and the smallest, and I begged the others, do leave a sip for me, I am so thirsty. The woman whose turn it is looks at me maliciously, or so it seems, her eyes narrowing as she lifts the bowl a second time to her mouth and empties it. I thought I wouldn't last the night, I was so thirsty, but that was self-pity. In the end I did fall asleep.

I never went back to Auschwitz as a tourist and never will. Not in this life. To me it is no place for a pilgrimage. I am told that they exhibit my Auschwitz poems in their museum, against my express wishes. That doesn't make me furious anymore: one gets old and indifferent. I could be proud to have survived what some have called the asshole of creation, proud that it held me and couldn't keep me. But it is dangerous nonsense to believe that anyone contributed much to her own survival. The place which I saw, smelled, and feared, and which now has been turned into a museum, has nothing to do with the woman I am.

And yet in the eyes of many, Auschwitz is a point of origin for survivors. The name itself has an aura, albeit a negative one, that came with the patina of time, and people who want to say something important about me announce that I have been in Auschwitz. But whatever you may think, I don't hail from Auschwitz, I come from Vienna. Vienna is a part of me—that's where I acquired consciousness and acquired language—but Auschwitz was as foreign to me as the moon. Vienna is part of my mind-set, while Auschwitz was a lunatic terra incognita, the memory of which is like a bullet lodged in the soul where no surgery can reach it. Auschwitz was merely a gruesome accident.

On July 7, 1944 the remaining inmates of the Theresienstadt Family Camp entered the gas chambers. I have read up on it in the relevant publications.

FORCED LABOR CAMP

1

It was a lovely summer day in late June. We got gray, uniform prisoners' clothes, were loaded into wagons and sent away from Auschwitz. The clothes spelled relief: they meant that we were really going to another camp, not to a place of execution. Whatever awaited us now, I was confident to survive it.

Even our hair had only been cut short, not shorn as was common. Perhaps because we would occasionally have contact with the civilian population, and bald women are bad public relations for the shearers, even in a totalitarian state. Again it was a trip in freight cars, but this time it was pleasant. We were only twenty women, not too many for the space, and everyone was relatively young and relatively fit. And we had no luggage to crowd us. We owned nothing, only our lives, which was perhaps a little less than nothing under the circumstances, but it felt irrationally good. The doors were open and fresh air came in. We were leaving Birkenau behind. I was happy.

And yet everything looked different. I had come from a death camp and was looking out onto a normal landscape. Another girl told me later that she was sure she would live when she saw the first hillside with wildflowers. It was a sort of bet she had with herself: if you see wildflowers again, take it as an omen, you'll be okay.

It's a beautiful country. The Germans who were driven out of what they still call Upper Silesia rave about it, much as the Cuban exiles do about their homeland, and on that summer day it was picture postcard pretty, as if time had stood still and I hadn't come directly from Auschwitz. Bicyclists on quiet country roads between sunbathed fields. How I wanted to join them, though I didn't know how to bike. Would I ever learn that skill? The world hadn't changed. Auschwitz had not been on a foreign planet, but part of what lay before us. Life had gone on without a hiccup. I pondered the incongruity of this apparent carefreeness existing in the same space as our transport. Our train, for all our temporary relief, was part of the camps, part of their independent and peculiar world within a world, while out there was Poland or Germany or Silesia, whatever its geographic name, home of the people we were passing, a place where they felt at ease. What I had gone through hadn't even touched them. Thus I discovered the secret of simultaneity, a mystery that seemed unfathomable and therefore related to timelessness, eternity.

We passed a summer camp for youngsters. I saw a boy in the distance energetically waving a large flag. It was a gesture affirming the sunny side of the system that was dragging us along in the blood and excrement of its underside. So much light out there— how could that be? Later I freely associated this boy, whom I barely glimpsed on my way from Auschwitz, with my German friend Martin, who became and still is, for me, the epitome of the postwar German intellectual. I know this is unfair. But I still see myself rushing past him: I see him and he doesn't see me, for I am inside the train. But perhaps he sees the train. Passing trains fit into the image of such a landscape (part photography, part illusion); they convey a pleasant sense of wanderlust, the urge to travel. It was the same train for both of us, the same landscape, too, yet the same for the retina only—for the mind, two irreconcilable sights.

2

In the late afternoon we arrived in Lower Silesia, in a forest. The nearest village was called Christianstadt, and so was our camp. Later we learned that it was a subdivision of Gross-Rosen, a place that remains fairly obscure, even though it was one of the largest concentration camps, if you include its many subcamps, or *Aussenlager*. The forest was idyllic, quiet, and the camp seemed bearable with its empty wooden barracks. The buildings had actual rooms, unlike the large stables of the barracks in Birkenau. Six to twelve women slept in each room—not too bad.

We were received by uniformed female guards, who addressed us in a normal, if somewhat strident, tone and used the polite form of address for the grown-ups. It is hard to convey to English speakers the difference in respect or disrespect that is inherent in a switch from the formal to the intimate form of address. In the camps the prisoners were *du*, thou, and now this sudden return to a normality, a reminder of civilization. It was unsettling rather than reassuring, but hypocrisy is better than brutality. We remained the charges of these women during our stay in the camp, although occasionally men turned up, who were obviously the real power. Female guards are often called "SS women." It's a misnomer, since there were no women in the SS. The SS was strictly a men's club. Everybody knows this, and yet the term remains in use, as if to make sure that women get half the blame for an organization that was never theirs.

Much has been said about the cruelty of these women, but only recently has there been any real research on them. I am the last to say much good about them, but the evil they did shouldn't be overestimated. The Nazi evil was male, not female. Our guards came from families with little education and were put into uniforms since they could hardly wear civilian clothes to work in the camps. I believe on the basis of my own experience, as well as from what I have heard and read, that on average they were less brutal than their male counterparts. It is hardly news that women are less violent than men. If later on the world's judgment condemned them as much as the men, this makes a convenient alibi for the real culprits.

But as soon as I say this, I meet with bitter objections. Nazi women, I am told, were just as wicked as the men; they just didn't have as much opportunity to commit crimes. Which still leaves us with the fact that they committed fewer, whatever the cause. We don't condemn people for what they might do under different circumstances, but for what they actually did. Certainly German women were ecstatic about their Führer and cheered him wherever he went, but as repulsive and ridiculous their enthusiasm looks today on extant video clips, it was no crime. And what about Ilse Koch, the wife of a Buchenwald thug, and her famous lamp shades of human skin? It seems that we always pull the same names out of the hat when it comes to women, while the names of the men who committed the atrocities are legion. No women were charged in the great postwar trials at Nuremberg or later at the Auschwitz trials at Frankfurt. Again, this is no attempt to exonerate the women who committed crimes, but how are we ever going to understand what happens when a civilization comes apart at the seams, as it did in Germany, if we fail to see the most glaring distinctions, such as the gender gap?

The women guards of Christianstadt were moderate in their authoritarianism. When they were in a bad mood, they showed it and took it out on us. Why not? They had no reason not to. They were arbitrary, and they liked to pick protégées. But they weren't egregiously cruel—not that I can remember.

During our first days in the camp, before the work started, the guards chose a few children, including me, to go into the woods berry picking. It was strange enough to engage in this quintessentially idyllic activity under the eyes of those powerful, friendly women. A Hungarian child—Shari was her name—puts on a skillful act and clowns around, amusing and flattering the women. I am disgusted, purist that I am. She acts like a monkey, I think. But I, too, become a kind of a mascot for an afternoon or two. Because of my thick black hair they called me Black Peter, which is the single unmatched card in a game that is the counterpart of America's Old Maid. Cute, only I don't feel cute—these Germans were my enemies. I was all in favor of not being tormented by them, but for intimacies it was too late. This was not a kindergarten. Enemies who pretend to be kind and yet don't help you. If at least there had been a concrete advantage for us. But wasn't I the calf with which you play, knowing it's still going to be slaughtered before it gets to grow into a cow? I didn't want to be a calf. (This recurring tendency I have of comparing myself to likable animals later on cured me of my meat-eating habit.)

But at first there was mostly the sense of recovery from the terror of Birkenau and of being alive in the sunshine of the late summer of 1944. It took a while before the work groups were organized, and so there were hours when I lay in the grass, free from the terrible confinement of the death camp barracks, and enjoyed the privacy of the open air.

As the year wore on, the guards became irritated and their reactions unpredictable, and therefore dangerous. Sometimes they would shave a prisoner's head, a punishment that filled the women with a despair I couldn't comprehend, since I was too young to grasp the deeper and symbolic significance of this despoilment. And there were cases where a woman disappeared, was sent away, and didn't come back. But violence is something else again. They may have seen us as animals, but useful ones. Sometimes it occurred to me that one ought to be able to remind them of our common humanity. For example, through speech. If they would only listen, they would hear that I am no different from girls my age on the outside. And yet even if they had listened, what then? Wasn't there already an immeasurable distance between them and me? Did I want to be perceived by these uniformed Germans, after all that had happened, as a German child? At the same time, it didn't occur to me that I, too, had changed and that even in different clothes I might not look or act like the children "outside." That test was still to come.

3

Since I had lied about my age, I lived in Christianstadt among grown-up women who had had a life before the war, which they could use as a yardstick for the future. They exchanged recipes the same way I recited poems. At night a favorite game was to surpass each other with the recital of generous amounts of butter, eggs, and sugar in fantasy baking contests. I didn't even know many of the dishes they cooked up and listened with a growling stomach, just as I listened with a hungry imagination to their tales of travel, parties, dates, and university studies—their "estates of memory," as the novelist Ilona Karmel has called them. Yet a certain unease crept into my efforts to make sense of the unknown world I might someday inhabit. I was nagged by the twin questions: How could I ever catch up with these natives of a saner universe, and secondly, How could the past have been so rosy if it had led to Auschwitz and Christianstadt? What was really out there?

At first we were the only prisoners in Christianstadt: Czech, German, Austrian, and Hungarian women from the Theresienstadt Family Camp at Birkenau. Then some Eastern European Jews arrived who spoke Yiddish and had been selected directly at the ramp in Auschwitz. And right away we had a caste system. The new arrivals were dirty, we said, and kept our distance. Personally I kept less of a distance than my elders, because among the new inmates there were girls my age. They had made it because they wore several layers of clothes on top of each other, which made them look older. The selection on arrival went so fast, one of them told me, her eyes still clouded with the terror, or the sadness, of recollection. And this is how I learned a passable Yiddish.

The season turned wet. Then it got cold, very cold. No one who lived through the winter of 1944–45 in Europe is likely to forget it. The paratrooper whom I later married was fond of telling me of the hardship he suffered because of this cold. I respected his suffering, as I respect all suffering, and it was a long time before I had the heart to tell him that I was cold, too, during those months, and that no army provided me with blankets. He seemed surprised. He had forgotten that we lived in the same world, though worlds apart. In the fifties the Holocaust hadn't yet been enshrined, and it was not proper to talk about it in any detail.

In the mornings we were wakened by a whistle or a siren, and then we stood in rows of five for roll call. My dislike of standing in lines dates from this experience in the camps: to stand, just to stand. Sometimes I leave a line when it's almost my turn, out of revulsion for the bovine activity of simply standing.

We got a black, coffeelike brew for breakfast, a ration of bread to take along, and marched off in rows of three. A guard ran alongside us, trying to make us keep in step by means of her whistle. Her whistling was quite useless, however. Despite all her annoyed frustration, she never got us to march properly. Try to teach Jewish housewives—and that's what most of them were, of course—to act like army recruits! Men could be trained more easily, I thought with a grin, touched by an early whiff of feminism.

Even in those days I was struck by a thought which I confess has more of a hold on me than moral outrage about the great crime. It is the absurdity of the whole thing, the senselessness and waste of those murders and deportations which we call Holocaust, Shoah, "Final Solution" (in quotation marks), the Jewish catastrophe—new terms, one after the other, because the words decay even as we use them. The irrationality of it all, how easily it could have been prevented, how nobody profited from my carrying rails for a railroad that was never finished, instead of attending school. Again and again I think: chance, accident. I know as much as the next person how this catastrophic breakdown of what we took for European civilization came about, but the historical backdrop doesn't really explain how a twelve-year-old girl ended up in Christianstadt, sentenced to do men's work, and of course doing it poorly, so that her contribution to the war effort was worthless to the exploiters. Our explanations amount to no more than a shopping list of previous events. And the sum under the bottom line is made to be the inevitable result of what stands above. There is a kind of intellectual game that examines every famous German of the past to determine what he may have contributed to the Holocaust: Bismarck, Netzsche, the Romantic poets and philosophers, Luther and the Christianity of the Middle Ages. Every child has a great-grandmother whose genes we carry, so it's convenient to blame the old woman in her grave (who certainly wasn't free of sin) for the mess her posterity has caused. But the equation doesn't work. If it were correct, one would have to conclude that without a few, targeted old writings and artifacts in libraries and museums, the Nazis couldn't have run amok. The truth is a truism: one can't predict the future, just as one can't predict the next number on a roulette wheel. And the more "civilized" we become, the more our societies come to resemble roulette tables, because no idea is so ludicrous that it can't be carried out where the taboos have broken down and values can be changed at a whim. It is often said that the Nazis were a throwback to barbarism. That is, first, an insult to so-called primitive people who tend to stick to the rules with which they were brought up, and second, a simplification of the modern situation, where science, once the carrier of enlightenment, has turned out to be also the carrier of a virus, the virus, that is, of its own superstitions—racism, for instance—which are more dangerous than those of the religions that have been discredited. If I fantasized that I should be able to have a rational talk with the victimizers, didn't that imply that an "open sesame" would wipe this ghastliness off the face of the earth and allow us to return to normal? As if there had been merely a mistake instead of a set of decisions.

Before we left Auschwitz there had been a "gynecological" exam carried out by female prisoners, which was not for or about our health, but served the purpose of discovering whether we hid any precious items in intimate parts of the body. I find it difficult to write this down and notice that I have done so in a rather circuitous way. Yet it was not a traumatic experience; it was just humiliating. Later, in college, I was oddly relieved to find similar scenes in that great satirical classic, Voltaire's *Candide*. Any event you can turn into literature becomes, as it were, speakable.

Everyone was so undernourished that no one menstruated. But perhaps the cause was not only hunger, but imprisonment itself. Even well-nourished animals seldom have a litter in a zoo. Prison is bad for us living things, from the lower to the highest links on the food chain. Some women thought the Nazis had put something into our food to prevent menstruation, which only goes to show how well-off they had been before, since they didn't know the effects of starvation.

We were assigned to do men's work: we cleared the forest, excavated, carried the trunks of trees, and laid railroad tracks. Obviously something was supposed to go up in Gross-Rosen, but I was not interested in what it might be. It is in the nature of slave labor that the worker either ignores or hates the purpose and end product of his work. Karl Marx would have appreciated us and, I hope, turned in his grave if he could have seen us prove his thesis.

Sometimes our keepers lent some of us out to the village population, and then we would sit in some attic and string onions. That was better than the cold air. The villagers stared at us as if we were wild animals. (But I speak your language, I wanted to say.) Sometimes my friend Susi and I had to work in the quarry. That was the worst of all, because no other place was so desolate and cold. What exactly did you do there? my son asks, and for the life of me, I can't remember what we did with those rocks. We clung to each other, but that didn't help much. There was no protection against the cold, our clothes were too thin, and though we had wrapped our feet in newspapers, which was some help, I still felt helplessly exposed. We longed for the next rest period, for time to pass. Perhaps I can stay in the camp tomorrow as part of the cleaning crew. How can we hold out much longer? (About twelve years later I watch Susi, who is like a sister to me, as she plays with her small daughters in the sand. I hear her soothing, superior-sounding voice: do this or don't do that, she says. Suddenly I see us as we were, Susi's arm around me, the two of us crouching in the quarry in the cold wind. I turn away from her and the children, for the sand has solidified to Silesian granite and the children's game has become threatening. Why doesn't she go home with her children? All this sweetness is a lie.) I still dream of Silesian granite. It's a kind of wasteland where I look for warmth, but there is none.

I didn't work in the munitions factory, but usually in the open air. We women were the cheapest, poorest work force, most easily replaced and therefore least worthy of food. I marched to work with my eyes glued to the ground, hoping to find something edible on the road, because someone had once found a plum. I fantasized about an apple. It didn't have to be ripe and could be partly rotten. But there was never anything. Naturally not. We marched in columns and I was somewhere in the middle. Why should I find what others had overlooked? The best thing was to be assigned to the cleaning crew. Sometimes I was lucky that way.

The girl who thought she would live if she saw wildflowers on a hillside became my role model in Christianstadt. Her name was Vera. She was Czech, and she demonstrated and expressed a total and uncompromising contempt for the Germans, even when they were nice. It was an attitude I tried to imitate and make my own. It gave you something to live by. Once I helped unload vegetables for the kitchen and was able to stay in the cellar storage room a few extra minutes, which gave me the opportunity to steal some turnips and a head of cabbage, with Vera's help. It was common to steal from these provisions if you had a chance to. Everybody who could did it. Nobody had questioned this practice in my hearing. I handed Vera the stolen items through the grating of a small window and afterwards was quite proud of the risk I had taken and of my achievement. To my astonishment, Vera was not impressed with either of us. Good socialist that she was, she had a bad conscience. She told me that we had done what we had done because we were hungry, but the bottom line was that we had stolen from the community of prisoners. This was a new thought, and unfortunately it made sense. My thirteen-year-old brain had, up to that point, only understood that you mustn't steal from individuals, and of course, not from an ideal community like the Eretz Israel of our dreams, which was still the goal of all my wishful thinking. But it had not occurred to me that the soup for the others would be a little less nourishing because of our stolen turnips. It would be too much to say that Vera's reflections made me feel bad, but they did expand my horizon in matters of right and wrong. I admired her for harboring such ideas, knowing how rare they were.

I learned a few Socialist songs from her in which workers figured who brought the world to a standstill by resisting exploitation. I tried to impress her with my knowledge of poetry. A few years ago I found her again. She had survived the last death march and become a journalist in Prague and, her conscience still fine and active, now blamed herself for having served the Communists beyond the first period of hope in a new society and at a time when she should have known better. When I told her how much I had wanted to impress her in Christianstadt, she replied to my astonishment that I had succeeded, but not with my poems, rather with some character traits, some stubbornness or self-assurance unusual in a twelve-year-old, and thus precisely what I had wanted to learn from her.

In October 1944 I turned thirteen, and in a fit of mystical introspection I decided to fast on Yom Kippur for the first time in my life. Of course that didn't mean I was going to throw away my food. It meant keeping my ration until the evening and eating it only after sundown. It was a gesture of solidarity with the observant women in the camp, and it was a profession of Judaism and my entrance into the world of the grownups, since children aren't required to fast. Looking back, I find myself rather unmoved by any of these three motives. What does seem right is the self-assertion which is involved in voluntarily assuming a difficult discipline like putting off a meal when you are genuinely starving.

People say pityingly, "You didn't have a childhood. You lost your childhood." But I say, this, too, was childhood. I grew up, and I learned something, as every child does who grows up, who grows older. I would have learned differently and better and would have learned different and better things under other, more normal circumstances. And I wish it had been different. I would give a lot if I could look back on a different childhood. But it was as it was. And, I repeat, this, too, was childhood.

5

My friend and foster sister, Susi, adopted my mother, or was adopted by her, in Birkenau when we were moved from the family camp to the women's camp. She sort of ran along with us, the way a stray animal, a dog or a cat, will show up at your doorstep and stay. I knew Susi by sight from our games at the Jewish cemetery in Vienna, where she hung out with the older children and impressed me by picking up spiders and allowing them to run over her hands and arms. She was an orphan who was taken from her grandmother's apartment and deported to Theresienstadt. There she lived in the same house as I, but in a smaller room with only fifteen girls who were known for their pronounced camaraderie and exclusivity. And now she was in Birkenau, disturbed like the rest of us and without a soul to turn to. So my mother said: "Come along and join us."

Now this is the best and the most unusual thing that I can say about my mother: she adopted a child in Auschwitz. She decreed without any fuss that this girl belonged with us, as if it was the most natural thing in the world. Susi stayed with us until an uncle from St. Louis provided her with a visa after the war, which meant she could emigrate before we did.

In Christianstadt I had only a single friend, and that was Susi, whom I still call my sister, for there is no other term to describe our relationship, which seems absolute, although we share few, if any, interests. What is absolute about it? Nineteen forty-four, nineteen forty-five, the black hole at the center of the century.

Susi always thought that my mother saved her life. Certainly my mother's care and concern saved her from a certain degree of psychic damage: the mental self-neglect that sets in when nobody gives a hoot whether you exist or not. For us, Susi was not only a presence, she was important. And thus she existed for herself, too, simply because my mother made her feel that she mattered. Without us she would have remained isolated; with us she was part of a family, and thus valuable. We had nothing else to give her. I can't tell whether she would have stayed alive without my mother. But I suspect that perhaps all three of us can claim a share in having saved each other.

Dear reader: don't wax sentimental. We are a family, which means we are like other families, only perhaps a bit worse. In later years my mother often rejected the woman whom she had once treated as her own child. I would come for a visit to my mother's small, unattractive house in the San Fernando Valley, where she lived contentedly for more than thirty years, and I would make a date with Susi. I tell my mother energetically, because I expect her resistance, that Susi will pick me up. My mother sulks: "If you want to go out with her, that's your affair. But don't have her come into my house. I don't want to see her. And now I am going to bed." Susi, aged more than sixty by now, and who has often been a better daughter than I, stands in front of the gate and waits for me to exit, since she isn't allowed to enter. It happened once, it happened again and frequently. Susi put up with the humiliation because she hoped it would ultimately pass.

And it did pass. My mother was afraid of Susi, who had been trained as a psychiatric nurse and sometimes assumed the condescending tone of her profession. That was a big mistake. To this day Susi treats me the same way, using childish nicknames and a know-it-all attitude. I see this as the privilege of an older sister, and while I sometimes get annoyed, my mother reacted in panic and terror. Susi, she argued, wanted to send her to a mental hospital. The paranoia which has probably haunted her all her life met its objective correlative during the murderous Hitler years. Afterwards she found it harder than ever to judge the danger potential of her environment. For example, we would drive past a police cordon and she would say: "There, you see. I told you they were after me." I tried to remind my mother that, in fact, Susi had once saved her from a psychiatric clinic, but that reminder was another mistake. Susi had simply slipped into the wrong pigeonhole in my mother's mind, and we couldn't convince her that this daughter would go a second time through hell for the woman who had saved her from hell. Susi, who is no more religious than I am, would complain that it's particularly hard on her to be excluded during the High Holidays. In the end, old age did what reason had failed to achieve, and my mother was friends with Susi once more. She welcomed her visits, and nobody heard a harsh or down-putting word from her anymore.

6

In the forest we had some contact with German civilians, for example the foremen who directed our work. Once during a rest period I sat on a tree trunk next to a fat, squarish man, who must have invited me to join him, for I would never have done so of my own accord. He was clearly curious. I probably didn't match his ideas of forced laborers—a dark-haired, emaciated child prisoner, a girl at that, who spoke flawless and presumably native German, and was unsuited for the work, a kid who belonged in school. He wanted to know my age. I wondered whether to tell him the truth, that I was thirteen, or to continue the old lie, which had saved my life so far, and pretend that I was three years older. What I really wanted was his lunch. He was eating a sandwich of lard on rye, a delicacy not to be found in the camp, and I wondered how I could get him to give it to me. To have obtained this bread with lard would have been an achievement, and I wanted it for this reason, as much as from hunger. I wanted to share it with my mother and Susi. Susi maintained contacts with the kitchen personnel. She would occasionally turn up with extra food, and I wanted to compete. I figured if I told the guy how young I really was, it might soften him up, but from the point of view of safety, the lie that had saved my life was better. I don't remember how I decided in the end, only that I didn't get his bread and lard. To give him his due, he cut off a large bite for me, but all one could do with that was eat it on the spot. He asked me a series of questions about myself, which I answered with much reserve. Even if I had wanted to, I wouldn't have known what words to choose to describe what was happening to our people. But of course, I didn't want to anyway. Nothing could have been farther from my mind than to take risks with a stranger, a German.

The fat man, for his part, told me that German children, too, didn't go to school anymore. They had gone to soldier, everyone. Did he want to persuade himself, or me, that all was fair and just in Christianstadt? He stuffed himself while telling me about the starving German people.

In today's Germany there are many well-meaning men and women of about my age whose families employed forced laborers. *Employed* is too good a word—let's say who *used* forced laborers, non-Jews, imported from all over conquered Europe. They think back on these unpaid servants with pleasure, even affection. Our Poles were well off in our household, they'll say: they used to play and laugh with us kids and they had enough to eat. They liked us. And I listen and ask myself, what about the anxious alertness, the suspicion, the over- and underestimation of the enemy which must have burdened the minds of these deportees? Didn't you notice then? Don't you remember now? Shouldn't you revise your judgment? If the Germans who were children then haven't considered these questions, it is because no one sees himself as an enemy. The enemy is always the other. How can I be an enemy, when my parents love me and I am a friendly, civil child? And so they never talk about forced laborers, and they shrink visibly when I don't shy away from saying "slave labor."

Here is my contribution to the topic: I didn't want to be friends with the fat man, I wanted his food. And I wanted it not just for myself, but to bring back to my mother and Susi as a token of my skill, not only because I loved them, but also because I wanted to say, here, look, I am good for something. Be that as it may, I didn't get his sandwich.

I imagine that in the mind of the fat man, if he is still around, I am a little Jewish girl who wasn't all that badly off, for she didn't tell any horror stories, though he encouraged her in a friendly way to be honest and to chat about her life. And she wasn't afraid—that was clear from the way she talked—and therefore she had no reason to be afraid. And perhaps he uses this encounter as evidence that Jews were no worse off during the war than the rest of the population.

The first weeks of 1945, and by now there was so little to eat that you couldn't think of anything but food. When I got my daily bread ration I stuffed it into my mouth as if I had to swallow it all in one swoop. Once in a great while I saw myself as I must have looked to an outsider and was ashamed.

As the food supply decreased, the social differences between the prisoners increased. Economic class distinctions, like everywhere else. The cooks and their children grew fat—actually fat. The less there was to eat, the more eagerly the keepers of the food ate it. Since they cooked not only for us but also for the guards, they had access to whatever there was, and they helped themselves. When the winter clothes came (used stuff that had belonged to the dead), the cooks chose first and took what was best. I am standing in front of the central building, and there is light in the kitchen, so I can look in the window: a cook shows off her plump daughter to another woman, who is wearing worthless rags; she shows the ragwoman what a good skirt her daughter is wearing, and the daughter preens and poses as if this were a fashion show. Ragwoman admires Kitchendaughter in her new secondhand getup because she is hoping for food, for a second helping.

One evening Susi told me that the kitchen staff had some leftovers, which they were saving for the children. I ran to the back entrance of the building and stood around for a while; a few women who must have heard the same rumor joined me. I got impatient, thinking that perhaps these latecomers would push ahead, though I was there first, and so I went up a few short stairs and then walked along the narrow, well-lit hall to the back door of the kitchen. Suddenly a door to the right opened. A tall woman guard appeared, and behind her an SS man I had never seen before. He calls to me with a strong northern accent, using the polite form of address. I stand before him, my metal dish in hand, and he asks what I want. I tell him I've heard there are leftovers. He says, "Now watch out." Idiot that I am, I still think he'll let me pass, for why would he want to waste the leftovers, if indeed there are any? You don't throw away food when it's so scarce, do you now? And before I know it he has hit me in the face, full force, so that I stumble backward along the hallway and see stars. My wooden clogs fall off my feet; the dish falls from my hands as I crash to the ground. When I recover my eyesight, the other women have retreated, and the SS man and his companion are gone (after some further verbal nastiness meant to send us packing). Susi helps me get up, and one or two of the others pick up my things with a bit of comforting tongue clucking. I feel that they feel that I provoked this scene, that it was my fault. Walking back to my barracks with Susi, I curse, "The pig actually used the polite form [*er hat mich gesiezt*]," as if that were adding insult to injury. My face still hurts, and the chance for additional food has evaporated.

We return and tell our story. My mother claims that if she had been there, she would have hit back. "Why, then we were lucky that you weren't there," Susi and I say in unison. My mother irritates me, because she stylizes herself at my expense: she is the potential heroine, unlikely as it may seem, and reduces me to poor-little-victim status. As if the humiliation of having been hit wasn't enough, she has to add her superior airs and her pity. And yet, reading this passage, Susi reminds me of something I had forgotten. My mother, oddly enough, was for a short time a kind of protégée, inasmuch as she got to work in the laundry, which was a privileged job. She achieved this position in an unlikely way: she complained to one of the guards that her children had been treated unfairly. The woman was obviously impressed by my mother's spirit and courage—I guess her Hitler Youth education had conditioned her to recognize these qualities—and so rewarded her. I recall this as an example of how anything that can happen will happen somewhere and somehow.

On the evening of my failed attempt to get some scraps of food, I recited one of my Auschwitz poems, a revenge poem called "The Chimney," to my assembled roommates. In this poem the personified death machine proclaims that when it has consumed all who have come its way, it will in the end consume those who built it. I recited these verses with much verve and the secret thought, "You'll get your comeuppance, you creep who hit me, just wait." That was a comfort of sorts, but of course it was nonsense, too, for we can be pretty sure that he didn't get his comeuppance. If he doesn't, or didn't, live in a luxury villa in South America, which he may have bequeathed to his children, then perhaps he lives, or lived, on retirement pay in Göttingen, and he may even be the old pensioner whom I overheard talking to a young saleswoman in Schmidt's drugstore the other day. He was carrying on about foreigners, especially the ones from Poland: "They should all go to the gas chambers and our politicians can join them there." I was about to choose between two tubes of toothpaste and almost dropped them at these words. I look at him, guess his age—yes, homeboy is old enough; he knows the score. He notices my glance, and now it's his turn to look me up and down. "Did I hear what you said?" I ask. We look each other in the eye: a look of recognition. And with a sarcastic undertone, he says, "You heard me correctly."

8

January 1945. We could hear the Russian gunfire approaching, as every day the front moved closer. The menacing noise was sweet music to us. We didn't have to work anymore: we starved, froze, and waited. Reprieve from hard labor was a blessing, but we paid for it by getting less and less food. During roll call an SS man yelled, "Don't imagine that Roosevelt will help you," which led me to conclude that American help was indeed imminent. Prisoners from other camps which were gradually being evacuated showed up at Christianstadt and slept for one night on the floor of the central building, which housed the kitchen and the eating hall of the guards (we ate in the open air or in our barracks). The next day they moved on. I talked to one of them and still see myself bending over her as she lay on the floor. She looked like exhaustion incarnate. I felt that strange sense of profound compassion for those who need sleep and also felt privileged, because as yet I hadn't been forced into that kind of exertion.

The younger prisoners made plans. We had warmer things to wear now that winter had come: civilian clothes instead of our prison uniforms, a motley legacy of the dead. We had had to cut out a square piece of cloth from the back of these things and replace it with a yellow patch. During our last days in the camp, the exchange of recipes for rich food was replaced by talk about means of escape. Some had covered the yellow patch with the original piece or even boldly removed the telltale sign altogether.

We hoped the Germans would simply abandon the camps and let the advancing Russians take over. But they didn't; they evacuated us. These last deportations, near the end of the war, the seemingly arbitrary moves from one camp to another that have entered the history books as "death marches," were often not meant as such, I have been told. The famous German organizational impetus had failed once again. It wasn't part of an overarching plan to let so many prisoners starve and freeze to death so near the end. It was the "accidental" result of an evil intent.

This time we had to walk. We had to carry our blankets and our metal dish, no more. We wore the rags that were our clothes, with the yellow patch that could be covered. Being on the road, we naturally dreamt of escape. But we moved in the wrong direction, away from the front. Those were the first days of February 1945, and it was still very cold. We dragged ourselves along the road, through the villages, slowly and on the edge of total exhaustion. Was there no end in sight?

That night the SS men, who were now in charge, commandeered a few barns for us to sleep in. I had a very modest notion of what I needed by way of space and comfort for a good night's sleep, but in this barn there wasn't enough room, not even for my limited requirements. We lay so close to each other that you couldn't get out to pee. We had tin cans and the place soon stank. I had had plenty of practice in living and lying down in unnatural proximity to others. But this night in the barn surpassed my adaptability, perhaps in part because the women were so burnt out, so close to cracking up. They disgusted and appalled me. Suddenly they weren't my people anymore—I have had enough, I won't, can't, take anymore.

Next morning our trek continued. The road stretched and stretched on in endless boredom. Boredom is an innocent word which seems to denote a minor evil. Yet it is a condition that is more than mere displeasure with luxury or inattention to uninteresting matters. Boredom, tedium, ennui, means that you want to escape from time itself. You can run away from a place, but you can't pack up and leave time; time has to pass on its own, as it were. Therefore tedium is awareness that you are a prisoner of time, and thus it is a close cousin of despair. Theologians know this. I probably felt this kind of lethargy all the more because I was physically so low. I had really arrived at the end of my strength.

And then we acted. On the second night we took off during the chaos of being herded into yet another container. It was again a village with barns, but this time, if I recall correctly, our keepers could requisition one barn only, because the owners were unwilling to have us. I still see the place: some light coming from the buildings, semidarkness in the crowd, which patiently waits for the next command, darkness and silence a bit further on. As I stood there, the last spark of energy seemed gone, and nausea at the prospect of a second night like the last was a lump in my throat. And then there was the lure which arose from the surrounding land. In spite of the cold of that February, there was the promise of spring in the air, a seduction I have felt every February since that time. February is purgatory time. There was a stillness, a type of security which didn't quite reach us and yet seemed to be within reach. You could feel it merely a few steps from the misery of the camps, which we carried with us on our backs together with the blanket and the yellow patch. Out there was the breath of nature, organic, silent.

Now, let's go, this moment! My mother wanted to wait for the next bread ration. I contradicted her bitterly, desperately. They're hardly giving us any food anyway; we can find this much on our own. Now or never, no one is watching, they are occupied and likely to be tired. Not another night in one of those dreadful barns. Three young Czech women were of the same opinion, and Susi sided with me, persuaded by me. My mother still hesitates, then agrees, albeit reluctantly: yes.

Most of what we call a decision hardly deserves that name. We tend to slither into life-changing situations, driven by this or that circumstance. But anyone who has ever made a real decision knows the difference between pushing ahead and being pushed. Our decision to escape was a real, a free, decision.

Last night I exuberantly wrote these sentences with memory bearing down on my mind, but today they seem false, an illusion. I want to erase them, but should I? I see how wrong it is to start with the assertion "Anyone who has ever . . ." I speak of a moment in my own circumscribed life as if it was more than a personal epiphany, as if it had been a valid revelation giving me the authority to generalize. Like saying, "I have a secret that I'll share with you"—childish stuff. What do I really know about free decisions except that I sometimes have been able to overcome the lethargy which I see as the true ambience in which we, or I at least, usually vegetate? Lethargy is not the same as laziness. If you are lazy you try not to make an effort, at whatever, work or play. Lethargy, on the other hand, can involve quite a bit of strain. For example, marching on until you drop instead of running away is still lethargy.

So much to limit my claim to the knowledge of freedom. And yet: on that evening I experienced the unforgettable, prickly feeling of what it means to reconstitute yourself, not to be determined by others, to say yes or no as you like, to stand at a crossroad where there had been a one-way street, to leave constraint behind with nothing in front, and call that nothing good. Certainly there were reasons and causes why we found the energy to act—as there were reasons and causes why we could have continued on that desperate, doomed march. We made a choice: inebriated with hope and despair, a heady cocktail, I chose the freedom of birds that can be shot down by any hunter.

I believe the farm at which we were supposed to spend the night was on a small elevation. Or perhaps it seemed so because now our movements were so fast and light, downhill, as it were. As the last spark of energy blossomed into a firework in my head, we six turned on our heels and ran down the street.

Part Three

GERMANY

Wo Deutschlands Himmel die Erde schwärzt,
Sucht sein enthaupteter Engel ein Grab für den Hass . . .

Where Germany's heaven darkens the earth,
Her angel, beheaded, seeks to bury her hate . . .

—INGEBORG BACHMANN, FROM "FRÜHER MITTAG"

ESCAPE

1

During the next minutes, as we six ran down the street, away from the freezing, hungry prisoners and their enforced wait for shelter, we passed the barrier from the world of the camps into Germany. Of course the concentration camps were within the German Reich, and their brand name would forever bear the label "Made in Germany," but they were, or seemed to me, encased in a capsule we had shattered. We were free—free to be hunted down if our luck should turn. But I remember the exuberance, the euphoria, of these moments.

Leaden fatigue and physical weakness had turned into their opposite. I felt an enormous burst of energy, and wondered, while running, whether I had really been as exhausted as I had imagined. How come I am suddenly moving so fast, when I had thought I was incapable of another step? It seemed a miracle then. Today I know that this "miracle" goes by the simple chemical name of adrenaline.

Out of breath, we stopped at a crossroads and split up. The three young Czech women were planning to make their way to their homeland, which was relatively close. We three hoped to find shelter in a village and wait for the Russian army. A hasty good-bye, eager good wishes and blessings. No more dull eyes and sagging features: the faces were alive, ready for any exertion.

My mother, Susi, and I turned to the right and walked, somewhat more slowly now, down a deserted road, looking for a place to spend the night. We found a small barn, or ministable, which wasn't locked, and where a couple of cows gazed at us good-naturedly. I was delighted to have such a private bedroom, with lots of hay and no other people than those two, my nearest and dearest. I joked that I hoped we would have such exquisite sleeping facilities to the end of our days, for what could be more cozy than the presence of cows—and I fell asleep on the spot.

The next morning, very early on, my mother, who always maintained she could do everything, tried to milk a cow. The cow was friendly, but uncooperative. Instead of milk we found water and a washbowl. An inveterate superstition of the camps held that if you kept clean you'd stay alive, and since we had become fetishists in this respect, a chance to wash seemed even better than a chance to eat.

As we stepped out onto the road, the countryside seemed freshly washed, too. Nature had thus far been largely a matter of cold and heat to be endured during roll call and work. Now it was full of gleaming objects. The land seemed to welcome us, as if asking us to live up to our new roles. It wasn't home, but it was approachable, not terra incognita. It was earth, not hell; nonjudgmental, not sinister. (I have been back to that part of the world, both when it was still the other Germany, East Germany, as well more recently, after reunification, and every time I feel pulled back into the peace of that early convalescence.)

Simply to walk down a country road of one's own volition was like conquering the world. Freedom meant getting away, rather than getting somewhere. Getting away from the lethal march, from the bedraggled crowd, from slavery's constant invasion of ego and identity. The air smelled different, more springlike, now that we had it to ourselves. Who knows what the next day is going to bring, what any next day will be like, so why worry?

Freedom, says a friend who has read this far, can be cold as ice, especially if it's the kind of absolute freedom without security that I have described. The transition, she says, is too fast to be believable. Surely, she says, you must have been scared at times? Perhaps I have forgotten the fear, because fear wasn't a new sensation. What was new was that life could be light as a feather, where it had been leaden the day before, and I wasn't thinking "You can be blown away," I was thinking "I am flying." My hopes, what I had been waiting for all these years, had come true all of a sudden.

Our general intentions were simple. We wanted to reach the Allied Armies and in the meantime eat and find shelter, especially when the weather turned to hail, sleet, and a very cold rain, as it did during the first days after our escape. But then it got warmer, and never again cold. In my entire life since, it hasn't been cold, not really, not even when you have to cover your face against the wind in Cleveland or feel that it will blow you away on the corner of Times Square and Forty-fifth Street. No matter how and where I have shivered since 1945, it's only been a reminder of what it means to be cold. On rainy February days I have an unpurged vision of steel gray Silesian skies and the purgatory of bad weather that led from inferno to sweet earth.

But the land that offered itself up as a cornucopia of life was in reality a country on the move, of villages about to break up. It was a period in those borderlands of the former German Democratic Republic and what is now Poland when the houses emptied out and the roads filled up with trekking refugees. Many of my German friends remember those very same roads, on which they, too, were children fleeing with their families. But their memories are not joyous like mine. It was our luck to be caught up in the general dismemberment of the old Germany, and we followed the train of the newly homeless who were choking on their own misery and hadn't the stomach to ask suspiciously where we came from. They were mourning their losses, the possessions they had had to leave behind, and grieving for the homeland they wouldn't see again, while we were happy to have left our prisons and to have gained so much, that is to say, our naked existence.

Here is the source of my precarious bond with Germans of my generation, here where our paths joined. Comparisons arise spontaneously when we remember those last months of the war, and they are not only differences. For example, we have in common the memory of the delicious taste of rutabagas, which for some older Germans retain the odor of nourishment per se, sustenance in times of famine. I have known young Germans who have never eaten a turnip, a vegetable that is too plebeian for the bloated society of today's Federal Republic. But some who are my age or a little younger will occasionally cook some for me and each other, and we eat this humble meal as a kind of ritual, in celebration of peace and survival.

The mother of one of the students whom I have compared to Tom Sawyer's friends whitewashing the fence was born during this evacuation from today's Poland. Displacements of long ago that impinge on today's lives.

Now comes the problem of this survivor story, as of all such stories: we start writing because we want to tell about the great catastrophe. But since by definition the survivor is alive, the reader inevitably tends to separate, or deduct, this one life, which she has come to know, from the millions who remain anonymous. You feel, even if you don't think it: well, there is a happy ending after all. Without meaning to, I find that I have written an escape story, not only in the literal but in the pejorative sense of the word.

So how can I keep my readers from feeling good about the obvious drift of my story away from the gas chambers and the killing fields and towards the postwar period, where prosperity beckons? You cannot deduct our three paltry lives from the sum of those who had no lives after the war. We who escaped do not belong to the community of those victims, my brother among them, whose ghosts are unforgiving. By virtue of survival, we belong with you, who weren't exposed to the genocidal danger, and we know that there is a black river between us and the true victims. Therefore this is not the story of a Holocaust victim and becomes less and less so as it nears the end. I was with them when they were alive, but now we are separated. I write in their memory, and yet my account unavoidably turns into some kind of triumph of life. All I can say, helplessly to be sure, is that these are not the adventures of Huckleberry Finn and Nigger Jim, floating down the river on their raft, experiencing a somewhat sinister but mostly humorous journey.

Having said this much, I paradoxically have to add that on those roads of eastern Germany we three were full of good humor: we were elated and in love with existence. It was a subjective state of mind and doesn't decrease the staggering number of the victims by a single digit. Yes, we laughed a lot, for humor thrives on danger, for whatever reason. (A friend says it's because jokes are a vent for fears—hence gallows humor. He says neurotic people make the best comics, vide Woody Allen.) And then there was the thrill of adventure, for Susi and I were children. We were not intimidated because of our long imprisonment. On the contrary: we enjoyed what we had. It was all ours, and for the first time really our own. It must have been harder on my mother, but she, too, became witty and inventive. One reason for our well-being was, without a doubt, that soon we were no longer starving. We begged, we stole, and both were relatively easy. The peasants and farmers who had to leave their homes often had more food than they could carry, and they were generous. They were slaughtering their pigs and clearing out their cellars, so that now and then we would get a genuine meal, even meat. In any case, there were potatoes, turnips, apples. We acquired secondhand clothing and soon looked less suspicious.

We had invented a plausible tale, one much more believable than our true story, when I think of it now. We pretended to be refugees from the eastern part of Germany with an ailing family member, who was me. For my sake we had left our trek in order to search for a doctor. But while we were still looking for medical help, we said, the others left without us, together with all our belongings. Lo and behold, the story worked. We had made it so far, so why shouldn't we make it to the end? Every right step made us more sure-footed. Susi and I still talk about our minor achievements, which added up to the major one of survival. Two old women, we sit giggling, "Do you remember the time when . . . ?"

Do you remember the policeman who looked at us askance, and though my mother wanted to walk faster and get away in a hurry, you walked up to him, munching on an apple, and asked him for directions to the next village? How I admired your chutzpah! But Susi counters that this was my idea, that I had picked up this bit of psychology from some book, and that she just followed my suggestion. In any case, the policeman, nonplussed, told us which road to take and let us take it.

And do you remember the time we decided we had a "right" to ask for help from the authorities? And how my mother was aghast when you reasoned, correctly, that the village folk wouldn't know that there were red-haired Jews—that's a refinement that only the racists in the cities know about—and that you could therefore easily pass for an Aryan girl with your flaming red hair, and you swore that you could act like one. So you stormed into the office of the village mayor and laid our refugee story on him, a tearjerker, but you told it indignantly: " . . . And now we have no papers, not even ration cards for food, no money, nothing, Do you understand how hard this is for us, what with my little sister so sick, and is *this* the German community spirit [*deutsche Volksgemeinschaft*—a buzzword of the Third Reich] which the Führer expects of us all?" "Look at me," said Susi, rising to new heights of improvisation, "I have done my year of social service [*Pflichtjahr*, required of all young girls], and this is how I am treated?" Dear Susi, you must have kept your ears open in Vienna for the slogans of the Hitler Youth, for you could deliver them on demand, as if you had just been waiting to try them out. And you put the stored rage for what we had really lost into those phony demands. Later you boasted that you heard the mayor's secretary whisper to him: "When we were that age, we wouldn't have dared to speak in that tone to our elders." Revenge for past humiliations! They gave you what you came for, and you came back to us, laden with clothes—even shoes—and ration cards.

And I remember when a pack of kids ganged up on me as I was sitting alone in a shed where the two of you had left me after decreeing that I looked too Jewish to come along for whatever it was you were trying to pull off. Emaciated, ragged, and very black-haired, I probably looked plenty weird to these lighter-skinned, brown- and blue-eyed children. They decided to test me. Where was my father? I answered, he is at the front, of course, a soldier. So how often has he been home on furlough? And for how long? Well, of course I failed that quiz question. I had no idea how often daddies in wartime came home. Mine never did and never would. I guessed blindly, and my answer was too generous, I believe. The children, confirmed in their suspicion, left contentedly to report to their elders. Then the two of you returned from wherever you had been, and I bitterly blamed you and then blamed myself: you should never have left me alone—so what if I look Jewish? Now see what has happened? I have spoiled everything, stupid as I am. For suddenly it looked as if the whole village was after us. People emerged right and left from their houses, as if we were witches or worse, and we, of course, simply ran.

We ran as fast as we could, slowed down by what we carried. "Throw away the blankets," I yelled hysterically. "They weigh us down, and they make us recognizable."

"But we'll need them in this weather," my mother replied.

I prevailed: in our anguish we threw away what kept us from freezing and got out of that village unscathed and empty-handed. And we didn't die of cold, for not all people were that hostile, and we did find shelter. Throwing away the blankets has stayed with me as a kind of vital metaphor for decisions where I sacrifice something I need for something I need even more, hoping the gods won't reject the precious gift I offer. Like getting divorced or quitting a job is like throwing away my blanket in February 1945 in Silesia.

2

Because we could rest whenever we pleased and choose whether to go to the right or the left, Susi and I felt far more secure than was justified. We had a sense of mastering our destiny that was belied by incidents like the one I have just mentioned. Occasionally we were recognized as "convicts" who had escaped from a prison camp. The front was close, and we continued to hear gunfire every day, but we had no idea how to cross over, especially since the roads were crawling with military police. Before we had new clothing, we once fell into the hands of a policeman who politely approached us asking for our IDs. The cover-up of new material which we had sewn on our backs was a primitive disguise for the former patches that identified us. Since we had no papers, my mother "confessed," admitting everything, there being no point to lying. So much for that, I thought, and felt not so much afraid as saddened. The old heaviness of mind and limb returned. What next? (Later, in college, I read about fugitive slaves and thought, I've been there, I know many variants of what they felt, better than the historians and the novelists. Only Toni Morrison, much later, got it marvelously right.)

The policeman took us back to his station, where he was going to let his superior take care of the case. On the way my mother started a conversation with him, as if this was a normal social occasion. The two walked ahead of us children, and the scraps I heard seemed odd, since both the tone and the content were so inappropriate. My mother had decided to play the lady and demonstrate to our captor that she was a member of the educated bourgeoisie. So she talked culture and music. He was a gentleman, she said later.

At the police station there was nobody to take us into custody. We waited. The policeman, who was friendly and a little confused by the peculiar fish he had caught in his net, gave us some food. My mother said he was impressed by how we shared and shared alike. We waited some more; nobody came. Our man got nervous. He had other duties and probably didn't like this particular one. What was he to do with us? Our transport of prisoners was long gone, and he wasn't the sort who would shoot three women with whom he had been talking and whom he had fed. Susi says he liked my mother, and that's why he allowed her to persuade him that he needed a piece of paper, signed by her, certifying that he had helped us escape, which the Allies, in my mother's scenario, would appreciate. But, I objected afterwards, anyone can make up such a claim. Sure, said my mother, fully convinced by her own specious argument, but I signed my full name and added our address in Vienna. Perhaps the real reason he let us go is that we spooked him.

Sometimes we stayed for days in a place, sometimes we got out fast. Something was obviously wrong with us—for example, that we had no luggage. But most of the people in that area didn't care anymore who was who and who was on the road. They were themselves about to be uprooted. And we were an unlikely trio of convicts and foreign enemies: a woman with two teenage girls, all of whom were native speakers of German. I tried to make myself scarce, since I looked so unmistakably Jewish, as my mother and Susi didn't tire of telling me. And indeed, I largely conformed to the stereotype, not only in appearance but also because I had spoken a lot of Yiddish in Christianstadt, and if I didn't watch out, would easily slip into a Yiddish expression. The other two criticized my movements as quintessentially Jewish, for example, walking with my hands clasped in back. "Like a *bokher* in a *cheder*" (a Jewish boy in an orthodox school), they would mock me, to my considerable annoyance.

We spent a few peaceful days in a village of Sorbs, or Wends, a Slavic minority. We were taken in by a farmer to whom we could tell everything, since these communities had no love for the Nazis. Their language is so close to Czech that my mother could communicate with our host without using German. And he was a real host. The victims and enemies of the Germans were his friends. He wanted to hide out on his farm till the Russians came, because as a Slav he claimed their kinship. Nevertheless, he had sent his wife and daughter westward. You couldn't trust the Russians with women, he said, not even with Slavic women, and he warned us against staying.

Two or three weeks after our escape we gave up our plan to wait for the advancing army or even to make our way in its direction. There was no way of getting across the front line, and the evacuation of the villages was thorough. Even our Slavic host, who was at home here, had to arrange for a hiding place. In addition, there were the stories of systematic gang rapes, the Russian revenge for German atrocities. As victims of those same Germans, we should have been spared, but victors who exact justice by committing crimes against civilians aren't necessarily that discriminating.

One day my mother had a fit of hubris, of sinful pride, due to our success. We needed papers, she said, IDs of some kind, and she would see to it that we got them. How? Simple: go to a village pastor, tell him our story, and ask him for help. Perhaps she was inspired by Susi's triumph with the village mayor and wanted to compete. (My mother was both great, in the sense of heroic, and petty, in the manner of a spoiled girl. Often both qualities merged in her actions.) Susi and I had not seen many examples of Christian love either for neighbor or for enemy in our short lives, and so we were skeptical. But my mother was of the opinion that the churches and the Nazis couldn't abide each other, and that Protestants were more open-minded than Catholics—this in spite, or because, of the fact that she had experienced Catholic Austria. She argued that no minister would denounce us to the police or the military, even if he wasn't willing to help. Therefore she wasn't risking much. I suspected that she had once read a novel in which a Protestant minister played a positive role. It was a far-fetched and rather crazy idea but, as it turned out, it paid off. The man of God to whom she entrusted herself and us was really a Christian, as the Christians would say. The Jews would call him a *zadik*, a just man, or in post-Holocaust language, a righteous gentile. There were such Germans.

She didn't take us along on this expedition, much to my chagrin. Perhaps she didn't want any critical witnesses to her rhetoric. I am sure it was a theatrical event, and she may well have embellished our gray and dreary history with some invented anecdotes. For she always lied, often just for the fun of it.

She was herself astonished at the effect she had had, when she returned with trembling hands, in which she held our papers. "Look what I got here!" Now we were officially and until the end of the war a German family. She said that the pastor had been practically speechless and didn't hesitate for a moment. He didn't consider whether he was breaking the law, but rushed to his files and feverishly started to look for the right thing. He had baptismal certificates and other documents which were deposited in churches, and he gave us papers for a mother and two daughters. There were some improbabilities, like imperfect dates of birth. But these papers struck us as a godsend.

My German friends are happy when they get to this part in my story. One of them, the daughter of a pastor who belonged to part of the Lutheran church that really did resist, says with a shrug, well, it wasn't such a big deal. It didn't take all that much courage, since ministers of the church had the right to issue ID cards and retained that right under the Nazis. Her father, she said, would have done the same. So much the better, I say, if there were more men like the one who helped us.

And so one evening we boarded a train to southern Germany, to Bavaria. We had had to decide quickly, because trains were rare and you couldn't tell whether and when there would be another one. At the station, and later inside the train, the atmosphere was friendly, unbureaucratic, and matriarchal in the best sense of the word. The train happened not to be crowded, at least by our standards. Once again, we were lucky. There was an air of equality; everyone was caught up in the same mess.

I stretched out on one of the wooden benches, delighted with the space and the warm clothes I was wearing, including a good pair of long pants. A woman, herself a mother with children, came over to me with a smile and covered me with a blanket. I was astonished and naturally grateful to be tucked in by a stranger. It's the most quintessential of motherly gestures, so who wouldn't be grateful? And yet: she thinks I am one of theirs, and she's covering me because she takes me for a German, an Aryan, child. And then again, no. She is giving this blanket to me, three-dimensional me, and to no one else. She can see me falling asleep fast, because thinking makes you drowsy, and she does see me and no one else, nor has there been a mix-up. Therefore it was me whom she meant to cover. Am I taking something that wasn't meant for me, or am I receiving a gift? It didn't make sense, or did it?

3

Trains were slow and often didn't move at all during the daytime, in order to avoid the bombers. So the trip took days, gradually taking us, it seemed to me, farther and farther away from the world of the camps. In reality, Germany was dotted with these excrescences of human suffering, but subjective experience superimposed itself, and still does, on my knowledge of the geography of evil. Nowadays the German rapid train system is a marvel of efficiency and comfort, and I have crossed the country many times from one end to the other in a matter of hours. Memory refuses to accept the fact that this is the same country through which our refugee train crawled when I was thirteen years old.

Susi remembers death and illness on that train. I don't. I only remember sleep after exhaustion, and a kind revitalization. We received some food at the train stations from the National Socialist women's organization, the NSV—sandwiches that were pure manna, they were so good. The NSV was a charitable group, which didn't prevent the Soviets from deporting the women who had belonged to it. Those who had helped distribute the food landed in starvation camps because the Nazi letters *NS* were evil, and wherever the Russians found them, revenge was called for. A good friend of mine, a German who was four years old in 1947, almost lost his mother because she was among those who had handed out bread and cheese and sausage to the refugees like those on our train. He says his mother's deportation was stopped only because an aunt of his, who had been gang-raped by the Russians so often that she had lost all fear of them, put on a great, tearful scene, holding her little nephew in her arms to demonstrate that the child's mother, who stood by on the ready with her suitcase packed, was needed at home. The Russians, he says, were touched, especially since the aunt spoke a little of their language. My friend kept his mother and grew to normal adulthood. A point of convergence between us.

We finally arrived in Straubing, a small Bavarian town. Today it is larger and considered a "jewel" of Bavaria because it's pretty. I was still carried along by a dizzy sense of happiness, the very opposite of what the genuine German refugees experienced. For they had lost everything, that is, all their property, while we hoped to have gained everything, that is, the rest of our lives. So this arrival in Straubing was for me sheer euphoria and for the others a low point, a leave-taking from home. Here we were among free men and women who complained about this and that, and were entitled to their complaints—unimaginable behavior during those other mass transports we had endured. We were fellow citizens and treated as such. We had a place to stay assigned to us and ended up on a small farm at the edge of town, where we three had a room to ourselves, a sheer luxury.

But there is another side to this coin of triumph, and it is a sense of having committed a betrayal, not to say treason. Here are two examples, the first somewhat comical: my mother made friends with our landlady, who one evening looked deep into my mother's green eyes and asked how come one of my mother's daughters looked so Jewish. My mother, thinking how her two "daughters" didn't look one bit alike, figured that this difference in appearance could best be explained through paternity. And so she confessed in sisterly confidence, as between two women who have seen a bit of the world, that she had once had an affair with a Jew, and she begged the other woman not to talk about this weakness and sighed that it had caused her much grief and regret. It worked and in a sense it's a funny anecdote, but it's not quite the stuff of comedy, and there is a bitter aftertaste in the retelling.

And here is the other example: I went shopping, and suddenly the prisoners of an evacuated concentration camp occupied the street, guarded by SS men and their dogs. And I stood on the sidewalk. I had never seen "us" from the outside. What separated me from them was a matter of a few weeks, no more, after we had been together for years. They looked so tired, as if there was no place on earth left for them. The dogs looked alert, well fed and purposeful. My previous comrades walked slowly and with all their strength gone, whereas I had acquired a firmer step in that short time. I had become a German girl, who occasionally went to church on Sunday, where I had learned to cross myself awkwardly, and helped out in the potato field. For the rest, I came and went as I pleased. And now here they were, my people. I stared at them with intense concentration and knew that if they noticed me at all, it was only as part of a hostile population.

That was an hour where the sense of having committed treason was not part of any comedy. Not that I wanted to be back with them—but that is the point. I wanted to remember seeing them, wanted to remember this one-sided meeting, yet I did not feel that I had to share their fate. Survivor guilt does not mean that you think you have no right to live. Speaking for myself, I never believed I should have died because others were killed. I hadn't done anything bad to anyone. Why should I pay? It's a question of debt rather than guilt, though these ideas are closely bound together, as in the Lord's Prayer ("Forgive us our debts") or in the word *debit*, and in German the words are related, the one *Schuld*, guilt, the other *Schulden*, debt. One remains a debtor and yet doesn't quite know to whom one owes the debts. One would like to take from the victimizers to give to the victims, but one doesn't know how. For you owe me—I am a victim—but I owe them—for they are dead, more victim than I. One is debtor and creditor at the same time and is doomed to perform surrogate actions, alternating between giving and demanding: senseless actions in the flickering light of reason.

That was my last contact with concentration camp inmates. They walked right through the middle of town, in broad daylight, and there were townspeople to my right and my left who looked away. Or closed their faces so that nothing could penetrate. We have our own troubles, kindly spare us yours. We waited on the sidewalk until the train of "subhumans" had passed. When a few weeks later the Americans occupied the city of Straubing, none of its citizens had seen anything. And in a sense no one had. For you haven't seen what you haven't perceived and absorbed. In that sense, only I had seen them. I still do.

4

The period of our escape was the time of the last and heaviest air attacks. Germany, the scourge of Europe, was scourged in turn, her great cities set afire. Together with their bombs, the Allies dropped leaflets, asking the civilian population to surrender or to resist the Nazis. Nothing could have been less effective than these slogan-filled messages, delivered by the hated, screeching, anonymous death machines in the sky. People shrugged their shoulders and contemptuously tossed the leaflets aside, even though they had ceased believing the propaganda line about a German miracle weapon that would lead to final victory.

The Allies had not bombed the concentration camps, and so I had no experience with death from the air. At first I paid no attention to the sirens: I was so convinced that the Americans wouldn't kill me if the Germans hadn't succeeded that I usually failed to go to seek cover when the alarm sounded. We didn't have a proper air-raid shelter anyway, just a cellar for storing cabbage, potatoes, and apples, a cool place to turn milk into buttermilk. I only started to understand what air attacks were all about when I was surprised on the potato field by low-flying planes. We lay down flat, and when I looked up, I noticed that we were as unprotected as if we stood in our nightgowns with arms akimbo before a cannon. My heart beat like a drum, and I had to take a deep breath to calm myself once I saw only clouds in the sky. I had a similar fright one quiet day when suddenly the windowpanes crashed into our room. That time I rushed into the despised cellar in a great hurry.

I know fear of death only as a kind of childhood disease, like measles, and only in its most acute state, like a raging fever, or what I imagine an epileptic fit must be like. I have never experienced the other kind, the insidious rebellion against the limits of life, the terror of being wiped out slowly and inevitably. I only know the sudden attack in a situation of actual danger and the hunted rabbit's reaction: how do I get away from this, now, today, or at the latest the day after tomorrow? Not every danger causes panic. There has to be a trap without an exit, where the two natural responses to danger, that is, flight or defense, are not available. Having to sit still. To be incapable of doing anything when your life is imperiled—that's what can drive you crazy. This kind of fear is the fear I experienced twice, the first time in the extermination camp and the second time during a bombing attack shortly before the end of the war.

We lived close to a railroad, which may have been the reason why we were frequently bombarded. This time there was a massive attack and for once everyone in the house had gone into the cellar. Our hostess whimpered quietly, while her husband crouched behind a barrel as if it could shield him. Occasionally his head popped up above the rim, and when he heard the next explosion, he ducked again. In spite of my terror, I thought he was funny. Danger, I repeat, is fertile ground for humor.

Finally the bombs seemed to fall directly on my head. Several times I was convinced the end had come. For minutes at a time I must have lost my mind: I yelled and clung to my mother, who remained perfectly cool, as usual. (Years later I met some British youngsters who proudly told of their courage during the Blitz. I felt cheap and inferior by comparison and have often wondered whether the difference was one of temperament or context.)

When the all-clear signal sounded, I could hardly believe that the house was intact. A bomb had fallen on the chicken coop, and the chickens had been prematurely slaughtered. I stared into a giant hole, and while the terror ebbed and my heartbeat steadied, I triumphed in the thought that once again I had escaped by the skin of my teeth. I no longer believed that the good Lord had meant to save me, and gave the credit to chance or luck, except that chance by definition doesn't deserve credit. We looked, shook our heads, went our way, and didn't talk again about our hour in that dark underground place. What could we have said? These border situations between life and death are not easily accessible to words. Human speech was not invented or meant for extremes.

Apart from strictly military situations, Americans have no idea what it is like to be bombed. Neither their personal nor their historical consciousness has stored that experience, and yet it is we Americans who do most of the bombing in today's world. We are surprised by the less than grateful response of civilians whom we are ostensibly helping, because we have always been up in the air, not down on the ground. In 1945 I knew that I was being bombed by friends, and yet it was unforgettably wrenching.

And then one day they came, the "Amis," the Americans. It was April, and in May the war in Europe would be ended. We had spring weather, and they had taken over the streets by advancing with their tanks and jeeps. There hadn't been a battle of Straubing because someone in City Hall had shown some sense and surrendered. The long nightmare, the seven lean years since Hitler's army invaded my homeland—that, too, without a battle—were suddenly over. We had arrived.

We hadn't planned any further than this moment. The three of us walked to the center of town, looked at each other in amazement, and asked: "What now?" My mother, determined to try out her English, walked up to the first American uniform in view, a military policeman directing traffic, and told him in a few words that we had escaped from a concentration camp. Since I knew no English, I couldn't understand his answer, but his gesture was unmistakable. He put his hands over his ears and turned away. My mother translated. He had had his fill of people who claimed they had been in the camps. They were all over the place. Please, leave him alone!

There was warm sunshine on my bare arms, which from now on I didn't have to cover up to hide the Auschwitz tattoo. And I could use my real name again. It was a great occasion, but I was glad that we had freed ourselves and didn't depend all that much on the victors. Because my imagination had provided a more colorful picture of the great hour of liberation. Here was my first American, and he deliberately closed his ears.

One thing, I figured, was certain: this war hadn't been fought for our sake.

A DEFEATED COUNTRY

1

"Not for our sake" was only half the truth, but still a valid half. The free world didn't welcome us as brothers and sisters, long lost but found again, liberated from evil forces and now to be jubilantly included in the Family of Man. That was the picture my childish yearning had painted. In reality we were a burden, a social problem.

In occupied Straubing you could easily conclude that most American soldiers, with the exception of the Jewish ones, had rather diffuse ideas about why and for whom they had risked their lives. Of course, that's always the case: men go to war because they are drafted. They usually go with enthusiasm, which lasts as long as their side is winning, never mind if their cause is good or bad. A minority know their own minds, and the rest mistake the collective mind for their own. The individuals who composed what we are now urged to call "the greatest generation" were on the right side partly by accident. Their enemies, if they were not in leadership positions and didn't participate in atrocities, were by the accident of birth on the other side. They—the Germans and their allies—have not exactly been encouraged to boast of the acts of physical courage and the risk-laden comradeship of soldiers in the field that the winning side took and takes pride in. They are arguably the most despised generation, the flip side of the "greatest." And yet, like their counterparts on the winning side, they have done very well in the economic boom that has graced the industrialized world since the war, and they see themselves as the architects of the new, democratic Federal Republic of Germany.

Their success creates problems for the national psyche, even when—and perhaps particularly when—the fatherland was so egregiously in the wrong. Young Germans often insist that their identity is European, but no one else in Europe substitutes the continent for their country.

We were lucky: my mother was hired as an assistant and interpreter to a Jewish officer and helped with the DPs, or displaced persons, people the likes of us, who had escaped or been liberated or come out of hiding. They either wanted to get back home or to emigrate. We had been the first DPs in Straubing. The others came by and by, if they didn't live in special DP camps. Hardly a one was older than thirty, and most were Jews. Each had his own tale of suffering and survival. The normal fate had been death; every one of us was an exception. The military government and various international organizations, including later the United Nations, saw to it that they had a place to stay and fed them.

The Germans hadn't lost their hatred and contempt of Jews, but it had become subliminal. It simmered on, as stew in a high-quality saucepan continues to simmer after the gas has been turned off. And the heat itself lingers even longer. What else could you expect? We survivors reminded the population through our mere existence of what had happened, and what they and their people had done. Perhaps they were afraid of our revenge, or they thought we were like dogs that have been regularly beaten and can only snarl and bite. If you hadn't been there yourself, you could make believe that only criminals had survived the camps or those who had been brutalized while they were incarcerated. Never mind that this view was in direct contradiction to the equally widespread opinion that the camps couldn't have been all that bad: witness how many survivors we (poor Germans) now have.

Honor the dead, but mistrust the living.

2

At first we got to live in a large, luxurious house which had apparently belonged to a high Nazi functionary. To live in such a place was surreal and dreamlike—the reversal from misery and cold and violence to safety and a warm summer with a garden and lovely books was so sudden. I loved living there, not wanting to own any of it, but riding on a heightened sense of temporary enjoyment. I figured we would soon emigrate.

That summer in the early peace of 1945 was an enchanted time, like floating on air, beyond calendar and clock.

Susi and I learned to bike and to swim in the Danube. The current took us downstream, and we would run back up along the sunny bank, applauding when the boys and young men of our small Jewish community tried to impress us by swimming upstream for a bit. Those of us who had been stranded in Straubing came to know each other quite well during that long, deep breath of the first postwar summer. Years later I returned for a visit and expected the river bank to be crowded with swimmers and sunbathers, but of course the Danube was polluted, and the riverbanks looked drab and forlorn.

Life in the DP camps, in contrast, was far more hectic and more confined. The closest was Deggendorf, where Susi liked to hang out because there were lots of boys and much dancing. There was a craze for dancing in the immediate postwar period, among Germans as well, I have been told. Some tacit, life-affirming principle at work, I guess. I found Deggendorf depressing, because it was yet another camp. I wanted privacy. All my life it was to be my main luxury, and I have remained aware of it as a privilege one mustn't take for granted. Susi, for her part, is virtually addicted to company and totally unhappy when she is alone. Do both of these preferences go back to the crowded misery of our childhood environment? Visiting Deggendorf I earnestly asked myself whether I would be able to stand living in a kibbutz, the goal of all my dreams. Perhaps I would have to live in a city in Eretz Israel in order to have a place of my own.

The natives were anything but pleased that the occupying army was confiscating their houses and apartments. If the conquerors used them for their own convenience, that was bad enough, but then, to the victor belong the spoils. It was beyond endurance, however, to see German property given away to tramps and vagabonds who came from God knows where—though it had to be endured.

A friend of mine who was born in one of the Baltic states as a member of the former German minority called *Volksdeutsche*, or ethnic Germans, remembers how the Nazis gave her and her family a house in Poland during the war, as part of the German effort to colonize the region to the east. She says the Polish owners had been forced out so quickly that the dishes were still on the table, and the cats still ran around the house, meowing with hunger, because their humans had been gone only a few days. It was those plates on the table, says my friend, that made her grandmother realize that what they were being given had been taken from other civilized persons who knew how to eat with a knife and fork.

The owner of our first house soon got it back, probably because he managed to put together a good enough case that he hadn't been a genuine Nazi. We got an apartment closer to the center of town. I didn't care where we lived, as long as it wasn't a camp.

Some Jews of our acquaintance discovered in the rather elegant place to which they had been assigned some object that could only have come from a synagogue. Thereupon they deliberately and carefully destroyed everything in the house which they couldn't use. I didn't think this was a good idea—since there had been ample destruction, why add to it? But I had to admit that if vandalism could be justified, then this tasteful, upper-class, synagogue-enriched villa was a case in point.

One day I was on my way to the American office where my mother worked, to pick her up. Suddenly an angry stranger grabbed me, tore me off my bike, and began to curse and insult me. At first I thought I might be riding his bicycle, which had been confiscated like everything else we used. And since I valued my bicycle, I could well understand that its previous owner valued it even more. My attacker, however—a tall, skinny man who spoke with the cultivated Bavarian accent of the upper bourgeoisie—tossed the bike aside into the bushes, proof that there was something else that made him tremble with rage. I screamed and pulled but couldn't free myself. He: "You are coming with me." No indication of where to. In the nick of time my mother comes around the corner, with her light, quick step, assesses the situation, and throws herself on the man like a fury from hell. Compared to her venom, his is a mere fit of pique. Her tongue-lashing is spawned by murder, the murder of her family, to be precise; his merely by a temporary expropriation. In addition, her threats are backed up by the power of the occupation forces. So naturally she wins within seconds.

It turned out that the enraged Bavarian had seen me with the young men who had disfigured his apartment. He thought that I, too, lived there, or at least had easy entry to their place, and therefore I, too, could be held responsible for the havoc. He wanted to force me to let him into the house. As if I had a key. Now it was my turn to be outraged. I figured his old-man's fantasies were painting a picture of orgies, in which my still premenstrual self played the role of a scarlet harlot with my brotherly older friends. After that scene I was no longer sorry for his demolished knickknacks and furniture. He had heroically picked on the smallest and weakest of the despised kikes. But he had not counted on my mother.

Only recently I found out that Straubing did not have a Jewish commander. I was convinced we did, partly because we were hated, seen as the protégés of a Jew-infested American military government.

3

Newspapers, like everything else, were hard to come by in the summer of 1945, and they consisted of a few sheets only. I read the paper, whenever I could find one, and followed the war bulletins from the Pacific and the first official reports about the liberated concentration camps. I decided to submit my two Auschwitz poems, which of course I knew by heart, to a newspaper. I copied them carefully, eight stanzas for one, four for the other, and added a letter in which I described the circumstances of their composition, mentioned my age, and boasted that in my thirteen years I had lived through more and worse than most old adults. There was no answer. I was disappointed. Then, just as I stopped being disappointed, someone said to me, "You are in the paper," and told me where I could get a copy.

Tanned and happy I jumped off my bike at the address he had indicated. House and garden belonged to one of the natives whose faces turned to stone when they saw a Jew. With the joy of a freshly printed author I asked him for the paper. He thrust it at me: "So that's you," he said, with a look as if my appearance and my allegedly horrendous past didn't gel. "You can keep it," he added, not so much giving me a present as removing some seemingly malodorous thing from his home.

Instead of a modest column I found half a page that dealt with me. In the middle was a photo of my cover letter, which had been carefully ripped, so that the jagged edges, together with the awkward handwriting of a girl who hadn't spent much time in school, evoked the impression of an emergency SOS, a kind of message in a bottle. To make matters worse, they had added a drawing of a ragged, terrorized child, who accidentally happened to look a little like me. What I minded most was that they had eviscerated my poetic output without asking, omitting one poem altogether and printing only two stanzas of the other, and these two were embedded in a maudlin, hand-wringing text, in effect asking the public for pity. Now I understood the man's reaction to the girl poet.

I had imagined that if you send a poem to a newspaper, you get a polite answer, even it isn't printed. And if it is printed, you get a few copies of the paper, and maybe even a few marks in payment. One shouldn't have to scour half the town to find a copy. The fact that the editors hadn't contacted me afterwards also irritated me—it so clearly contradicted the sentimentalities of the writer, who was shedding ink like tears, but didn't bother to find out who or how I was, and (most crushing) if I had written anything else. I wanted to be a young poet who had been in the camps, not a former child prisoner who had written some heart-wrenching verses. I felt humiliated, and therefore ashamed, and wanted to put the matter behind me. But for a few weeks the local DPs made a fuss over me, especially the former "politicals," who wanted me to recite my poems in public and then resented it when I chose others than the published ones. I felt manipulated, regretted having sent the poems to the paper, almost regretted having composed them.

Yet these verses, left behind with a past I was soon to shed, in a country I wouldn't see again for sixteen years, continued to lead a stubborn life of their own, unknown to their progenitor, who had abandoned them. They were reprinted, recited on radio shows, and finally got into an anthology of verse by Germans in exile and prison. A copy of that volume landed fifteen years later on my California doorstep. The editor, though again reprinting my truncated poem without permission, had at least given me notice ex post facto.

One of the other contributors to that volume was a professor of the Berkeley German department, who was curious to meet me, and who persuaded me to go for a Ph.D. in German. Thus the poems were ultimately responsible for a long career.

4

The story of my poems is an anecdote from the early stages of Germany's attempt to come to terms with its Nazi past. Much has been written about the Nazi years, but the history of German consciousness and gradually dawning awareness, of acknowledging and rejecting the dark years, is still shrouded in a mass of reproaches and counter-reproaches, children accusing their fathers and parents blaming the circumstances and some members of all generations hating those who remind them.

"But who can tell," said one of my Tom Sawyers, who sported a large wooden cross on a leather band around his neck, "how any of us would have acted or would act today, if we were living in a police state. Would I, though I am a believing Christian, have had the courage, would I have it now, to hide an escapee and endanger my own life, not to mention my family, if I had one?"

I answer, that's right: you can't demand courage as a matter of conscience and a matter of course. Courage is beyond and above normal behavior, or we wouldn't admire it. Therefore cowardice is an acceptable reason for sins of omission. Cowardice is both normal and the norm, and you shouldn't condemn anyone for having acted normally. But you can't claim that you didn't know about the Nazi atrocities and at the same time claim that you didn't do anything to oppose them because of fear and cowardice. Either you didn't know about concentration camps, or you were afraid to land there yourself if you didn't toe the line. You can't have it both ways. He nods. That's grist to his mill. My two conscientious objectors needed no lessons on the subterfuges and evasions of their parents' and grandparents' generations. They are the experts in that field.

What I liked about this boy with his wooden cross is that he doubted his own integrity. I keep pondering the question we've raised. If cowardice is a normal element of self-preservation, and therefore deserves a better name, for example precaution or foresight, then we ought to condemn only what lies below cowardice, that is, the active participation in evil, the extra homework beyond the assignment. So I ask him: "What do you expect of your conscience? What are the limits of cowardice that you would accept for yourself? You mightn't have the gumption to help someone in need, but surely you wouldn't kill because of the ethnicity or nationality of your opponent, because he is Jewish, Swiss, or black?" "Certainly," he replies. "If I couldn't expect this much of myself, I wouldn't be a conscientious objector." "Well," I say, "that's a good beginning," and reflect that I have to believe him, or I couldn't talk to him, and I have to believe it of myself and of my children. But is it true?

In a mystery novel everyone is suspect, simply by virtue of being there. It's a kind of moral realism, which is the main attraction of these books. (Only the detective is exempt, since he—or she—is the fairy responsible for restitution and retribution.) The certainty that all problems can and will be solved is essential to this kind of fiction and makes even the best mysteries inferior literature. That is why most readers read them only once. I am usually disappointed and bored by the end, whether I have guessed who the culprit is or not, but the beginning and the middle delight me. They confirm my expectation that you can never know what sin anyone is capable of committing. Theologians have always known that freedom cuts both ways, since it means that we can change our minds, learn to be different from what we were, and thus overcome early influences. There is no certainty, even in the case of someone who's my own son, that allows me to say: "I know him. This is how he'll act in a given situation. He is incapable of doing this or that." Anyone may change simply by deciding to, for better or for worse. The more highly developed we are, the less predictable we become. Freedom means, among other things, unpredictability. Animals can be imprinted when they are little; humans never cease to learn. You can tell what the little chicks will do for the rest of their lives, but not the ethologist who discovered their behavior and made them treat him as their Mother Goose. Because Konrad Lorenz became a Nazi and one of the Party's privileged professors, yet after the war became a reasonable citizen again and was awarded a Nobel Prize. Lorenz himself denied that there was such a thing as evil; there was only "aggression," a normal expression of animal behavior, and fixed action patterns, he wrote. The title of his bestseller, *On Aggression*, is in the original *So-Called Evil* (*Das sogenannte Böse*). A morality derived from science in the service of denial.

5

When the survivors were among themselves, they either outdid one another with stories about their suffering, or they wanted to leave all that behind in order to focus on the future. Some were proud of what they had gone through; others didn't want to spend their lives thinking about injuries and injustice. I mostly belonged to the latter group, especially after my experience with my poems. The DPs who wouldn't stop talking about the Nazi years seemed to me pathologically introverted. Their tirelessly repeated memories seemed to stand in the way of the future. Wasn't what really mattered to find out how one lives in peacetime? If you'll only let me find out. And yet I, too, was still fascinated, and of course burdened, by what had happened. By turns I was curious about the past and shrank from it. (Come to think of it, I am still riding the same seesaw, now that I am almost seventy.)

I read whatever I could find about the Nuremberg trials—news items which our German neighbors treated with distaste, as if the investigators and observers were guilty, and as if turning away from the ugly facts were a proof of innocence. Germans didn't acknowledge or inform themselves of the crimes that were documented there for the first time—crimes that had been committed in their name, by their relatives and by themselves. It was easier to argue that the trials were nothing but a deliberate humiliation of the German people. Sure, the World War hadn't been a picnic, so the argument ran, but war never is. Germany faced up to the Holocaust only in the sixties, with the Auschwitz trial in Frankfurt, when Germans were standing in a German court of law, being judged by Germans.

I slowly realized that my brother and father were among the six million murdered Jews. (In those days it was common in Germany to say "six million humans [*Menschen*]," for Jews are human, too, don't you know, and we are no longer anti-Semitic. Later only the Communists insisted on diluting ethnicity to the point where you couldn't tell anymore who had been persecuted and why. The rationale was that it could have happened to anybody. But it didn't. It happened to me and my brother, not to the blond Catholic children next door.) For as long as possible, I tried to disconnect what I read in the papers from the expectation of being reunited soon with the men in my family. Only gradually did expectation turn into disappointment. Hope evaporated undramatically, almost unnoticed, as it had once before in Vienna, prior to our deportation. First there was impatience, then resentment. Why weren't they here yet? Hadn't I held out long enough? Is there never a happy end to waiting? In those days I accidentally killed a little dog I had and was fond of. I failed to turn off the gas in the kitchen where he slept, and though I heard him cry at night, I didn't get up and look. Of course I was mortified the next morning when I found his lifeless body and was despondent for days. Accident or symptom? And if the latter, symptom of what?

Since my sixteenth birthday I have lived in America. In April 1945 I couldn't know that I would have to spend another two and a half years in Bavaria. The old story: What country was ready to accept us? The United States had a jumble of requirements and quotas that seemed quite opaque to us. But then, I didn't want to come to America. Some of my friends in Straubing had survived a death march on which they had been strafed by low-flying Allied aircraft, though the pilots should have recognized that they were not attacking the enemy, but the exhausted, starved victims of the enemy on their way to yet another concentration camp. Or hadn't they been informed of our existence? The postwar denazification program was notoriously corrupt and inefficient, and in liberating the concentration camps the Allies had often been so careless and unprepared that people died because they couldn't digest the heavy food that was indiscriminately shoved at them, or because of a lack of medical care. You might say that wasn't the fault of the Allies, who couldn't foresee what they would find, but to me it seemed as if these last victims had died of Allied sentimentality. Their liberators had been better at taking horrifying pictures of the living skeletons than at rescuing them.

Photos as an instrument of sublimated voyeurism, the victims helpless objects of the camera. The British, I remember, made a documentary film about a liberated camp showing naked young women taking showers. The justification of the voice-over: look at these Jews, whom the Nazis accused of being dirty—how eager they are to wash up. What thinner veil for visual exploitation? The more you wash, the less you deserve to be murdered?

But these are minor infringements, compared to those of the Soviet liberators. I heard from Jewish women who were almost raped in their liberated camps and saved themselves only by threatening to jump out of windows and the like. Those were the lucky ones. Their stories strongly suggested that there were others who were unlucky, and who endured the trauma of rape as a kind of coda to their persecution by the Nazis. Stalin's army didn't always make fine distinctions between the women of the enemy side and their female victims. From a patriarchal point of view, the mass rapes and gang rapes of German women that occurred in the Soviet occupied zone were an act of revenge, not necessarily just, but understandable, in view of the atrocities the German forces had committed in the Soviet Union. To that way of thinking, rape is an encroachment on male prerogatives, getting at Uncle Siegfried through Auntie Gudrun, as it were. And Auntie Gudrun had better shut up about the dishonor that has been done to the family. An act of violence that dishonors its victim will not bring her attention, let alone sympathy. Language favors the male, by putting the shame of the victim into the service of the victimizer. We abhor these attitudes in non-Western cultures, but when a brave woman filmmaker recorded this chapter of German history, she was virulently attacked by a knee-jerk reaction from the German left, which wouldn't tolerate a chronicle of German women as victims. Yet the memory of rape by invading armies is a substratum among German women, swept aside by prosperity but lingering on in occasional outbursts of rage and grief. Those who have been tortured and those who have been raped have this in common, that time doesn't eradicate what they have suffered, as it does with illness and accidents.

I wanted to emigrate to Eretz Israel, to Palestine, and help build a country inspired by socialist ideals, where justice and humanity would prevail. But in Palestine the British had the whip hand, and they were as stubborn as ever regarding Jewish immigration. We could have sailed illegally, via Italy. That seemed doable to me, merely a further adventure; but my mother saw only the risk. If the boat fell into the hands of the British, we would have to sit it out in yet another camp, in Cyprus. And, she said, she had had her fill of camps. In the end she made the final decision without consulting me. I could hardly blame her and was not exactly used to having things go my way, but still it was a severe blow. She hadn't fared badly with the Americans, and she thought that America would offer her a good future and maybe another husband (she was to find two more of those). But in the meantime we had to wait. I got to be fourteen, then fifteen, and my mind was stocked with German books and ideas. I lived among the ruins of German cities and German culture. By the time I left, a part of me was irreversibly German, albeit in an offbeat way.

6

And what was to be done about school? I had never been to high school and hadn't even graduated from elementary school. My education was so rudimentary that I should have studied with children much younger than me. Yet due to the war I emotionally belonged to an older generation. I would have been intolerant and intolerable within any school, but particularly a German one.

So to catch up, I took private lessons in the various subjects you take when you go to school. I liked that, because I was hungry for knowledge, and studying a bit of Latin, math, English, and ancient and medieval history helped me escape from the haunting past. Either the teachers came to us, or I went to their place; my mother paid them officially with worthless German currency and unofficially with precious American cigarettes, the currency of the black market. She had no respect for school knowledge—she never did—but she did believe that studying was the path to upward mobility. Susi joined me, but haphazardly, since she preferred the dancing and the boys in Deggendorf. Her grandmother, who had managed to hide during the war, turned up and stayed with us for a while. Susi was the first of us to emigrate, after her uncle in St. Louis had found her. But suddenly Hanna was with us, my closest friend from Theresienstadt, the daughter of the wild-haired math teacher, who had not survived.

Hanna mentioned that her father once sent a mathematical paper he had written to Einstein, and that to his delight, Einstein had responded. We were duly impressed and advised her to send him a letter, reminding him of her father. Soon there was an answer with the Princeton postmark, typed by Einstein's secretary but signed by the great man. We handled this letter carefully and inspected it with awe. Einstein remembered Hanna's father and would be delighted to do what he could for her. Why didn't she go ahead and ask—don't be bashful—even if it was only for a Care package. We figured that he didn't know we had enough to eat.

If Einstein, one of the most famous Jews in the world, wants to help the daughter of a murdered fellow mathematician, maybe he can get you into an American university, we told Hanna. Hanna wanted to be a medical doctor, which wasn't such a big deal in Europe, where most doctors didn't make a lot of money and, unlike in America, there were plenty of women in the profession. So she wrote a respectful letter with lots of help from everyone we knew and asked not for food but for some help with her future. This time the answer was signed by the secretary, who wrote that apparently there were people who thought that Mr. Einstein had a magic wand, that he was not in possession of such an object, and that it took a good deal of nerve to ask such favors. Hanna was devastated for days. How could we have given her such bad advice? We apologized; we had meant well. Shortly after that Hanna's relatives in Australia found her, and that is where she lives today.

Thirty-five years later when I joined Princeton's German Department as its first female full professor, someone pointed to a very old lady and said in hushed awe that she had been Einstein's secretary. And I thought: "So she was the one who wrote the letter that was a transatlantic slap in the face to a child who had been badly hurt and was therefore doubly vulnerable, all in order to shield the world-famous mathematician from the importunities of an unknown, murdered mathematician's daughter." Why didn't she simply send a college catalogue from a state school and explain how the system worked? I was repelled by this small, unassuming, white-haired woman, as she had probably been repelled decades earlier by the thought of greedy, unwashed survivors wanting more than food, wanting a future.

The teachers were Hanna's and my chief contact with the German population. They were a mixed group: some were elderly high school teachers, some were young men who had been soldiers and wanted to go to the university. The Latin teacher was a retired, old-fashioned Bavarian, whom I liked for his grandfatherly manner and because he was the only one who occasionally asked a question about the war years. Perhaps he had been a party member like the English teacher, who admitted it unhesitatingly, adding he had had to join to go on teaching. Now, due to denazification, he was out of a job and available to give private lessons. They all denied having been convinced Nazis, but for me that distinction was too abstract. It was not something I could judge, for I hadn't spent those years in Nazi Germany but among persecuted Jews.

The math teacher was a different matter. He was a refugee from the East and had the nerve to tell me that the Americans shouldn't have meddled in the war between the Russians and the Germans. I tried to argue, didn't succeed too well, came home in a rage, slammed doors, and yelled that anyone who held such opinions should at least not utter them in front of Jews. He didn't teach me much math, just as the English lady in Vienna, who sympathized with the Nazis, failed to teach me her language.

Another of our teachers, a veteran who was doing his first year of practice teaching at a local school, complained about the discipline problems he encountered. He told us that boys at least had a sense of honor to which he could appeal, which was lacking in girls. Morality concerned all people, so why was this man telling me that honor was beyond my ken by virtue of my gender? It made no sense, except as an insult. While Germans had to revise their judgment of Jews, however reluctantly and sporadically, they didn't even try to revise their Nazi-bred contempt for women. I learned so little from this man that I don't even remember what subject he taught. I was also told that Rilke, whose poetry I had just discovered, was too feminine. No man should write such verse, which was only good enough for poetesses.

After a year of instruction, I underwent several days of exams at the local high school, at the age of barely fifteen. Standards were loose, and many veterans who had missed years of schooling were getting so-called emergency diplomas. I passed, but hardly because of my intellect and knowledge, though I did give it my best shot. Rather it was because of my mother's position with the conquerors. She went to the principal of the school and asked him to admit me for examination. Perhaps she bribed him and his colleagues with cigarettes, or perhaps she intimidated him, or tried to touch his heart strings with stories about her poor child who had suffered so much. Or she may have convinced the officials that they had nothing to lose if I got a diploma from Straubing High School, since we were going to New York pretty soon.

7

In 1947 I moved to nearby Regensburg, where my mother now worked for UNRRA, the United Nations Relief and Rehabilitation Administration. She lived in a house with other women workers from this agency, wore a nice green uniform, and enjoyed her work. Since no dependents could live there, I found a room in town and enrolled in the only institution of higher learning in the area, which happened to be a Catholic theological seminary. My high school diploma entitled me to enter. Regensburg now has a proper university, but the choice of courses in the second semester of 1946–47 was rather limited, and so believe it or not, according to my matriculation book, which I still have, I was taking courses in logic and epistemology, in the history of medieval philosophy, and in early modern history. I was a fifteen-year-old with no academic background sitting in a large lecture room with older students, many veterans among them, as well as a few Jews. Of course I felt uncomfortable, both because I was Jewish and because most of what I heard was over my head or dry as dust or too arcane to interest me and had no bearing on the questions of war and peace and violence and discrimination which occupied me compulsively, even when I tried to turn away from them. Almost all the professors were Catholic priests, and just how would these conservative men of God have treated us a mere two years earlier? I couldn't shake the feeling that I wasn't welcome, just tolerated, and moreover that I was here under false pretenses. I couldn't have taken an exam in these subjects, except for history, to save my life.

Defeat bred its own variants of nationalism. When the history professor mentioned that the Poles consider Copernicus one of their own, a general protest ensued. Scraping feet voted for the German blood of the astronomer, whose German name is Nikolaus Koppernigk. (As I write this, I check him out on my computer encyclopedia. For Americans he is a Pole, simply and unequivocally.) My male Jewish fellow students didn't relish the fact that their new instructors were the old oppressors and yet were their superiors in the classroom. Provocation hung in the air on both sides. Or was it just me? When one of the Jewish students asked a question, I heard him with the ear of a German, noting how his formulations didn't fit the schematic language of the classroom, and how his German harked back to Yiddish.

But I learned a lot in the freedom and quiet of my little room, where I greedily devoured history and literature—whatever I could lay my hands on in those days when books were hard to come by. In class I was out of place because I could so easily be distracted from concepts by metaphors and facts. Clearly, I was less intelligent than I had hoped, and I felt frustrated by an inarticulate notion that something was wrong if old material was processed as if the immediate past and the uncertain future had no bearing on it. And yet, perhaps philosophy could provide the tools I needed, if I could only get the hang of it. I didn't get the hang of it, but I made a friend.

His name was Martin, he was a young veteran, and we had started talking in a class that we both liked, and where I was actually taking notes. The lecturer wasn't a cleric; he was a refugee from Breslau in the East, and he taught early modern history. He was the only one who raised questions and posed problems that made you sit up. He spoke vividly about the Peasants' War in Germany and Erasmus's ambiguous attitude toward the Reformation. These were my subjects, and in fact, they were anybody's subjects—just and unjust war and oppression and questions of conscience and allegiance—even if they were displaced onto the sixteenth century. It always amazes me how much stays with you from what a good teacher can teach you. Martin, in a novel he wrote decades later, has a hero who is obsessed with the Peasants' War, which would have changed the history of Germany if the rebelling peasants, who tried to expand the religious upheaval of their day into a social revolution, had only won it.

I seldom took notes, but I came dutifully provided with note paper, and I often tore it into small pieces. It didn't occur to me that this nervous tic could make a bad impression, until Martin raised the point. I maintained that I could concentrate better when my hands were occupied. He rejoined mildly, with a brand of irony that slipped unobtrusively into sympathy and is to this day a hallmark of his writing style and his conversation, that it looked like the opposite, inattention rather than concentration, and professors are sensitive.

So for once I was writing and not tearing up paper, when my poor-quality postwar pencil broke. (No ballpoints yet.) From a back row someone courteously offered a metal stylus, a definite upgrade. I had noticed Martin before: he stood out. His clothes were formal, unlike the other students'. He wore a jacket and a tie to class and looked around disdainfully before he chose a seat. That he in turn had noticed me was flattering and nourishment for my insecure ego. He leaned forward with an urgent gesture, as if the loan of a writing utensil was an act of supreme significance, and with exaggerated emphasis urged me to accept it. I returned it gratefully after class.

That is how a conversation started that is still ongoing and will never, can never, have a satisfactory end.

8

Martin Walser is today one of the most respected and controversial German writers of his generation. His name is second only to that of Günter Grass. A southern German from the area around Lake Constance, near the borders of both Austria and Switzerland (at that time the French occupation zone), he was someone with a sense of identity, at home in a specific landscape, as I had not been at home in Vienna, a fellow who knew who he was and where he belonged. I only knew that I would soon emigrate to a strange place.

Students in those days used the formal *Sie*, even if they knew each other well. Nowadays they use the informal *du*, even if they have just met for the first time. With hindsight it seems ridiculous that Martin and I never got around to that *du* on our many walks and at the readings and plays we attended. And yet the other was the correct form for us, for it signaled distance, and distance, both geographic and mental, became the conserving marinade of a lasting relationship.

I wasn't in love with him, unless love includes any kind of fascination with someone of the other sex who is very unlike you. It was as if the boy on summer vacation (or was he at Hitler Youth training camp?) who had waved a flag, and whom I had glimpsed a little over two years earlier in passing on the way from the death camp to the forced labor camp, had become my companion in exhilarating literary conversations. Of course Martin wasn't that boy, but at different times they each signified the essence of Germany to me.

Martin lent me books, among them Kafka's stories, which he had just discovered for himself. (He was to write a dissertation on Kafka that is still worth reading.) Kafka wasn't yet the most widely read German-language author in the world, though his clique of followers was rapidly expanding. I was haunted by the stories and not much bothered that I didn't understand them. In one of the books I found a handwritten poem by Martin, in serious, dreamy, and regular cadences. The poem spoke of a woman who came like the sun of her country (presumably the Near East) and lit up to the speaker's dusk. "Traces of strange journeys were on the hem of her garment," it continued, "but I didn't look at them." I responded with a sarcastic poem, which surprised him, and I hoped he was impressed with my ability to versify, though I carefully refrained from mentioning my ill-fated publication.

After I had been seen in Martin's company, some of the Jewish students took me aside for a serious talk. A Jewish girl with a goy, and a German at that? No way. It wouldn't do. I got indignant. And you, with your notorious affairs with German girls, where do you get off telling me whom to date? That was different, they answered smugly; they were men and could fraternize freely. I was insufficiently socialized in the nuances of gender roles and heard only contempt for women in their words and the arrogance of an authority which they didn't have, but presumed to have because they were male. First, in my childhood, there had been the contempt of Aryan children for Jewish children in Vienna, then the condescension of Czech children for German-speakers in Theresienstadt, and now the arrogance of men towards women. These three types of contempt may be considered incommensurable, but I experienced them within a few years in my own person, in the order mentioned. I am, so to speak, the guinea pig of the comparison, and so it has validity for me. As to the outcome, I took no notice at all of the other students, except that I gave them a piece of my mind, and Martin's company became for me a kind of rebellion against the arbitrary constraints of Jewishness.

He was to say later that I gave him no chance to talk about our common, and yet so dissimilar, past, whereas I think it was the other way around. One day, after Professor E's class, I remember talking about Martin Luther and his anti-Jewish tirades. The subject presented a dilemma for me, since Protestantism was historically the road to the German Enlightenment, in contrast to Catholicism, and because a Protestant pastor had helped us during our escape. And because young Luther had been an activist and a hero and a good poet, to boot. How could he compose the mindless, hate-filled curses against Jews of his later years? Martin, who was raised a Catholic, thought the subject was tiresome, which made me accuse him of being a closet anti-Semite. Not so, he responded. Kafka was one of his models, and besides, he had a strong interest in Jewish intellectual life. Could I tell him something about the kabbala? To my shame I had to admit that I could not.

Most German intellectuals have since had their say on the Holocaust, and Martin Walser is no exception. Inspired like many others by the Frankfurt Auschwitz trial, he wrote an essay he called "Our Auschwitz." "Our" referred to German guilt, but also to the gulf that allegedly separated the victims from the victimizers and their countrymen. I read that essay and thought he should have consulted me beforehand and asked my opinion. Perhaps I could have helped him close the gulf. And weren't novelists supposed to transmit empathy? Of course he was famous and lived in Europe, and I was nobody and lived in America, and we kept in touch through letters only. Still, here I was, an Auschwitz survivor of his acquaintance. And after many more years I asked him about this omission. He was surprised: he hadn't known that I had been in Auschwitz-Birkenau. Theresienstadt yes, Auschwitz no. That is improbable, I said, because I certainly told him when we were students in Regensburg, and even in those early years Auschwitz was a word that carried meaning. His teenage daughters chime in and agree that it's improbable. And yet it is believable, too, because our minds forget what our hearts won't remember. In addition, a concentration camp was something for grown men, not for little girls who weren't supposed to have vast areas of experience unknown to a returning veteran like Martin. As his poem said, he hadn't glanced at the hem of my garment.

In their California school my children told their classmates that their mother had escaped from a German prison camp. The other kids had laughed at them, they reported, not without some doubt as to my veracity. The other kids knew from TV that a Stalag was for American soldiers who tried to escape. But a girl? "Your dad, okay. But not your *mom!*"

Basically, Martin says, it is not abnormal to hate foreigners. It isn't right, of course, but it harks back to primeval thought patterns. Progressive education, he argues, can reduce this type of tribal thinking. Instead of blaming the haters, change their mind-sets. Sounds good, except that minds can't be set like clocks.

Someone who works in a lab will kill forty mice without batting an eyelash, whereas getting rid of one mouse running across a dining room in the middle of supper causes a stir. The point which a German professor of animal husbandry was making in my hearing was that there is no such thing as evil, there are only habits and primitive behavior structures. Variants on Konrad Lorenz's point of view.

Martin says, well, hatred of Jews was one of those variants of xenophobia which comes naturally to all men. No one wants to deal with differences if you haven't been brought up to tolerate them. I wonder, however: do I really act and look so different from him and his family, who have invited me into their house and at whose table I am sitting? Ever since I came back, their hospitality has been as genuine as the water of their lake on a warm day is sustaining and refreshing. As we talk to each other, the difference of language is a matter of minor nuances, yours Alemannic, mine Austrian and less noticeable, I should think, than the English phrases and syntax that sometimes discombobulate my German. Certainly less important than the web of common allusions and ironies which amuse us, sustained by the many books which we both have read. And as for appearance, your wife and I could be distant relations. "No, no," Martin says, "you look Jewish." I think so, too, and am glad that he acknowledges it, because I don't like people to say, "You could just as well be Italian or Mexican." But then, am I so unlike your family that you need sophisticated consciousness raising to prevent yourselves from persecuting me? Am I such a stranger here at your breakfast table where one of your daughters is pouring a third cup of coffee for me, and we remembered the summer when an army of ants invaded Papa's study? Didn't our friendship come easily? Or did it really take virtue, courage, and deep insights on your part?

"But of course we didn't mean . . . and how can you even think . . . ?" I think that the Jewish catastrophe can't be explained with abstract arguments taken from ethology or the mice of the veterinary science professor or Konrad Lorenz's views on the strutting rivalry of male animals. Nazism was the product of a highly developed civilization which was rotting at the edges and fell apart, and no one knew when and how that would happen, while you can predict with a certain amount of accuracy which way primitive behavior will go. What happened in Germany was advanced and therefore fortuitous, arbitrary. Put differently, freely chosen.

I call him from California, while I am writing this. His wife and I talk about children and grandchildren. He is finishing a novel, but he doesn't talk about his new fiction. The newspapers are upsetting him: he is attacked by the liberal intellectuals; they wrongly accuse him of nationalism and associate his ideas with Nazi ideas. He has written an autobiographical novel—his best, I think. But he doesn't talk enough in it about the Nazis, according to his critics. In fact he has put himself into the line of fire by arguing in public that Germans have to move on and put the Nazi past behind them. My old friend is a convenient target, to be sure, for simple-minded generalizations, but also a far too convenient rallying point for those who want to swear allegiance to the entire Germanic past, from Tacitus, who held up the Germanic tribes as a model to the decadent Romans, to the postwar "economic miracle" fueled by the Marshall Plan. He is the focus of a controversy that has at its core the question of how to be a German patriot.

The best of the young Germans shrug it off; the worst of the old Germans blame the Jews and the foreigners. Then there is a broad middle section with Martin Walser as their spokesman. I admit that sometimes I avoid him for months. There have been times when I never wanted to see him again. Or read him again. He leaves out too much and defends the omissions. He doesn't whitewash the past, but he straddles a fence. Not untypical of his countrymen. Then I do read his latest book and love the way he strings words together. Then I do visit, and there is both the distance and the human warmth. Now in his seventies, he is still what he was in his twenties: the epitome of what attracts and repels me about his country.

9

Even after all our papers were okayed and accepted, there were delays before we could embark on our long trip across the ocean. We were on our way when a strike in New York (Teamsters, I think), nailed us down in crowded quarters, first in Munich, then in Bremerhaven. It made me aware how miserable I would have been in a DP camp. I read, or tried to read, whatever English books and magazines I could get, strolled through the ruins of downtown Munich, and went to makeshift theaters where they were playing O'Neill and Thornton Wilder for an audience hungry for the literature it had missed out on during the insulation of the Hitler years. In Bremen I looked at landmarks, including a supersize statue of Roland, the nephew of Charlemagne (Karl der Grosse in German), which ironically guarded the destroyed city. I was in limbo, where the air smells of hope and farewell.

We sailed on the SS *Ernie Pyle*, a somewhat creaky old warship. She was not in the best of conditions, and the captain was more respectful of the weather than of her capabilities, so we were afloat for about two weeks. We slept cramped in steerage, but that was all right: comfort has only become of interest to me with increasing age. During the day I would sit for hours on deck on a pile of ropes and stare at the ocean. (There were no chairs; this was not a luxury liner.) Gradually I let go of Europe, as you might slowly open a fist and gently drop what it held. Before I returned, I had gotten twice as old.

For dessert we usually got ice cream in small closed paper cups. The insides of the lids sported photos of film stars, male and female. They looked overly groomed and decorative, and every day I looked forward to whatever quintessentially American face, famous though still unknown to me, I would get to see with my ice cream, all the while gaining weight through lack of exercise and intake of fattening food.

On board there were some Ukrainians who would spit out an occasional anti-Semitic remark. An American sailor said: "These people don't count in the United States. They stay all the way at the bottom." And to illustrate the low social position which he foresaw for them, he bent down a little and held his hand flat above the boards of the deck. This demonstration left me with mixed feelings. Much as I approved the notion that the anti-Semites wouldn't achieve much in the New World, I was worried by a creeping suspicion that we, too, might end up with those who stayed at the bottom. Would I be judged, before I had had a chance to show who I was? It was a bothersome thought, given where I came from. Illustrated ice cream and friendly sailors—that was America on the *Ernie Pyle*.

As we approached New York harbor, the Statue of Liberty and Manhattan Island were wrapped in a warm mist. It was one of those typical humid October days, a strange climate for us Europeans. Too warmly dressed in our clumsy German postwar coats, we stepped ashore. My mother asked a harbor official, much as she had asked the first MP we saw in Straubing, "Where do we go now?" He answered: "Wherever you like, lady. It's a free country." We had been emigrants for many years. Now we were finally immigrants, and the immigrant city New York took us in.

Part Four

NEW YORK

Either you will
go through this door
or you will not go through.

. . . .

The door itself
makes no promises.
It is only a door.

—ADRIENNE RICH, FROM
"PROSPECTIVE IMMIGRANTS PLEASE NOTE"

1

New York in the late forties was, as always, the quintessential city of immigrants, meaning a place where the natives know how to keep the newcomers at arm's length and see to it that the wretched refuse of God knows what teeming shore recognize their immigrant status and do not overreach. At the same time it was (and is) a city with room for new-comers, even elbow room and a playing field—not a level one, but a play-ing field nonetheless. Or there wouldn't be ever-new waves of us immi-grants. A playing field where neither togetherness nor apartheid is fully practiced.

Emboldened by the freedom of the postwar years and no longer hun-gry for food but all the more hungry for life and learning, I stumbled shortly after our arrival into the admissions office of Barnard, the female pendant to Columbia University, to inquire whether I could conceivably enroll there. I thought I mightn't have the academic credentials, but was surprised to find out, though indirectly and through tasteful hints, that it was a matter of money and status. I didn't know about private univer-sities, since in Europe they were (and are) state-owned. Here I was Oliver Twist asking for more. The smiling condescension that covered a steely refusal to so much as look at my case contained its own, albeit unspoken, rationale: you are just off the boat, you obviously have neither cash nor clout, and yet you want to take advantage of Ivy League glam-our. You belong with the huddled masses yearning to breathe free. So go breathe. New York was showing its teeth. I felt humiliated, but got one good piece of advice: try Hunter College.

We spent our first few nights in a repulsive shelter provided by a Jewish organization, where I had my first opportunity to compare that most indomitable of New York tenants, the Manhattan cockroach, to the Viennese bedbugs of my childhood. Soon we managed to rent a tiny, affordable walk-up in mid-Manhattan, which an uncle and his wife, pre-war immigrants, were about to vacate to move to better lodgings.

My mother, who detested living off charity, soon found a job. There was still an acute food shortage in Europe, where she had helped reunite scattered Jewish families, but in New York she earned a dollar an hour massaging fat women who believed they'd lose weight through the physical exertions of someone else. "More, more," they demanded energetically, if my mother flagged in her efforts.

We were poor. I hadn't known poverty, for money had played virtually no role in my life. We had lived in Germany before the currency reform of 1948 created the deutsch mark as a viable means of exchange, and had used American coffee and cigarettes to pay for whatever was worth buying. Since she worked for the Americans, my mother had access to these items. Money had been worthless. Here it was a never-ending headache.

The refugees of our acquaintance had little in common with the famous intellectuals and exiles whom a latter-day nostalgia has endowed with an aura of wisdom and noble suffering. Ours were white-collar folk, with a few physicians among them, whose intellectual horizon had never lain far from the shore. They had escaped in the thirties, and now that they earned more than they had a few years back, they felt it only fair that those who came after should have a tough time, too. You have to start from scratch, work yourself up from below. (But how much time would that take? Time was slipping by so fast.) They were proud of having weathered so much hardship and of the elbow grease they had demonstrated. The wives had earned a pittance cleaning houses. We had spent the same time as slave laborers, not earning anything, but that was a different story and didn't count.

They showed off how Americanized they were. They corrected each other's English and mocked each other's accents. And they despised themselves because they hadn't been born here. They used such phrases as "so-and-so sure didn't come with the Mayflower" and explained to me what the Mayflower was, thereby intimating their knowledge of American history. But they were also proud of Justice Felix Frankfurter, the Viennese Jew on the Supreme Court, and they tried to compensate for their low self-esteem by inflating their former positions in Europe and then made fun of their own exaggerations. Since they were uprooted and displaced, they laughed at the self-importance of the uprooted and the displaced. They had a popular German song about a small dog, who claims at the end of each stanza to have been a St. Bernard "over there, over there, over there." They wanted to purge themselves of the poisoned past and only cut into their own flesh, ignorant of how to perform such delicate surgery.

My uncle, who had arranged for us to take over his old apartment, including some basic furniture, was a bookkeeper. He coped with the problem of uprootedness by clinging to the new culture as the epitome of goodness and resented any criticism of the American way of life, like the incipient Cold War hysteria, which might threaten his still somewhat shaky certainties. (But I felt that I, too, had ideas about good and evil, hammered out in the fires of destruction which would later be called the Holocaust, and that I wanted to add to them, but not exchange them for shallower views.) My uncle looked a lot like my dead father, and I would have liked to see in him a father figure. But it didn't work. I was too uncivilized for him and my aunt, too wild, too unmannered and unwilling to compromise: in short, too much of a social liability, too un-American. I must have seemed sassy and brash, for I lacked the deprecating, soothing ways which American girls of my generation learned to equate with good manners from kindergarten on. (And against which they later rebelled, I might add, but the women's movement was far in the future.) I didn't know how to dance, giggle, or talk the kind of sweet nonsense expected of female teenagers. And in my European way, I was intolerant of euphemisms. Quite apart from *bathroom* for *toilet*, I questioned why it was vulgar to say *belly* and balked at using the baby word *tummy* or the anatomically wrong *stomach*. Wasn't it enough trouble to learn the correct English word, without then being told I shouldn't use it? I couldn't understand why I should put on a different dress every day, when yesterday's dress was clean. These are trivia, but they were typical of my bad manners, which stemmed partly from genuine ignorance of how to behave and were partly a rejection of the anxious approval of everything that could be labeled American. My upbringing had taught me to be antiauthoritarian, skeptical, and inclined to question and contradict. It was an attitude that I had needed in order to maintain whatever shred of self-esteem I had managed to salvage. Our circle took due notice and disapproved, even though my socialist criticism of American capitalism was no more than a childish game. Had I been a boy, no one would have minded my long, lonely, nightly walks through Manhattan or the fact that a couple of years later I hitch-hiked with a few other girls to Canada and afterwards camped with them on an island in Lake George (the best vacation I ever had). In a girl such self-assertive conduct was unforgivable.

We also had some genuine American relatives—a family who had lived on Long Island forever, whose mother tongue was English, and who treated us with the same patronizing goodwill as our Austrian and German grandparents had shown to the Polish and Russian Jews who fled the pogroms in the East to Vienna and Berlin, and whose German had easily slipped into Yiddish, as our English slipped into German here in New York.

We spent our first Thanksgiving at the home of these New Yorkers just a few weeks after our arrival. Prior to dinner I was assigned to the company of a younger girl, who clearly considered the task of entertaining me an imposition, especially since it was a strain to talk to someone who was still learning the language. To make some use of the wasted time, she asked me to brush her hair. She liked having her hair brushed, she explained, because it was good for the hair, and it felt great, too, especially if it were done long and vigorously. So I did as asked, wondering whether this was an American custom and whether I was being treated as a guest or as a maid.

My sigh of relief when we were called to dinner was premature. The feast began with celery stalks. Our relatives were amazed and, I believe, somewhat indignant, at our lack of enthusiasm for this strange, unknown vegetable. Instead of inviting us to leave it alone if we didn't like it, they urged us to get used to it. There was a suggestion that they had expected us to look more emaciated (did they feel cheated because we had normal body weight after more than two years of freedom?) and to show more gratitude for their Thanksgiving bounty. They had paid our passage, but they hadn't provided an affidavit for my father when he was in France. They would have had to guarantee that he wouldn't be a burden to the state—purely a question of money. They weren't related to him, but rather to my mother, and at that late date he would have had to come without us, his family. Not something an American head of family would ever do. They talked about this issue. It was on their minds. And while I didn't understand everything with my rudimentary English, I understood that they had a clear conscience. They could have saved him, I thought, as I chewed the fibrous, probably indigestible, and in any event repulsive, stalks: with a promise of dollars they could have saved him. And we would have him now.

Who has a right to live? Sure, I know that I am supposed to be forever grateful to the Allied soldiers for rescuing me, but I am only half ashamed to say that I am not. I reason, if you are born, you have a right not to be murdered. "But they shed their blood so that you might live," I am told. Well, the truth is, I didn't need their blood; I needed something much cheaper, an affidavit to get out in time. If I had been allowed to emigrate before 1939, I might be grateful. But after the war I wasn't in any danger and might have lived in a number of places. I didn't need to come to America to stay alive. Besides, who knows whether the Holocaust would have occurred if there hadn't been a war to camouflage the atrocities? Maybe, maybe not.

The dinner was long, the food was rich, the condescension unrelenting. Jobs were plentiful, they said. I should look for one, learn English, earn some money, and take some courses in night school, because with my pitiful English I wouldn't get into college anyway. My mother got on her high horse. I was plenty smart enough for college, and she would earn enough for both of us. And what did I want to study, our relatives inquired. I had no idea, but in order to say something, I asserted that I wanted a Ph.D., ignorant as I was of the American college system. Since the others were ignorant of the continental system, where you go straight from high school to a professional school, they were indignant at my presumptuousness. How could I talk about a doctorate when I didn't have a bachelor's degree? I assured them that I didn't want anything that was easy to get, and I did mean to study hard. This remark was graciously received: for once I had given the right answer.

After dinner they took us home in their large and showy new automobile. There was still a shortage, and they had had to wait to get one. While I sat in back in the dark, snug and comfortable, my aunt at several removes lectured me: "You have to erase from your memory everything that happened in Europe. You have to make a new beginning. You have to forget what they did to you. Wipe it off like chalk from a blackboard." And to make me understand better, she gestured as if wiping a board with a sponge. I thought, she wants me to get rid of the only thing that I own for sure: my life, that is, the years I have lived. But you can't throw away your life like old clothing, as if you had another outfit in the closet. Would she want to wipe away her own childhood? I have the one I have, and she has a different one—I can't invent one for myself that's more respectable. Struggling with foreign words that seemed to lurk behind seven veils, I told her why I had to reject this invitation to betray my people, my dead. The language was recalcitrant. My aunt hardly listened to my alien gibberish.

Later, when we were invited to visit them again, I refused. My mother wanted to go. I made a scene and didn't give in.

2

Hunter College was indeed the answer to my impecunious desire to be a real student. It cost nothing, and you could even borrow the textbooks.

Susi, or Susan, as she now called herself, had written from St. Louis, warning me that I'd need an American high school diploma to be admitted, but the opposite was the case. Hunter's admissions office counted not only my Straubing diploma but also my semester at Regensburg, where I had merely been an auditor, not taking any exams. Hunter took everyone and hardly pretended to evaluate the foreign credentials of immigrants seriously. New students were admitted on probation, and if they didn't fail their exams during the first year, they got credit for what they claimed to have learned elsewhere. It was a slapdash policy that gave us an opportunity, and as a group we were hard-working and scraped by, though not always with glorious grades.

But first you had to take an English language exam, written and oral. I prepared by reading books which I got from the New York Public Library, one of my favorite institutions in the world. I discovered the local branch in my first week in the city and couldn't believe my luck when I got a card from a friendly librarian without a fuss or a fee and was allowed to select from a cornucopia of books right away. Our friends and relatives predicted that I wouldn't, couldn't, pass the entrance exam after only three months in the country, stammering and stuttering over every English sentence. I did poorly and realized it. The cutoff point was 65 percent, and I came home despondent, climbed up the five floors to our apartment, where my mother was waiting at the door, and told her I had flunked. Now I would have to wait until fall instead of starting in February. What would I do for the next half year, if she didn't want me to apply for a job? She believed me and was as crestfallen as I was. A few days later I got a notice from Hunter: I had scored sixty-seven points, two points above the minimum. Once again, skin of my teeth: essence of success, precisely because it had been so close.

Hunter, today coed, was still a women's college, though due to the overflow of incoming veterans on the GI Bill, we did have a few men. They tended to huddle in the back of crowded elevators and classrooms, probably ashamed that they weren't at CCNY with all the guys planning to have serious careers.

I had spent my life among women, and this didn't change in New York. In my family, in the camps, and even after the war, men had been at the periphery of my life. It was true that from that periphery they called the shots because they had the power, and my mother never ceased to assure me that a woman needed to marry someone who'd provide for her. But her own example was different. From the beginning of the Hitler period until the time I left her, she was without a husband. Before and after she was a wife. But I knew her in the postwar time as a working woman, and under the Nazis her men had been powerless and had perished.

Engraved on one side of our building, between Lexington and Park Avenues, were some high-minded words of compromise by Emerson: "We are of different opinions at different hours but we always may be said to be at heart on the side of truth." I read this daily and it didn't make sense to me. Either you are wrong or you are right. How can the truth go both ways? Though our college song contained the immortal lines, "Fame throughout the wide world / Is the wish of every Hunter daughter true," in reality Home Economics was a popular major, and no one pretended that it was a path to glory. Apart from housewife, the choice of acceptable careers, if any, was among teacher, librarian, and social worker. I wanted to take languages, maybe French or Spanish, but was told that I already had a foreign language and didn't need another one. Instead, I had to take a number of meaningless, even childish, required courses, such as hygiene, where we were instructed to keep a straight posture when on the toilet, and a test question might run, "What soap should you use when washing your hair?" (The answer was "liquid soap.") There were animated, even agitated, discussions on the use of tampons (relatively new at the time) and whether to shave one's legs. But side by side with this nonsense, and for the same number of credits, there were offerings of a high academic caliber—especially the English literature courses. Many of the best professors were women, an advantage that can't be overestimated. Access to the great English authors, from Chaucer to Henry James, with elucidations by women trained in the New Criticism was the real gift that Hunter bestowed. I don't think I would have trusted myself to aspire to a college teaching career if I hadn't been trained by women in how to read Shakespeare and Faulkner. (And yet, no women writers, no Virginia Woolf, no Emily Dickinson!) In graduate school I was to have no women teachers. New York, odd as it may sound, is still for me the capital of the English language.

But there was the discomfort of the clothes, the shoes, the manners of the forties in America. My mother spoke disparagingly of girls and women who were clotheshorses. That was good socialist parlance, and fine with me, for I wanted to dress unassumingly, just blend in, and not spend much on it, since we had no money. (Forty dollars a week, of which seventy-five dollars a month went on rent.) Like so many new immigrants, we bought our clothes on Union Square, at Klein's, I believe. My mother had been an athletic and rather elegant woman before the war, and she was still (or again) good-looking. At first I trusted her taste, but soon I became suspicious. She forced me into little girl dresses for which I was too grown-up and too plump. She gave me a purse decorated with golden ponies and a red jacket to wear over a dress of a different red. I knew that was wrong but didn't know what was right. Red goes with everything, she said.

My hair grew wild and no permanent could tame it. In the late sixties, my son felt that a similar mop of hair that had come to him in his genes was a gift of nature, expressive of an up-to-date state of mind. But in the late forties, my appearance fitted all too well the image of the young savage that our immigrant friends and relatives had formed of me. When I asked my mother to help me, she mocked me: "Use your comb," she would say, and then watch my frustration and rage. Just as she had alternately kissed and slapped me when I was a child, she would now shower me with exaggerated compliments and without transition criticize my appearance. One moment she would tell me out of the blue how pretty I was, the next moment exhort me to try harder to find a boyfriend. Both instances of motherly love seemed to me uncalled-for and embarrassing. In retrospect, I am sure she sensed competition. She was looking for a husband, and here I was growing into a young woman.

My mother consistently pretended to be six years younger than she really was. Six years is the length of World War II. Perhaps she didn't want to have aged in those years. She pretended that the Nazi years had washed over me, as if, being a child, I hadn't been quite conscious of what was happening. I was a stage prop, her property, at most a minor figure in her drama. Teenage vitality and energy bothered her. When she said, "You are all I have," I felt that she meant I shouldn't grow up, shouldn't grow away from her. And yet it was true: she didn't have much else besides me. In her very last year of life, when I was trying to be a considerate daughter but nevertheless went on a trip, she said sadly, "You have always run away from me."

3

The Holocaust had no name as yet, and hence it wasn't even an idea, only an event: among the other disasters of the Second World War, a lot of Jews had died. A concept without a name is like a stray dog or a feral cat. To domesticate it, you have to call it something. The word *holocaust* for the Jewish catastrophe came into general usage in the seventies. Since then many have objected that it is derived from a nonapplicable source, since mass murder isn't a burnt offering to the gods (which is what the word *holocaust* traditionally meant), and that *Shoah* is a better term. I don't care particularly, as long as there is a word, any word, that unambiguously refers to what we are talking about without the need for a lengthy circumlocution to pinpoint a particular catastrophe and distinguish it from others.

The president of Hunter College, who had the German name Shuster, gave a talk in which he strongly protested the Nuremberg trials. The victorious Allies, he said, had the power but not the moral right to hold the vanquished responsible for what was done during the war. I had often enough heard this argument with its false rationality from Germans, who had a vested interest in the equality of the combatants. And perhaps the difference between war crimes and the new indictment of crimes against humanity wasn't altogether easy to grasp before Hannah Arendt taught us. But what was unpardonable was that Mr. Shuster spoke without any consideration of his audience. The "Hunter girls" were overwhelmingly Jewish, and many of them were recent European refugees. On the Jewish High Holidays the classrooms were almost empty, and the students who did come were, for the most part, also Jewish but not observant. Or was it precisely we, the generation of survivors, whom he targeted, we for whom the Nuremberg trials had not simply been an act of revenge against a handful of leading Nazis, as he implied, but the first major public acknowledgement of the Jewish catastrophe?

I wasn't the only one in the audience who got hot under the collar.

Other Hunter graduates say that he was known to be anti-Semitic. Maybe so. But the form that the denial of our prior lives took was complex, and it was pervasive. Our teachers talked about the Coventry and London Blitz, but none ever stopped to ask the class if any of the students had experienced bombing raids and what they had been like. It was as if we had lived, and yet not lived, through those years. Consider that only three years after the war there was a British film production of *Oliver Twist* with Alec Guinness playing a splendid, stereotypical Fagin, emphasizing his Jewishness. It is odd that the sheer indecency of depicting a Jew as a victimizer of little Christian children so soon after our children had gone up in smoke in ostensibly Christian countries didn't strike the producers. Even more interesting to me was, and is, the film *Gentlemen's Agreement*, considered a masterpiece of social consciousness in 1947, and one of the first American movies I saw in New York, when I still couldn't follow the dialogue with ease. It dealt with a Jewish veteran who returns from the war and can't find a suitable house or apartment because of restrictions against Jews. I watched the film with mixed feelings at the time. The discrimination was real, yet at the same time seemed trivial. Recently I saw it a second time and was struck that the entire film doesn't mention the Jewish catastrophe—not once, even though its protagonist has fought the Nazis. His, and the film's, only concern is that Jews should be allowed to live next-door to gentiles, not that a third of them had been murdered—though obviously a reference to Hitler's war against the Jews could have strengthened the argument against ethnic discrimination. There is mention of Zionism and a Jewish state, but not of the Holocaust. Perhaps if it had had the handle of a moniker, it could have been integrated. The reluctance to deal with it is perhaps comparable to the relative silence about the Vietnam War after the shooting and the shouting had died down. A diffuse sense of shame had set in.

In the fifties my husband, who had parachuted into France on D-Day, taught European history at Berkeley. When he came to the Hitler period, I offered to talk to his students about the concentration camps. (Later I would frequently teach Holocaust literature courses, but in those days I was a housewife and part-time librarian.) A drawbridge in his eyes pulls up: you can hear the chains rattling, and the water below is a greenish yellow, probably rich in algae. He flatly says no. No explanation. I want to say, "But I didn't propose to do a striptease in your seminar," though perhaps it was the same to him, something improper that reflected poorly on his honor as a decorated veteran who had fought evil. We were like cancer patients who remind the unafflicted that they, too, are mortal.

Once we were invited over by some veteran friends of my husband's. One of them, who had been a pilot in a low-flying plane—like the one who had strafed the death march column of my friend in Straubing, I thought—recalled how much fun it was to have that power. One time he had targeted a single man on the ground and had chased him and finally let him live, on a whim, because he deemed that the man had "earned" his life by nimbly running back and forth between the road and a ditch. The pilot had hunted him as he would a rabbit and had finally given up, admiring and laughing at his prey, and he claimed that in the end he had cheerfully waved to the man with the wings of his plane. I tried to raise his consciousness by pointing out that the German on the ground may not have understood this as a friendly gesture, because he was in a rather different state of mind, not having had the alternatives of killing or not killing, but only those of staying alive or being killed. In other words, we were talking about the terror of death. I didn't say all this from love of Germans, but because this ex-pilot didn't know the rules of comparison, because he saw a player in a game where he should have seen a victim. Sure, the roles could have been reversed. Perhaps the two men weren't dissimilar in character, and the victim could have been victimizer. Possibly he really had been the victimizer on some other occasion. But at that moment, the one was at the mercy of the other, and the quasi-comradely "greeting" of wings was out of place, since they weren't equals. In the end, my husband's friend is irritated and taken aback by my words. He isn't prepared for serious objections to his merry memories. I realize that women are tolerated in these circles only when they keep their mouths shut. My husband, to whom I have been married for less than a year, is annoyed with me. I have embarrassed him.

Like all newcomers to New York, we were warned about street crime and when and where one shouldn't risk going. I disliked the patronizing smile behind these detailed descriptions of the perilous status of young women, "especially in Central Park and after sundown." Of course they were right, but there was a sort of male pride in this talk and a secret bonding with the would-be rapists ("I, too, could under certain circumstances . . ." and "I know how easily . . ." and "A girl can't know how a man feels"), as if the problem were merely a matter of the different anatomy of the sexes and not of the perversity of power and violence, which always victimizes the weak. I wanted to make the point that I had faced greater risks in my life than taking a walk in Manhattan, but the remark would have been undesirable because unfeminine, and besides, I knew it to be superstitious and illogical, since past perils are no inoculation against future ones. But shouldn't these people have realized that, while I was new to New York, I was no stranger to the ABCs of violence? It was a putdown, no matter how well meant, rooted in denial.

And there were, in fact, both men and women with whorehouse fantasies who wanted to know whether I had been raped. Like the college doctor who saw the Auschwitz number on my left arm and called sundry nurses and colleagues, as if, now that I had washed up on these shores, the natives could invade my privacy at will. I was shaken but I'd answer, no, not raped: they merely wanted to kill me. I'd explain the concept of *Rassenschande*, the rule against miscegenation Aryan style, because I found it interesting that a malicious idea could serve as protection (albeit not a foolproof one) against sexual abuse. When my audience stopped listening, I knew that their intimate questions had not been prompted by sympathy or even curiosity. There is a thriving cottage industry of pornography based on the camps, which must have started about that time.

One of my friends reads this, shakes his head and says: "You complain that no one asked questions. But you also complain about the questions they did ask. You are hard to satisfy." There is a fine line between indiscretion and sympathetic curiosity. Damn right, I *am* hard to satisfy.

When my children were small, I caught the German measles from them. That was in the fifties. Their pediatrician expressed astonishment: What, I had never had German measles as a child? No, I hadn't. "You must have had a very sheltered childhood," he says, wisely shaking his young head. The medical profession is often at the forefront of those who know the answers before they ask the questions.

4

In New York the fear of death which had haunted me in Auschwitz gradually turned into its opposite, into depression, the temptation of death. There is an apt German legend about a winter so cold that Lake Constance was frozen solid, which never happens in reality, since the lake is much too large. One night, according to the story, a horseman unwittingly crossed it. When he got to the other shore and had firm ground under his feet, he looked back and realized where he had been, what he had done, and how unnatural his survival was. Tradition says he died of shock on the spot. I sympathized with that horseman.

I felt inferior, saw myself through the eyes of others, and there were times when it seemed that instead of having been liberated, I had crawled away like a cockroach from the exterminator. To be sure, this image owes more than a little to Nazi propaganda, but at a time when women were constantly put in their supposed place, it was natural for a young refugee to question her own value. In my family the women had survived, not the men. And that meant that the more valuable human beings had lost their lives. I was now the same age as my dead brother when his life ended and would soon be older. I would have liked to be a man, and preferably not a Jew.

Much of this deep malaise, which repeatedly turned into paralyzing depression, was what we now call culture shock and is due to the pain of having to reorganize one's life and thoughts to fit another nation's habits. But the rest was the recurrence of the losses and the question of one's own worth. I developed a pathological fear of the frequent quizzes and midterms at college. I wasn't used to regular exams and was obsessed by this anxiety; for days I wasn't able to think of anything else, even when I was fairly well prepared. That was the immediate cause of my mother's sending me to see Dr. Lazi Fessler. He was a psychiatrist and had been a close friend of my dead father. To talk to him, she said, would do me good. I had no idea what a psychiatrist does for a living, only that he was the man to see if you had nervous complaints. So he might well be the person who could help me sort out my various problems. And wouldn't he be glad to befriend a dead associate's daughter?

This man, Lazi Fessler, had asked my mother out to dinner a few times, and I suppose she told him a little about the two of us, leaving him with the impression that I was difficult and that she was patient. (Of course, I thought the opposite was the case, that I was an undemanding, if not an exemplary, daughter, and that it was she who was alternately unapproachable and prying.) Maybe she would have liked to marry him—he was single—and devotion to a difficult daughter would indicate a capacity for devotion to a husband. The operative term is the same. He married another woman in the end, an intellectual, we were told. My mother complained that the successful emigrants tended to marry American women. She couldn't compete with American women, my mother would say.

Fessler had an office in midtown Manhattan and was doing well, for psychiatry was a field in which a Viennese accent was an asset. The garden-variety psychiatry which flourished in New York in those days avoided all social criticism and any connection between individual suffering and historical evil—it was in full flight from the excess of history which we had just managed to put behind us. Hence all psychic suffering had to have its origin inside, in the mind of the patient. No cold winds from the outside could affect the hothouse of the psyche.

Susi, for example, went with her nightmares to a psychotherapist, a woman who told her that the camps in which Susi had spent her early teens could have no permanent effect on her, because she had been older than six when she got there. According to this logic, I point out to Susi, the camps haven't harmed anyone who is now alive, since children under six generally didn't survive. But were we dealing with honest opinions or with deliberate (conscious or unconscious) recriminations? For there was also the opposite opinion, held with as much fervor and no sense of a contradiction to be resolved, namely that the camps had inflicted irreparable damage on the lot of us. (One for the column "Don't forget who you are"!) When Susi first applied to nursing school, and a Jewish one at that, they turned her down in spite of excellent high school grades and a good performance on the entrance exam. The reason: a girl who had been in a concentration camp is unfit for nursing. What she had experienced must affect her ability to take care of patients. She'd be lacking in sympathy, the letter said. Fortunately she was admitted elsewhere and got the training she needed to become a psychiatric nurse and later a clinical psychologist. One of the great features of America is that you don't have to succeed on your first try. A closed door is just that: one closed door. It doesn't mean that all doors are closed.

So one evening I went to see Dr. Fessler in his office. Actually, I thought he had invited me to his apartment, since the address was Fifth Avenue. But he never did invite me to his apartment, this friend of my father's, though he had come to visit us in our shabby two rooms. During that visit he had snapped at me—I forget why. Perhaps because I had tried to take part in the conversation instead of just smiling sweetly. This reprimand from a stranger had come as a total surprise. I reacted by finding something to occupy my hands, as I tend to do to this day whenever I am ill at ease, like tearing up paper during lectures in Regensburg. I began to braid the tassels of the tablecloth. He wouldn't leave me alone, but now reprimanded me for the braiding, a discourtesy to him, who was our guest, he said. As if it was courteous to criticize my behavior in my own house, I thought. At the same time he used the polite form of address, the German *Sie*, while I would have taken the familiar *du* as a sign of goodwill to the sixteen-year-old daughter of his murdered friend. My mother sat without saying a word and wore a tired smile on her lips which seemed to put me in the wrong and approve of his paternally punitive attitude.

After this encounter I should have thought twice before presenting myself to him with my problems. Today I understand (though still not fully) that these men had their own agenda: the Jewish catastrophe was mainly and merely a resounding humiliation to them, not the tragedy of saints and martyrs that our own propaganda has made of it since. (Though the other side persists: belligerent Israelis will say, "Jews don't walk into gas chambers anymore," as they get ready to counter violence with violence. The Jews who were gassed are the inferior Jews in this scenario, which doesn't sit well with me.) What these male refugees who had spent the war in America—my uncle, Lazi Fessler, all of them—held against us was that we were the mothers whom they had left behind, we were the women and children whom they should have protected. While I, who had no axe to grind with them and operated on a different wavelength, wanted them to share their memories with me. To fill in the gaps in my own. To tell me what I had missed. Basically I wanted my father from them: I was looking for men who could somehow stand in for him, a last attempt to resurrect him from a grave he didn't have. That was asking too much. But these men *sounded* like him. I could still hear his voice in those days; by now I have forgotten it.

We spoke German, Fessler and I. German was easier for me, and perhaps for him too. I don't remember his English. I told him about my difficulties in college. Learning the language wasn't too bad; I was getting along fine, not brilliantly, but improving with each day. Nevertheless there was this panicky feeling before every damned exam, even if it was an easy one. Did I have friends, he wanted to know. No, not yet, I said sadly. It was my first semester, and finding friends takes a while. Unwittingly, I had given him his cue: my disinclination to conform, my arrogance. No, no, I said, taken aback, I am not a bit arrogant. I was too ignorant to understand that I wasn't to judge my own characteristics, let alone character.

I wanted to confide in him, so I told him what it was like at home, the constant friction, how I couldn't ever satisfy my mother, how she wouldn't leave me alone and criticized my every movement. (She did it to the end of her life, but it got to be funny when she was in her nineties and I in my sixties.) When there were visitors she didn't allow me to withdraw (granted there wasn't much space in our apartment, but still we had two rooms), and she put me down in front of the guests. When I said, I have to work, she would say studying isn't working, you don't have to work, I work for you. That's why I didn't like to spend time with her but preferred to go to the library, to museums, or for walks. She claimed that I read too much and demanded that I find a date, a boyfriend, but I wasn't interested. And even if I should find some guy I liked, *she* wouldn't like him— I was sure of that. (At Hunter College we had little opportunity to meet men. That was okay with me. The stress of the present life and the past, as it impinged on the present, was enough without further emotional complications.) And she always misunderstood me, I went on to explain. Whatever I said would feed suspicions I couldn't even fathom. She would take a joke seriously, and put the wrong emphasis on a throwaway remark. I was losing any desire to talk to her, because what I said simply didn't get through to her. But then my silence would make her suspicious. She smelled secrets where there were none. What was his advice, how could I break down these barriers, improve this relationship?

I had thought out beforehand how I would impress him by telling the facts objectively and unsentimentally, with poise and clarity. For if I could erase the bad first impression I had made on him during his visit with us, I might induce him into some personal conversation. For example, what kind of friends he and my father had been. If he knew of my father's aspirations, doubts, hopes. That sort of thing.

My father's friend, Dr. Fessler, sat behind a huge desk, which may have appeared even bigger to me than it was, because it signified distance, remoteness. I had to sit on a chair, in a corner, facing him from far away.

I hadn't noticed that he had become angry during my "objective" analysis of my home life and was therefore as startled as if he had hit me in the face when he roared: "Do you think your mother is a cow?" The indignation may have been real, or it may not, but I can quote the sentence literally because it was so unexpected. In my short life I had witnessed behavior that was far more problematic than what I was telling him about my mother, and nothing was further from my mind than to insult a person by calling her an animal. Since I had been raised with the full scope of anti-Semitic diction, I was and am sensitive to linguistic slurs and try to be politically correct to a fault. How could I think that my mother was stupid, when she had saved our lives more than once? He should not have used that image, I felt. I begin to smell danger. Misunderstandings were multiplying all around me, as if to illustrate and expand my initial question: why can't I talk to my mother so that she understands me?

The hour was over. I learned that it was a rule that I shouldn't stay longer than fifty minutes, but that I ought to come back. He gave me some homework: next week I should recite the flaws in my character and what I could do about them. To make it easier he told me what they were: arrogance and lack of respect. Sinful pride, in other words. These, he said, were the reasons why I had no friends and the cause of my anxiety, leading to such symptoms as fear of exams. He had it figured out.

I didn't recognize myself in this portrait and tried for days to make it fit the person I knew I was. The more I pondered, the less sure I became. Maybe his diagnosis was right in some way, only I didn't get it. At the next session I talked about how I might seem arrogant even if I was not. But I insisted that it really wasn't altogether easy to get along with my mother. He was annoyed. I felt my throat constrict with the fear that I might end up doubting my own judgment and hence my sanity. I fell silent and let him rebuke me.

"And look at your appearance," he said suddenly, pointing to a mirror. I obediently looked at myself. I was wearing my German coat, which was not very fashionable, to be sure, but who would buy a new coat if she had one that was still good? Granted my hair was a bit of a mess, but it was a windy evening, and I had been walking, so my hair was windblown. I felt terrible about this new shortcoming, but I was honestly confused. In this house, he enlightened me sternly, you could run across ladies of the best society, and what would they think of you? I came from war-torn Europe, from the camps and from postwar Germany, and ladies of the best society were the stuff of old novels. Besides, at this hour of the day no one was to be seen in this building, I thought, and wondered whether he had given me a late appointment because he was ashamed of me. Neglect of clothing, he told me, was an expression of contempt for my fellow men. Had he never heard of ignorance and poverty? But I felt too humiliated to proffer this even more humiliating defense.

I basically don't cry, but I was struggling with tears as I left. "Why are you crying?" he said triumphantly, or so I thought. I felt he shouldn't have said that. I was upset and trying to hide it, and he should have respected my effort to stay in control. On the way home I gave him credit for wanting to make a better person of me, but surely he wasn't helping me cope with New York. He had instructed me to come back with a hat. A hat seemed (still does, except on the redoubtable head of the late Bella Abzug) the most unessential piece of clothing, barring cold weather. But this was not a question of temperature but of a civilized lifestyle, as represented by fashion. With my mother's approval I bought a cap at Woolworth's for eighty cents, the cheapest head covering I could find. It was baby pink or light blue, and the money seemed wasted, but I put it on when I went to see Dr. Fessler again.

"What is conscience?" I asked him as a way of saying that the dead, whom I had so undeservedly outlived, were troubling. I didn't want to come straight out with this, as I now know, typical concern of all survivors, for fear that it might sound phony, since he had accused me of blind selfishness. I would have liked to show him my poems. There he could have read the words I had found for my grief. For his part, he had not provided any other words. Not even the word *Trauerarbeit*, which he must have known and I didn't. The labor of mourning, the recognition that it's hard work. Only once was there a mention of concentration camps, and then only in connection with my mother. As if I hadn't been with her. (I fleetingly wondered whether he even knew I had been there.) And he never answered my question, What is conscience? (I talked to the ghost of my father. "There, you see," I said, "you had no friends. Not what I would call friends." And I resented the familiar ghost, because I had vainly tried to find him in the person of this soul expert who was no mind reader.)

I had to get away from these sessions, which were destroying me. He is dismantling my very identity, I thought: I no longer know what I mean when I say "I." I guarded my words carefully, anxious not to give away anything that might boomerang. Of course he noticed and turned impatient with my silences. I was wasting his time, he said, precious time— ten dollars per session, which he let me have for nothing. At that moment two things happened. First, I didn't believe the sum he had mentioned. I was astonished but certain that he was lying. He can't be earning as much in four hours as my mother gets all week, I reasoned. And second, he had revealed that these painful meetings were a gift of charity, measurable in dollars, when I'd thought they were a gift of friendship, something you can't reject. I didn't have to accept charity.

I was to call him to make another appointment. I let it go. The telephone rings, there he is, and I stiffen. What does he want? He wants to know why I don't come to see him. I stammer and stutter. He wants me to assure him that he has helped me (for why else would I stop coming?). So I lie. I don't care. I don't owe him anything. Least of all do I owe him the truth. I just want to get off the phone. No, I am no longer scared of exams (I hadn't had any since I saw him last). He demands that I thank him. Why not? I thank him for his help. I never wore the Woolworth cap again and continued my nightly walks through Manhattan bareheaded.

I wondered whether I could make myself drown in a river like the Hudson when I had learned to swim in a river: the Danube. I'd probably stay afloat. I also reflected that the Hudson was pretty polluted. And so I stumbled through days of psychic imbalance with suicidal thoughts, talking to my ghosts. I was now writing English poems. They were partly experiments in a foreign language, partly a way of coping—the usual entanglement of form and content. Here is one that I wrote some years later in California, but its general tenor is that of my New York days.

> Choose of the many spirits
> a companionable ghost.
> Walk by his side in silence
> along the brown coast.
>
> Don't tell him your fears and forebodings,
> though the antechambers of hell
> deafen your ears with their roaring.
> Hold your breath and don't bore him
> where sound is whorled in a shell
> among seaweed, slippery to handle
> unlike your table and bed;
> where the sand won't cling to your sandal
> and the wind would not suffer a candle
> to burn all night for the dead.
>
> Taste him like salt beside you—
> a companionable ghost.
> Let him blind you, let him guide you:
> You won't get lost.

Dr. Fessler left an impression. I went to see him only three or four times, and he has been dead for many years. And yet I am still rejecting him and get angry when I mention him (as I have just proved in the preceding passages). By contrast, I have grateful memories from the same period of college teachers who took no further notice of me than that they taught me what they knew. Not only the brilliant ones, but others: the elderly scholar, for instance, with whom we did Anglo-Saxon in an early morning class (undergrads don't do Anglo-Saxon anymore, the more's the pity); I would simply apply modern German grammar to Old English, and because it was so close, I made fewer mistakes than anyone else. And fell in love with the mournful dirges of homesick sailors. So why can't I shrug Fessler off, be amused by the memory? He didn't inflict permanent harm. Or did he? It was as if, in the person of this Jewish doctor, the Nazis obtained a spiritual authority which they had never had for me in Germany, in the sense that here was a man who didn't let me be what I was (and that implies, does it not, a denial of the right to live and is a kind of death sentence) and who yet sounded like my father.

The worst was that, without asking or knowing anything about the people I had loved and lost, he doubted that I could make friends.

5

By the following summer I had conquered this crisis—I had made some friends. It was like climbing into a lifeboat.

At the University of Vermont you could go to summer school, leave the city, and get credit at Hunter. I spent the summer of 1949 in Burlington. I had a roommate who decorated her bed with stuffed animals, probably to denote a childlike and pliable femininity. She was a girl of the decade that was just round the corner, the fifties, and she wanted to find a good provider and be a good housewife—certainly nothing to sneer at but of no interest to me. She asked me what my nationality was, and I gave the only appropriate answer, that I was Jewish, born in Austria. "Well then you are simply an Austrian," she declared, "your faith has nothing to do with your citizenship." In a sense not, I admitted, and since the war was over, I could get an Austrian passport. But all the same there was a difference between me and the non-Jewish Austrians. To which she replied with the happy certainty of ignorance, coupled with a proud knowledge of the American Constitution: "That's not how we think in this country. We believe in the separation of Church and State."

"I know," I said, with a sigh of resignation, "that's why I am here. That's why I have applied for citizenship and already have my first papers. I don't want to be Austrian."

Since she was as well meaning as she was obstinate, I didn't bother to explain to her why I had dropped the blind date she had kindly arranged for me. He was a veteran who told me that he and his comrades had sometimes killed their German prisoners of war, when it was too much trouble to take them back. When I reacted more negatively than he had expected, he retracted a little, admitted that he had broken the rules, but so what, those had been merely Eisenhower's rules, and war is war.

So there was nothing to do but withdraw to the ivy-covered library, where I composed harmless poems to practice my English or lost myself in the balanced alexandrines of Alexander Pope or the biting prose of Jonathan Swift, assigned for my eighteenth-century English course. The idyllic New England setting reminded me of nothing so much as the garden of the Jewish hospital where I had spent my lonely last months in Vienna, only this time it was my own fault if I wasn't happy. Maybe Lazi Fessler had been right. I wrote a loving letter to my uncle and aunt in New York, didn't get an answer, and imagined that they had thrown away my mail as an insincere attempt to get into their good graces.

When I learned that there were some other Hunter students around, I decided to look them up. More than half a century has passed since then, and we still look each other up and gossip and worry about each other. And now three of us are left to mourn the death of the fourth.

My son says: "What were you like, the four of you?" He has known them from childhood on; to him they are like family, only more so. He says, "I see you at a table, like in an old black-and-white film, laughing and smoking cigarettes." What he means is that his take on this prehistoric friendship lacks depth and subtlety—for isn't everything that happened before we were born by definition prehistoric and pre-Technicolor? What did you have in common, he asks, when you are basically such different women? And it bothers him that we smoked, for he is an athlete and a health freak, and these fine people urged cigarettes on his mother when she was seventeen.

I found Kit and Liselotte at a table in the cafeteria, puffing away and in a good mood. They were taking a course on the New Testament, and I was interrupting a theological argument between them. But they were interrupting each other much more vehemently, assertion vs. counter-assertion: you aren't listening to me; yes I am, but you're absolutely wrong.

Kit and Liselotte were Jewish, and at the same time they were sincere Christians, albeit with some skepticism. They were forever questioning their own good faith in converting, as well as questioning Christian dogma. This was a new wavelength, terra incognita, for me. My Jewish liberal background decreed that Orthodox Jews were fanatics and baptized Jews were spineless assimilationists. I shed these prejudices quickly and quietly, as one takes off a pair of torn nylons under the table, secretly, so that no one will notice you've been wearing them.

They had rented a room in town, which was cheaper than the dormitory, and when they invited me to come along to their place, I knew that I wouldn't find any stuffed animals on their beds. Instead we found Monique, asleep. The others pelted her ruthlessly with a hail of pillows, so she would welcome me. She slept only out of laziness, I was told, and it is true that Monique regarded sleep as the best refuge from crisis and as a solution to most problems. She majored in math, and the other two accused her of not having as much work as humanities students did. Though irritated with her roommates because of the uncalled-for assault—she was the most reticent and private of the four of us—Monique showed her natural courtesy to me. The three were a curious mixture of exuberance and familiarity with grief, of vitality and depression. No wonder I felt I could belong with them, if they would only have me.

Liselotte, at twenty-five, was the oldest and the compass needle for the other three. When she had been barely past infancy, her parents had sent her from Frankfurt to a sanatorium in French Switzerland which specialized in a disease that a few years later could be cured with antibiotics. It left her with a permanent limp, though today she is the most robust of us. She and I had similar backgrounds in that we each had an unorthodox childhood that strained the imagination. Sickness as a kind of prison—I should have been able to imagine that, but I could not imagine how one grows up lying in bed. I asked her for details and didn't listen to the answers or didn't keep them in mind, so that I had to ask again. Not to get up for years, then to get up, then to have to do it all over again, and spend more time in bed. Liselotte says, "An unnatural situation becomes natural if it is the norm, whatever it happens to be." That's how it was in the camps, too, and still I was frustrated trying to imagine immobility. I tried to empathize honestly, then perhaps not so honestly, because it was bothersome and unpleasant. I reacted as others react to survivors of the camps, and thus assumed an attitude which I criticize in others. And learned slowly what you learn in friendships: to unburden yourself and inspect the bundle that you've had to carry, to find some tools that will serve to grasp and come to grips with what others have on their backs, instead of running in circles within an idiosyncratic enclosure of barbed wire.

I was at last integrated, if only within this small group of young women, for to integrate means to make a whole of parts, and thus each part must be less than whole, must be injured. Someone who has the same injuries can't help you, only someone who lacks something else. Friends fill the gaps: they are complementary to oneself, they do what you have missed, they have what you have lost. Family members, by contrast, share your genes; they don't expand your vista, except by chance. My new friends welcomed me and let me be as I was. I fervently hoped they wouldn't get tired of me, as I was the youngest.

None of us had grown up with a father, and all of us had problems with our mothers. In a way we were each other's parent replacements. Liselotte says to a professor in college: "I don't have time right now, I have to see Monique." The professor says, with the certainty of an older woman: "You are always running after one friend or another. You are not going to spend your life with them, you know." Liselotte, who made a success of her marriage and is by now a white-haired grandmother, pushes one knee forward, crosses her hands over her elegant cane, as she does when she wants to emphasize a point, and looking back over half a century's crises, says with conviction: "You know, that woman was wrong. I have spent my life with Monique."

Monique, a different type of refugee, was born in Paris—definitely a classier place than Fascist Vienna—and taken by her widowed British mother to London and then to Australia for safety, during the war. She had left her mother and siblings at seventeen on their way back to England, had enrolled at Hunter, found work to keep her going, and refused to let her family help her.

Monique grew up a Zionist, but unlike me she made a go of it. We had been in New York less than a year when Israel became a state and my mother came home bursting with the good news. My joy was mixed with disappointment that we hadn't waited long enough. Later I made some abortive attempts to go to Israel, but life interfered, and what was too often postponed didn't come about. But Monique took her social-worker training to Israel and worked there with delinquent children (Jews like to think they don't produce any, but they do, just like other societies), while in London her mother proclaimed, disapprovingly but also with pride: "My daughter eats institution food with flies." Monique later returned to California, if not disillusioned, at least with diminished enthusiasm about the character of a population that is ever ready for war, even if it's a defensive need. And then she quit social work and became what she always wanted to be, a pilot and a flying instructor.

"You see," I say to Liselotte, the least feminist of the four of us, "in a better world Monique would have become a pilot right away, since she loves flying. She got to it late and via detours." "But," says Liselotte, "you underestimate what she did for her clients in the course of her career, because you see wasted lives everywhere—you positively look for waste, so that you can wring your hands about it."

They all had part-time jobs. I didn't, except in the summer. Monique operated the switchboard at a girls' home. Liselotte had a room with a *New Yorker* cartoonist in return for baby-sitting. There was no prejudice here against entrusting kids to a handicapped foreigner. New York did have many faces. And Hunter was good for mavericks like us, though the education we got was a mixed bag.

Kit was our only American. She fled from a home situation that we hadn't yet learned to call dysfunctional. She tried out identities, changed her name from Catherine to Kit, later to Kitty, and in her last years she was Kay. She fled to us foreigners, with our deviant perspectives and languages. Kit's mother had told her two daughters that college was a waste of time, and instead they should have nose jobs in order to look more like film stars. Kit ignored the first advice and went on to a Ph.D. in English and a professorship in Canada, but she voluntarily underwent the torture of the second and had her nose broken as soon as she had the money. Liselotte lamented that Kit had spoiled her beautiful face in order to look like an average Jane Doe. But that was an exaggeration. Faces are a matter of character, not a matter of noses, even though a native nose is the preferable choice. Kit said Liselotte never told her she had a beautiful face, or she might have kept her old nose. Before Barbra Streisand's fame, a Jewish profile was scorned, and cosmetic surgeons all over the nation were breaking Jewish noses, especially female ones. Quotas against Jews were disappearing fast, and yet Jews were running away from themselves—that, too, perhaps a reaction to the undigested Holocaust in Europe. Or was it because restrictions against women got tougher again after the war, and there was a WASP standard? Black women straightened their hair in the days before black was beautiful, and Jewish women had their faces mutilated. In college Kit had converted to Catholicism to please a teacher whom she adored. Later she returned to her liberal, agnostic beginnings, chaired a local ACLU chapter in Canada, was a successful Shakespeare scholar, and died of cancer before she was seventy, whispering in an exhausted voice on the phone: "I never left a party early, Ruth, but I guess this time I have to."

The three of us who remain still struggle with Kit's absence in various ways. I, for one, can't get myself to delete her old e-mail from my computer. Ghostly writings in cyberspace. I could print it out and store it before trashing it, but even that would seem sacrilegious.

6

I fell on my feet and found my bearings because of these three. I could talk to them. They listened and answered, for or against, but always weighing what they had heard, unlike my mother, who used language for manipulation, not to express an opinion or state a fact. What sounded like a fact might be a lie, and every opinion was tailored for the moment. Language to her was like the makeup of an actress—you choose what your respective role requires—and so she listened for what might lurk beneath the surface, always speculating about the unsaid. But words will take their revenge when thus misused and played havoc with her mind.

She was jealous of my new friends. I invited them over and she disapproved: "With cripples and *geshmate* [baptized Jews] you hang out." When she said that I was sitting in a bathtub full of cold water, a tried-and-true remedy against the New York heat. (Since no one had air-conditioning as yet, you didn't have to feel bad about not being able to afford it. Who would have suspected that New York would ever be able to attract tourists in summer, of all seasons!) My mother is next door, in the kitchenette. She wants to spoil the new friendships that I am proud of. For no reason, just for the hell of it. I start screaming, I hate her. Another remnant of trust is gone.

We four took in whatever New York had to offer that was free or inexpensive. I learned what a joy it was to live in a city that has never been bombed. I loved going to museums and listening to Liselotte tell me what she liked about a painting. She would encourage me to dislike certain famous painters and to admire certain minor ones, in other words, to drift wherever my minimal understanding of art would take me. Museums convey a sense of permanence, the idea of "collection," as opposed to separation and loss. In a museum I feel that I belong, though nothing belongs to me. I lay claim to what my eyes take in. Libraries convey a similar sense of accumulated history and culture, but it's more a kind of promise, since you can't read all the books at once, whereas a museum offers you a ready-made feast. I can't be rejected by museums and books, except when the police interfere, forbidding me to enter the museum or burning the books. Of course that happens. But short of violence, that is, short of the ultimate abolition of meaning, art and literature can be a home for those without citizenship, because they remind us of our common race, the human race, and they sop you up, yet simultaneously feed you, like a magic sponge. They make you part of what you see and hear and yet let you stand back and choose.

The various Shoah museums and reconstituted concentration camp sites do the exact opposite. That's why I find them so hard to take: they don't take you in, they spit you out. Moreover, they tell you what you ought to think, as no art or science museum ever does. They impede the critical faculty.

In 1950, at the age of nineteen, I graduated. Hunter had given me a heap of advanced credits for stuff I never studied and didn't know. Presumably Hunter was trying to process as many students as possible as fast as possible. No one bothered to take a good look at my record. Nor did they think I was much of an intellect: in the students' counseling office, where I mentioned that I might want to go to graduate school, they strongly discouraged me because I had such poor grades, except in English, my major.

My mother had a better job now, as a physiotherapist in a doctor's office. She had gotten some money from her prewar Austrian property, had paid back our Long Island relatives the cost of our fare on the *Ernie Pyle* ("In America we pay our debts," they told her self-righteously, as if she planned to do any less), and with the rest had made a down payment on a pretty little house in Forest Hills. She thought it would be an enticement to make me stay with her. But it wasn't. I yearned to get away, the sooner the better. Just after I graduated, I learned that I had won a prize from the English Department for one of my poems. It may have helped me a year later to get admitted to the University of California at Berkeley with a waiver of the out-of-state fee. I was going to do comparative literature or English. American publicly funded schools have been good to me. I wasn't going to go back to New York, to my mother, ever, that was certain.

I worked for a year. I was a waitress, I worked in a factory, in an office, for a wigmaker, in a department store. The variety suggests that I wasn't a success at any of it, nor did I save much money. Most of what I earned went into the household. Since we never kept track of expenses, I still had to ask for money. My mother was not stingy. She just wanted me to depend on her, even if she was handing me the money I had earned. *Whatever belongs to me, belongs to you* was her motto. I interpreted this as "You belong to me, and therefore cannot own anything on your own." She spread a rumor among her friends that I was preventing her from getting married again. I would have been relieved to have a stepfather and to be able to leave with a good conscience. She must have felt that not finding a husband reflected poorly on her. Maybe for once she wasn't even lying, but sincerely believed that as I got older, I needed her more. I came home from work in the evening, and as often as not, I would turn around and get on the subway again, back to Manhattan, to see my friends who were still attending college. Though I was younger than they, I had graduated first due to the vagaries of the advanced credit system.

She went through my things; she never knocked at my door; she smelled my underwear. Later in life, when she came for a visit, she would often go through my wastebasket and read any papers she found there. I would confront her with this indiscretion, and she would defend herself: "What do you mean? If it's been thrown away anyone may look at it. At my place you can look through all the garbage."

No one is as dependent as mothers are on the dependency of their children.

7

And New York, that city of strangers, is in retrospect one of several places that I would hesitantly call home, even though none of them are. New York alternated between meanness and generosity: it invited everybody in, and when you got close, it turned a cold shoulder. Yet it was in

New York that I learned to speak English and memorized Shakespeare's sonnets and wrote English sentences and even verse. That's a kind of empowerment, as today's buzzword has it. I haven't lived in New York for decades, but when I visit the city, the very pavement reminds me that New York freed me from the incompetent silence of otherness by teaching me to understand its language—an English, by the way, which shares with my native Viennese German an insolent humor and an aggressive, colorful verbiage. In New York I attended college, not for very long, just two and a half years, but long enough to give some orientation to the confused map of my mind. And the friendships of those years have lasted until today. So when I come to New York, the city opens its parks and museums and says: "Remember, I gave you all this when you were a lost and unattractive kid with bad memories and habits, worse manners, and no one to turn to. Now don't you blame me if I look a bit rundown at the edges." On these short visits, New York puts the remnants of my teenage years around my shoulders, like a warm, if scratchy, cardigan. New York becomes a friendly, purring cat that once belonged to me (it was Franz Kafka who said of his native Prague, "This little mother has claws"), and I stroke old Mehitabel and act astonished: "Is it really you? Who fed you while I was gone? Did you eat mice and vermin, or even garbage? Shame on you!" And I add somewhat hesitantly, "Did you wait for me?" but glance furtively at my watch, because soon I shall leave the old pet to her own devices and be on my way again.

8

I sometimes dream that I am a hit-and-run driver. To run someone over with a car and not stop is a commonplace crime. Happens every day. I can empathize with the driver, and I wake up shaken by the dream and relieved that I am still innocent. The living forget the features and the eye color of the dead (other matters crowd our brains); children pack up their belongings and leave their parents. Unpaid debts remain, because like Shylock's daughter, Jessica, we have always taken a few things with us that didn't necessarily belong to us, even if they weren't ducats. And you can't clean up a relationship like a kitchen after the meal is over and the dishes are washed. I wish it weren't so, and yet I have no regrets.

Let me skip a few years. It is 1955, and I live in Connecticut. In California I married a graduate student of history who was a war hero.

Now my husband has a one-year appointment at Wesleyan University, where he is badly paid and has to plow a large percentage of that pay into the rent for an apartment in an old barracks owned by the college which stints on the upkeep of the place. We now have a child, the boy to whom I haven't given my father's name. The birth has cost us a full month's salary, since we weren't insured. In the meantime my mother has landed in a mental hospital in New York after a failed suicide attempt, which was probably meant to fail. They give her electric shock treatments; she resists, so they give her more. I have visited her with my husband and find her in a state of terror. What can I do? My husband is no help. He is horrified and probably sorry he married me. Relatives and friends blame her husband—her third husband, for she has married since I left her. But I can't get rid of the thought that I am the cause, I and my baby. She was on the way to visit me after my delivery. She took the bus, but got off before arriving in Middletown, rode back to New York, and called from there to tell me that certain red-haired men had followed her. Subliminally, I figure, she must have been thinking that her child was taking her place, the daughter becoming the mother: she takes my place without asking permission. And because this switch took the meaning out of her life, she felt that the world had become dangerous again, on the bus, at home, everywhere. It's a crazy idea, I admit, but I know her, I know her paranoia.

The phone rings. It is my uncle, the bookkeeper, and I think he is calling out of sympathy, but no, he is angry. He speaks in German. Viennese male voices resemble each other—it's my father on the line. I am standing in our temporary, scantily furnished apartment and cringe at his words. He says I had no right to get married, to leave my mother. His voice is shaking. I believe I know what's behind this reproach, but that doesn't help me, and I don't dare to voice the unspoken, the unspeakable, to yell back at him, "And you, and your mother, didn't you emigrate without taking her along, and she had a miserable end in Theresienstadt?" He had left his mother in Vienna, as I had left mine in New York, and in both cases there was a bitter end, and that's why he is now so mad at me. "You should never have left her," he says. But I had only moved from one U.S. state to another, and didn't leave her at the mercy of a terrorist government. I think I hear an undertone, something he doesn't say but implies: "You have no right to an independent life." He puts the receiver down, unreconciled, but he has told me his mind, and now he probably feels better.

I don't. I stand in the middle of the room and I scream. I just scream. As I did in Vienna when my cousin's neurotic terrier tore Grandpa's parrot to pieces. I don't shed tears. I just let go, top of my lungs, letting in the air or letting it out. How should one live in order to earn the right to live? And there was the newborn: you can't wish any child out of existence. The presumed justification for a woman's life, having children. Only in my case, this isn't a valid passport to life? And suddenly I know that I never counted on children to be my alibi. My husband has turned into a pillar of salt. He has become a stranger, as I am a stranger to him. Now he realizes what he got when he figured, this girl isn't used to much luxury, she'll be undemanding. I came with a lot of invisible baggage and expected him to share the burden. He wasn't equipped to do that. Our marriage was doomed from that moment on, though it lasted a while longer.

Four years earlier, when I left New York, everything was in a heap and a jumble at my mother's place. I packed poorly. It was late summer, and the heat was something, the external disorder a mirror image of inner chaos. I hardly knew what to take along. My friends were there and helped me pack, and my mother was desperate. She was aware that I wouldn't come back.

So this is the end of the story, the hit-and-run end, the living room with my stuff on the floor, my bad conscience, not bad enough to act on it though, and the disappointment of my mother, who had bought the neat little house in Forest Hills and would now have to live there alone. Until she found the third husband, who didn't pan out. After I left, she read my papers, discarded my correspondence, got rid of my books. At the end of the story there was a vacuum, in the rooms, in the people. At the end there was my betrayal: I had become Shylock's Jessica, abandoning an unloved parent.

EPILOGUE

The years
And cold defeat live deep in
Lines along my face.
They dull my eyes, yet
I keep on dying,
Because I love to live.

—MAYA ANGELOU, FROM "THE LESSON"

1

I have said that running away is what I am best at. And yet if you run not to get somewhere, but to get away, you may find yourself running in circles. Or, you hope, perhaps in a spiral, ending up not in the same place, but one floor farther up. By the early sixties, I was running away from a marriage. To make a living and support my two sons, I went back to graduate school and became a professor of German literature. For many years I had refused to have anything to do with the language, the two countries (Austria and Germany), or their people. But I was good at my new job. I taught Middle High German, wrote about the baroque epigram, and had some clever things to say about certain aspects of eighteenth-century literature. Nothing contemporary. And occasionally I went to Europe for a visit, just for a few weeks in the summer—maybe two weeks in Germany and the rest of the time hanging out with friends in England—though most years I taught summer school in the States to make ends meet. And that was okay, because these visits were more of a drag than a help: I carried too much baggage.

But in the late eighties I realized that I had unfinished business with a past that's an ongoing story. Something pulled me back. Perhaps the language. For language is the strongest bond there is between an individual and a place. German, strange as this statement may sound, is a Jewish language. Consider that until the Holocaust, most of the world's prominent secular Jews spoke and wrote it: Kafka, Freud, Einstein, Marx, Heine, Theodor Herzl (!), and Hannah Arendt, to name the first that come to mind. I had to go back to where it was spoken and give myself time enough to understand, if not the killer culture of the past, at least the next generation and a bit more of my own. By then I was fifty-seven, and it was now or never. I became the director of my university's Education Abroad Program in Göttingen, a university town in the state of Lower Saxony, which is as far as you can get from Vienna and still speak the language. That suited me fine: Göttingen held no Nazi memories for me, because memory is selective, and my memory is emotionally unimpressed by the fact that Hitler became a naturalized German in the neighboring Lower Saxon city of Braunschweig, or that the closest concentration camp is Bergen-Belsen, where I almost landed at war's end. To my childish soul, only the cobblestones of Vienna scream with hate.

I had been in Germany for only a few months when a teenage bicyclist ran me down one evening as I was crossing the street in a pedestrian zone. Suddenly I saw three bikes coming downhill from my right at what seemed a tremendous speed, one of them headed right at me. It was too close, too fast for me to leap back. I stared at the cyclist's lamp and stood still so he could bike around me, but he didn't seem to try (why doesn't the old biddy get out of my way?), and he comes straight at me. At the last fraction of a second I jump to the left, and he, too, swerves to the left, in my direction. I think he is chasing me, wants to injure me, and despair hits like lightning: I crash into metal and light, like floodlights over barbed wire. I want to push him away with both arms outstretched, but he is on top of me, bike and all. Germany, Deutschland, a moment like hand-to-hand combat. I am fighting for my life, I am losing. Why this struggle, my life, Deutschland once more, why did I return, or had I never left? I had become the victim of my own hit-and-run nightmares.

That's why I fell so badly, I had my arms in front of me and couldn't brace myself when I fell on the back of my head. The boy was sixteen. He wasn't acting out of ill will, I am sure, just feeling the exuberance of being on a vehicle that was fast—much faster than the old bikes used to be, more like being behind the steering wheel of a car—and perhaps some impatience with the old woman in his way. Someone other than he called an ambulance. I lost consciousness, came to, asked where I was. They told me. Then everything turned black again. I woke at the emergency room in the university clinic.

I vomit and am paralyzed. My body has become a threat, an embarrassment. I would like to leave it, rent another one or go back to where I was a short time ago. I am getting worse; now I can't move at all. I'd like to sit up, since my stomach is still rebelling, but I don't manage. Terror sets in: what's going on? The paralysis continues. Now I can't even lift my head anymore and whatever is left of vomit and bile runs back into my throat.

That was the low point. I hear the term *brain hemorrhage* and wonder who will help me die if I stay paralyzed. Presumably no one. The stench of death is in my nose, and in my mouth the taste of old putrefactions.

A specialist has been called and bends over me. I can smell his rich and spicy dinner. Then they stick my head into a machine in order to measure, to investigate—what do I know. Afterwards they talk about what to do. They talk as if I can't hear them. I try to catch what they are saying. Surgery or no surgery. They talk about me, not to me. They must think I am no longer sane. What sort of surgery? Open the skull, stop the bleeding. But the woman has a heart condition. She may not survive. This is crazy, it's all a mistake, I was merely on my way to see a play at the local theater with a student from California.

When I am not asleep, I try hard to get back to normal. I make a great effort, but helplessness imposes its own strains and pressures. The effort is yet another attempt to run away. To run from the headache and the paralysis, from an onrush of panic. I am hanging on to reason, which is the greatest of all goods, except love. Reason is a way of turning towards the world, even as love is. But the world has to turn your way, too. That's why I was grateful to my visitors, my new German friends who came in droves, appalled at the idea that I might die from a brutal accident in their country, where they're trying to redeem the sins of the past.

It was as if burglars had been in my head, as if they hadn't found what they could use, so had rifled through carefully wrapped papers in deepest recesses, and finding them worthless, had scattered them; or had gotten into all the drawers and cubbyholes, cut up my clothes (like the time when someone broke into my car and ruined some stuff I was taking home from the dry cleaner's), and left the closets open—and there are those ancient objects you think you discarded long ago, pulled back into the daylight. You feel dispossessed, because the house has been damaged badly by this wrenching disturbance and now seems an alien place. By and by you notice that there is more of your own self in the chaos than there used to be in the former tidy order.

People don't realize what's behind the symptoms they see. I try to speak coherently, like Gregor the bug in the Kafka story, and because I am trying so hard, my listeners don't know how much effort I have put into it. And I don't know how hard it is to understand me. They listen to what they assume I am saying. They comprehend that I can't walk like them and that I have to sleep a lot, but when it comes to thinking and talking, their empathy fails them. That's not a reproach, only a statement about limits. We expect from others more or less what we expect from ourselves, and as a rule of thumb that measure serves us well. But a gulf opens when someone is diminished by illness. Equality is gone, and different norms prevail for the patient and her visitor or caretaker. The gulf is deep; my friends bridged it as best they could.

It requires the greatest concentration to follow the simple instructions of, say, the physical therapist, because I have to consider very slowly and deliberately where left and right are and what these words signify. Tears come to my eyes from the strain and the frustration and the sheer effort of wanting my life back.

My thoughts whirled in a circle or in a spiral, formed the oddest geometrical figures, were never linear. And hung in the space of the repetitive hospital days. Time was splintered. I didn't experience it as a continuity but rather as a heap of broken glass, shards cutting into your mind when you try to put them together. I would forget by afternoon who had visited me in the morning, and the sequence of weekdays confused me, though I begged my friends, with teary eyes, to bring me the daily newspapers.

Every day is like a gate that closes behind me and leaves me outside. Searching for the past when it is nailed shut.

2

After a few weeks of hospital and rehab, it was over, and I was back at work. The blood had been reabsorbed. The doctors had refrained from surgery. They had been cautious, and they had been right.

But the memories remained, like cave paintings, which to the uninitiated eye at first seem mere scribbles, until they become figures and assume a spectral significance. They had at last caught up with me; in my hospital bed I had been their prisoner. When I was well, I had been able to escape them every morning by getting up, away from their shadowy assaults, and making coffee against their sound and fury and focusing on some immediate task.

How did I come to write this story? For a long time I had wanted to, but didn't because other urgencies interfered and because other books had appeared and seemed to have done the job. Now, while I still felt the presence of the angel with the ambiguous face, whom I have known all my life more intimately than I wished, I began. I first met him in the

Haggadah, the Passover text, and in a poem I wrote sometime in the seventies, had tried to envisage him as my constant companion. I tried out all the wings I knew, though angels in paintings have only birds' wings. I gave him bat wings, paper wings, no wings—birds' wings are too beautiful for a death camp. He became the suicide angel of my teens and the angel of the slaughter in Vietnam during my thirties. And in the end I welcomed him without being in a hurry. It's a sentiment I'll stick to, whatever the merits of the poem in which I expressed it. The secret was still death, not sex, the two collapsing into one.

TALKING TO THE ANGEL OF DEATH

What a fraud you were, liberator of the Jews who smote the firstborn
    in Egypt!
A Viennese grandfather but with practicable birds' wings,
amid the symbolic dishes, the prearranged questions and answers
and the orchestrated "Heil" on the streets, and upstairs the family
    tensions,
you were my Passover angel with your verses and scholarly wisdom.

But I saw you commit the ultimate obscenity in public,
chauffeur who drove the trucks with the naked corpses,
the pubic hair of the dead women piled high in the sunlight,
whoremaster of the camps,
wingless then.

In New York, bat-winged, you suffered from acne and masturbated on
    the subways.
Every time I crossed a bridge or looked out a tenth-story window you
    had an erection.
In the late forties, my pal, in museums and parks
and walking at night through midtown Manhattan we argued,
bilingually, whether or not to make love.

In the fifties you tricked me. A house without windows,
in a suburb I nurtured you like a blind embryo,
but gave birth to live children and packed up and left you,
deserted you like a burdensome husband,
buried you like a miscarriage.

You of the squashed cockroaches and the moth wings in the light
    fixtures,
in the sixties you returned with the six-thirty news, squatting
on the TV set in my temporary living rooms,
flapping celluloid wings against the two-dimensional war,
a celebrating bat.

Yet you were the angel of the small hours when I wakened with worry,
Guardian of the Garden, Tempter of Eve.
Everywoman's Orpheus with an offering of silence,
the great wings folded, butterfly-fashion,
and my own son's face.

Old friend, old adversary, most satisfying of lovers,
lifeguard as I swim my laps and my lungs give out,
as my hair thins out, as I hunt for my glasses,
as the dishes and papers pile up, you sit in my kitchen and classes,
wearing bright paper wings, an impractical joker, not a fraud.

    Now in the late eighties I sat down and wrote German prose for the
good people of Göttingen who had become my friends, who hadn't let
me lie in their clinic alone, but cheered me back into movement and
activity. I thought if I wrote in German, my mother wouldn't see it, as
she had no contact with things German and even considered my career
an embarrassment. But when my story appeared, more readers liked it
than I had expected, and so, perhaps inevitably, a bridge partner of hers
had a cousin in Switzerland who unkindly sent a copy. Even though she
was an impatient and infrequent reader, my mother easily found all the
passages that were critical of her and was badly hurt. All her neighbors,
she said, now knew she was a bad mother. There was no point arguing
that the neighbors didn't read German books. I just let it go and prom-
ised myself not to publish it in English until after her death. Let it
appear in French, in Czech, even in Japanese, but not in English. I owed
her that much. What you have been reading is neither a translation nor
a new book: it's another version, a parallel book, if you will, for my children and my American students. I began it when my mother's slow death
cut her contact with the outside world and prevented her from reading
anything but the headlines of the Los Angeles Times, and I am writing
these last words now that she is buried. I have written this book twice.

In Los Angeles they put the simple Jewish pine coffin into a hideous cement cast before they let you bury it; some health regulation from some department where they figure the dead pollute the earth. Dead humans, that is. Dead animals don't have to be packed in cement. Maybe the dead do pollute the earth, but if so, no amount of man-made material will stop them from it.

My mother looked small and shriveled in the hours I sat with her after she had died, not so much peaceful as spent. Life had drained out of her in those last days, and she just wanted to be left alone. I regret making her sit up and drink orange juice or cajoling her to come to the table to have some decaf and toast. She didn't want to. It was as if she was saying: I have put up with all of you for nearly a century, and now I want to be left in peace. It was a good death, as they say, for she was in her own home, her own bed, still able to move, and she even dragged herself to the toilet half an hour before she died. She was able to do that—a rare thing for a dying person, as the caretaker who was with her told me. But I think there is no such thing as a good death, because her body didn't obey her anymore, her mind was elsewhere or nowhere, and she was in a state of discomfort that I can only guess at. Not pain, but perhaps worse than pain: who knows?

Her mind had been going steadily, leaving her behind as it were, the same way that her eyesight and her sense of orientation and balance left her. Consciousness flitted in and out. She would snap to, and then again there would be only a flicker. Dying, I came to understand, is a drawn-out process, even if you are not in acute pain or in a coma. The thing that says "I" gradually steals away. In the afternoon when she ceased to breathe, she was only a little more dead than she had been at noon, when I saw her last. And for weeks her soul, if that's what it is, had been coming and going in a dilapidated body, so that she would stumble and mistake and ignore and recognize and turn towards and turn away.

When the men came to take her out of the house and I saw her shrunken body for the last time (for at the funeral the coffin was sealed), I felt a sense of triumph, because this had been a human death, because she had survived and outlived the evil times and had died in her own good time, almost a hundred years after she was born. And then again, I felt she had died like an old cat. In the end they just lie around and sleep mostly, they get up for water and a bit of food, and they drag themselves to their sandbox. For the rest, they are nearly blind, rather sweet, and have a variety of ailments. Both she and I had owned such cats.

She had lived in California nearly half a century. Susan, a better daughter than I, persuaded the New York mental hospital that she, as a registered nurse, could take care of our mother, and so they released her and sent her out to Los Angeles. My mother left Susan's house almost as soon as she got there and took her life into her own capable hands. She got divorced and sold her New York house, bought another little place, and found a fourth husband and a job. When they had institutionalized her in New York after her suicide attempt, she hadn't been any crazier than the preceding years, and that had never been enough to stop her from functioning rather better than many people who were of sounder mind. Her last marriage was long and not necessarily happy, since it was marred by the plague of her pathological suspiciousness, but it lasted nearly forty years. My stepfather died at the age of ninety-one, and she was buried next to him, as she had wished. I like to think that, on balance, the two had been good for each other. Her last eleven years she was again a widow.

I swore I would do everything in my power to prevent her from dying in a hospital, because to her all of them were concentration camps, and I found a helpful doctor and succeeded. Her paranoia caused her to dismiss cleaning women and caretakers. Once she put a new lock on the door because she feared a break-in from the capable and trustworthy household help she had just fired. She suspected her older grandson of wanting to turn her out of her house. (I would shout at her: "My children aren't criminals!") She mistrusted her neighbors, who liked her; her doctor, a native Pakistani, who treated her with his culture's respect for the old; and all authorities. She was afraid of being deported, because she had pretended to be six years younger. (I would remonstrate: "You saved them six years of Social Security and Medicare. They'll give you a medal if they find out.") As her mind became more unreliable, she mercifully returned to her childhood in the little Czech village she came from, where her father was the important director of the local sugar refinery. She would call me in a small child's voice by her older sister's name and ask me to help her with a zipper or some other item of clothing. Thus I found out that she had loved and relied on my aunt, while I only remembered the two of them fighting as adults. I would take her out to lunch, and she'd refuse at first, because she thought she had to go to school. When I assured her she didn't, her face would brighten, because she thought she had permission to play hooky. She would order cream of broccoli soup, fried shrimp, and blintzes.

To the end she loved to go for a ride and would exclaim at the beauty of the trees and the size of the buildings. She commented on the color of the cars and the color of the traffic lights, and was pleased as a toddler would be when she could coordinate green and red cars with the lights. During her last weeks and months, all memory of the Nazis seemed to be gone. She was back with her playmates on the Czech meadows of her first years. She had a pet goat and a cart pulled by the goat and was happy. There were only the village children, the fields and the animals, a doting father, bare feet.

None of her own generation was at the funeral. She had outlived them. But her last great love was there: my grandchild Isabela with one *l*, or Isabelita, as I sometimes call her, a little girl of four. Isabela had known her great-grandmother as someone who was in many ways on her level, and she wasn't fazed by a face that was scary to many children because it was as wrinkled as a mask, like a witch's. Little Isabela recognized the childlike spirit behind the mask and invented games and jokes for the old lady and cuddled and loved her. My mother's weak eyes shone when the child entered. As soon as she could walk, she'd toddle up to her with a bowl of fruit as an offering, and my mother would exclaim: "Ein Wunderkind!" Outside, they would walk hand in hand, neither of them all that steady on their feet, though for opposite reasons. In a restaurant, Isabela would feed my mother, as if she was a doll, and my mother obediently opened her mouth for a spoonful of chocolate pudding. At home, they sometimes threw food at each other, giggling, with my son—Isabela's father—commenting: "It's disgusting, but who cares?" Isabela was also friends with my mother's cat. Her own mother had taught her to sign before she could speak, and Isabela would make the sign of the cat (an indication of whiskers) when she came in the door for a visit. Then the cat died, and we had to explain the inexplicable. And Isabela would continue to sign for the cat, even after there was no more cat and she could say the word *cat*. But there is no sign for a dead great-grandmother.

Isabela was profoundly startled when she heard that she wouldn't see her Grandma Alma again. Strange as it seems, she had lost a favorite playmate and didn't understand how it could have happened. At the funeral she stared at the unfamiliar surroundings, frightened and unhappy, dry eyes wide open, having sustained a genuine loss, the first in her life of less than four years. She was beginning to understand the terror of time, the invisible thief with the force of a hurricane. I gave her some bric-a-brac from my mother's house, which she gladly and solemnly accepted, and a flower to throw into the grave (though the cement casing spoiled the effect of the traditional gesture).

I look at a snapshot of the two of them gleefully rubbing noses, a smile of total affinity on both their faces, the girl who'll be a woman of the twenty-first century, and the woman who was a girl in the early 1900s, sharing some genes, sharing affection. On one side, the child whose mind hadn't reached maturity, on the other, the old adult who had once lost a teenage son to anonymous murderers and whose mind had gone beyond ripeness. More than ninety years between them, but whenever they were together, chatting and touching, they met in a present that miraculously stood still for them, time frozen in space and space made human. Perhaps redeemed.

Irvine, California
Winter Solstice 2000

Credits and Acknowledgments

The excerpt from "The Lesson" by Maya Angelou is reprinted from *And Still I Rise* by Maya Angelou, copyright © 1978 by Maya Angelou, and used by permission of Random House, Inc.

The excerpt from "The Diaspora" by W. H Auden is reprinted from *W. H. Auden: Collected Poems* by W. H. Auden, copyright © 1945 by W. H. Auden, and used by permission of Random House, Inc.

The excerpt from "Früher Mittag" by Ingeborg Bachmann is reprinted from *Werke, Band 1* by Ingeborg Bachmann, copyright © 1978 by Piper Verlag GmbH, and used by permission of Piper Verlag GmbH.

The work of Tadeusz Borowski is quoted from *This Way for the Gas, Ladies and Gentleman* by Tadeusz Borowski, translated by Barbara Vedder (New York: Penguin Books, 1976).

The excerpt from "After a Hundred Years" by Emily Dickinson is reprinted from *The Poems of Emily Dickinson*, Ralph W. Franklin, ed., copyright © 1998, 1979, 1955, 1951 by the President and Fellows of Harvard College, and used by permission of Harvard University Press and the Trustees of Amherst College.

The excerpt from "Prospective Immigrants Please Note" by Adrienne Rich is reprinted from *Collected Early Poems: 1950-1970* by Adrienne Rich, copyright © 1993, 1967, 1963 by Adrienne Rich, and used by permission of the author and W. W. Norton & Company, Inc.

The work of Simone Weil is quoted from *Cahiers, Vol. 2* by Simone Weil (Paris: Gallimard, 1953) and translated by Ruth Kluger.

The excerpt from "A Dialogue of Self and Soul" by W. B. Yeats is reprinted from *The Collected Poems of W. B. Yeats, Vol. I: The Poems, Revised*, Richard J. Finneran, ed., copyright © 1933 by Macmillan Publishing Company, copyright © renewed 1961 by Bertha Georgie Yeats, and used by permission of Scribner, a Division of Simon & Schuster, Inc.